The Church in the Modern World

The Church in the Modern World

Gaudium et Spes *Then and Now*

Michael G. Lawler, Todd A. Salzman,
and Eileen Burke-Sullivan

A Michael Glazier Book

LITURGICAL PRESS

Collegeville, Minnesota

www.litpress.org

A Michael Glazier Book published by Liturgical Press

Cover design by Jodi Hendrickson. Illustration by Susan R. Lawler.

1	2	3	4	5	6	7	8	9

Library of Congress Cataloging-in-Publication Data

Lawler, Michael G.
    The church in the modern world : Gaudium et spes then and now / Michael G. Lawler, Todd A. Salzman, Eileen Burke-Sullivan.
      pages   cm
    "A Michael Glazier book."
    ISBN 978-0-8146-8270-8 — ISBN 978-0-8146-8295-1 (ebook)
    1. Vatican Council (2nd : 1962–1965 : Basilica di San Pietro in Vaticano). Constitutio pastoralis de ecclesia in mundo huius temporis. 2. Church and the world.   I. Title.

BX8301962.A45 C9746   2014
261'.1—dc23   2014010550

To Fr. Dennis Hamm, SJ,
esteemed friend and colleague

Contents

Prologue

The question of the relationship between the Christian Church and the world, understood as humanity in its historical existence with all the social, political, and economic structures which shape that existence, has not always been an issue for Christians. The earliest Christians took for granted that the Church was predominant, an attitude neatly summed up in the second-century *Didache:* "Comes grace and the world passes."[1] All that really counted was the spiritual world. When the empire became Christian, however, and the Christian movement had taken root, the question of the relationship had to be faced. At the end of the fifth century, it was forcefully articulated by Pope Gelasius I (492–496): "Two things are the principle of the rule of this world, the sacred authority of pontiffs and royal power."[2] Gelasius left no doubt about the relationship of these two things: "Though you [the Emperor] take precedence over the human race in dignity, nevertheless you bend your neck in devout submission to those who preside over things divine." This hierocratic prioritization was continued and solidified and promulgated as "tradition" well into the Middle Ages,[3] when there was the beginning of a profound change.

The twelfth century saw the first stirrings of modern science, that is, the study of the nature and the value of things in themselves.[4] Political rulers also began to reflect on their own nature and value at this time. They sometimes saw their power and their function of governance as entirely independent of pontiffs, a doctrine that led to several notorious confrontations: between the Holy Roman Emperor Henry IV and Pope Gregory VII, Holy Roman Emperor Frederick II and Innocent IV, and

---

[1] *Didache*, X, 6.

[2] Thiel, *Epp. RR. Pontif.*, I, 350.

[3] See Hugh of St. Victor, *De Sacramentis* II, 4, *PL* 176, 418; Also Boniface VIII, Bull *Unam Sanctam (1302)*: temporal power is subject to spiritual power.

[4] See Marie-Dominique Chenu, *La théologie au XIIe siècle* (Paris: Vrin, 1957).

1

Philip the Fair and Boniface VIII.[5] Theologians Albert the Great and
Thomas Aquinas participated in the development of the autonomy of
natural realities, including social and political realities, but their immediate disciples did not pursue this freedom of the natural from the
ecclesiastical,[6] and the predominance of ecclesiastical power continued,
though more and more challenged.

The growth of the autonomy of temporal realities and the consequent
emergence of genuine pluralism in the nineteenth century accentuated
the theological discussion of the relationship between ecclesiastical and
natural, including political, power. This theological discussion ended
with the Second Vatican Council, which boldly and clearly acknowledged
the autonomy of temporal and natural realities. This can be seen in the
Vatican II documents *Lumen Gentium* (the Dogmatic Constitution on the
Church [LG] 36) and *Gaudium et Spes* (the Pastoral Constitution on the
Church in the Modern World [GS] 36, 41, 56, 76).[7] For example,

> If by the autonomy of earthly affairs we mean that created things
> and societies themselves enjoy their own laws and values which
> must be gradually deciphered, put to use, and regulated by men,
> then it is entirely right to demand that autonomy. . . . For by
> the very circumstances of their having been created, all things
> are endowed with their own stability, truth, goodness, proper
> laws and order. (GS 36)

The debate on the relationship between the spiritual and natural
spheres was greatly advanced by the council: both spheres were autonomous but related. The specification of their relationship was further
advanced by the popes immediately succeeding the council, Paul VI and
John Paul II. The council taught that "a secular quality is special and
proper to laymen" (LG 31) and that the laity are "bound to penetrate
the world with a Christian spirit" and are "to be witnesses to Christ in
all things in the midst of human society" (GS 43). Paul VI repeated this
teaching after the council, asserting that the Church "has an authentic

[5] See Ernst H. Kantorowicz, *The King's Two Bodies: A Study in Medieval Political Thought* (Princeton, NJ: Princeton University Press, 1957), 97–143.

[6] See Etienne Gilson, "Pourquoi St. Thomas a critiqué St. Augustin," *Archives d'histoire doctrinales et litteraire du Moyen Age* (1926), 6–127.

[7] All citations for Vatican II documents are taken from *The Documents of Vatican II*, ed. Walter M. Abbott (New York: America Press, 1966). We have selected this transla-tion because of its precise translation of the original Latin texts.

secular dimension, inherent to her inner nature and mission, which is deeply rooted in the mystery of the Word incarnate."[8] Both the nature and the mission of the Church are rooted in the incarnation, that core Christian doctrine that confesses that God became man in Jesus of Nazareth. In the incarnation, Dermot Lane writes, "the gulf between heaven and earth, between God and man, between the supernatural and the natural, between the sacred and the secular . . . has once and for all been overcome, so that now we can glimpse heaven on earth, God in man, the supernatural in the natural, the sacred amidst the secular."[9]

The secular character of the Church and particularly of the laity is to be understood, John Paul II insisted, with a *theological* and not just a *sociological* meaning. "The term *secular* must be understood in the light of the act of God . . . who has handed over the world to women and men so that they may participate in the work of creation, free creation from the influence of sin, and sanctify themselves" (*Christifideles Laici* 15). The Church's service in and for the world, no matter what service it is, is not just *secular* service in the sense that it falls outside God's plan of salvation. It is also *salvation* service in the sense that it is for the sanctification and salvation of the world and its inhabitants. John Paul returned to this theme again and again.[10] A theological characteristic of laity is that they live in the world, know the world, value the world, and seek to permeate the world with the Spirit of Christ and Christ's Gospel. In the end, the Church and the world are one as the human person is one, the Church being the soul that animates the world to become its best self "as it is to be renewed in Christ" (GS 40). It is also, "by her relationship with Christ, both a sacramental sign and an instrument of intimate union with God, and of the unity of all mankind" (GS 42; see also LG 1).

The theological secularity of the laity was already common theological currency long before the 1960s and the Second Vatican Council. Pius XII described the essential mission of the Church as including the building up of the human community according to Christian principles. The lay faithful, he insisted, "are in the front line of the Church's life; through them the Church is the vital principle [the soul] of human

---

[8] *Acta Apostolicae Sedis,* 64 (1972): 208.

[9] Dermot Lane, *The Reality of Jesus* (New York: Paulist Press, 1975), 137.

[10] See, for example, John Paul II, "Unity in the Church's Mission with Diversity in Apostolates," *L'Osservatore Romano* 723, no. 8 (February 22,1982): 6; "On Liberation Theology," *Origins* 8 (1979): 23; "*The Church in Rural Africa,*" *Origins* 10 (1983): 23; "*Specialis Filia Romanae Ecclesiae,*" *Catholic International* 4 (1993): 5.

society."[11] In the 1950s, Yves Congar and Karl Rahner wrote in the same vein. After the ravages of World War II, the relationship of the Church and the world was even more pressing. Why, then, was there no document on that relationship among the preparatory documents of the council? The way the council developed clearly illustrates the answer to that question.

Pope John XXIII announced on January 25, 1959, he would convoke a council. The council convened on October 11, 1962. In the almost four-year interim between the announcement of the council and its opening there was a ferment of preparatory activity. The pope appointed ten commissions to sift the suggestions of topics that should be discussed at the council and to sort them into thematic documents to be debated and voted on. Sixty-seven such documents were prepared, most of them couched in condemnatory language far from the positive and reconciling approach enunciated by John in his opening speech, *Gaudet Mater Ecclesia* (Mother Church Rejoices). There was no document dealing with the Church in the modern world, but there were four dealing with issues that would eventually be incorporated in altered forms into *Gaudium et Spes*: the Moral Order; Chastity, Marriage, Family, and Virginity; the Social Order; the Community of Nations.

Even before the council began, it quickly became apparent that there would be serious disagreement regarding its content, tone, and shape. The text on the moral order, for example, had been composed mainly by a subcommission of Roman theologians and was classicist neo-Augustinian in structure. That is, it was based on the prevailing Catholic teaching of an objective, absolute, and immutable moral order. Theologians of a more historically conscious, neo-Thomist perspective were explicitly excluded from the subcommission. This preconciliar disagreement between classicist neo-Augustinians and historically conscious neo-Thomist theologians would serve as a paradigm for the disagreements that would occur throughout the length of the council itself.[12] Indeed, the debates over the schema and on the documents themselves, including one on the Church in the World of this Time, would repeatedly be played out along similar neo-Augustinian and neo-Thomist lines.

[11] *Acta Apostolicae Sedis*, 38 (1946): 149.

[12] For a discussion of the neo-Augustinian and neo-Thomist perspectives, see Joseph A. Komonchak, "Augustine, Aquinas, or the Gospel *sine glossa?*" in *Unfinished Journey: The Church 40 Years after Vatican II: Essays for John Wilkins*, ed. Austin Ivereigh (New York: Continuum, 2005), 102–18.

It should probably not be a surprise that there was such division among the Church leaders. By 1959, the historical situation of the previous several decades had left the world in a traumatized state. Europe had recently emerged from a war of unparalleled savagery and was still reeling from the horror of the "final solution" to the "Jewish problem" in Nazi Germany. The end of that war had given way to a "cold war" between the Western allies and the Soviet Union, a war that reached its moment of greatest anxiety shortly after the opening of the council in a standoff between the Soviet Union and the United States of America, the former seeking to install in Cuba nuclear missiles that could reach the United States, the latter resolutely vetoing such a move with a determined blockade. Colonialism was crumbling worldwide, with the former colonial powers leaving behind chaotic and poor countries. The former French colony of Vietnam collapsed under the strain of nationalism into a civil war which was already being waged when the council opened. The omnipresent scourge of racism was rampant, and civil rights struggles were being violently resisted in many places, the United States and South Africa being the most publicized. The world was living in fear and asking both what could be done and who could do it—ecclesiastical powers, political powers, or some combination of both.

The question of the most pressing problems of the modern world, however, was not confronted in any preparatory Vatican document, possibly because the Roman editors of the documents did not consider the issue of sufficient importance. By contrast, there was real unease among the fathers of the council about the absence of any discussion of the issue. Soon after the council began, Pope John appointed a new Mixed Commission to develop a document on "the Church in the World of this Time." That document would come to have a tortuous and evolving birth until, on the very last day of the council in 1965, it became *Gaudium et Spes*. It went through several tentative documents, a Roman document superseded by a Malines document superseded by a Zurich document superseded by an Ariccia document that became, after still more heated debate, the basis for the approved document *Gaudium et Spes*. The history of that development will be treated in detail in chapter 1. Suffice it here to note that, even after its overwhelming approval, *Gaudium et Spes* was still criticized as too optimistic in its outlook on the world, neglecting the evident widespread influence of sin on men and women. That critique continued and continues long after the council, but a careful reading of the document reveals that the critique is not sustainable. *Gaudium et Spes* gives plenty of attention to sin and its ravages in the human past, present, and (most likely) future (GS 10, 11, 13, 25). The document went on to become one of the most theologically and socially influential of the council.

Gaudium et Spes is divided into two main parts. Part 1, "The Church and Man's Calling,"[13] is divided into four chapters: the dignity of the human person, human community, human activity in the world, and the role of the Church in the modern world. These chapters have profound ecclesiological implications for how we think about "church" in the modern world, as well as important methodological implications for how we think about moral issues in the modern world.

From an ecclesiological perspective, *Gaudium et Spes* builds on the work of *Sacrosanctum Concilium* (the Constitution on the Sacred Liturgy), *Lumen Gentium*, and *Dei Verbum* (Dogmatic Constitution on Divine Revelation) to disclose a pneumatological center of a Church that only lives and functions authentically when it serves as the sacrament of Christ in the world. The emphasis is on the mission of this people to proclaim and bring to realization the reign of God on earth as it is in heaven. Accomplishing this mission presumes a deep belief in the Spirit who directs discernment of the signs of the times and a willingness to do all things in the manner of Jesus. Such a stance requires each member and the whole institution to demonstrate a willingness to speak and to listen in a generous context of dialogue that respects the other. Finally, as Pope Francis has pointed out, it requires the whole people of God to become a *practically* poor Church in service of the world, especially those who are on the margins of human culture because of their poverty or the oppression under which they must live.

Methodologically, *Gaudium et Spes* reflects a profound shift from the neo-Augustinian, classicist approach toward a neo-Thomist, historically conscious approach to moral theology. A classicist worldview asserts that reality is static, necessary, fixed, and universal. The method utilized, anthropology formulated, and norms taught in this worldview are timeless, universal, and immutable, and the acts condemned by those norms are

---

[13] The universal use of "man" and "men" throughout the Vatican documents might grate on contemporary minds accustomed to the liberation and equality of women. The use of the male noun, however, is not intended to suggest, as some have speculated, to embrace only males. "Man" is the English translation of both the Greek *anthropos* and the Latin *homo*, each of which embraces both females and males. While a gender-inclusive translation would be more desireable, any time we read "man" in the documents, we should read it as inclusive and not exclusive of women.

always so condemned. Historical consciousness, grounded in existentialism, fundamentally challenges this view of reality. According to a historically conscious worldview, reality is dynamic, evolving, changing, and particular. The method utilized, anthropology formulated, and norms taught in this worldview are contingent, particular, and changeable, and the acts condemned by those norms are morally evaluated in terms of evolving human knowledge and understanding.

Gaudium et Spes suggests four foundational themes that are central for ethically achieving the goals enshrined in those four chapters. First, it seeks to elaborate what constitutes the truly human (GS 26, 49, 50, 60, 73, 74) and human dignity (GS 19, 27, 39, 51, 66, 73), suggesting an objectivist metaethic that realizes that what is good or right can be defined universally in terms of human dignity or some cognate of it. Second, it offers clear indications of how human dignity is to be defined (GS 12, 24, 26, 27): right acts promote human dignity; wrong acts frustrate that dignity. Third, all men and women are called to discern what promotes and what frustrates human dignity. They are to realize that their pastors will not always be so expert as to have a ready answer to every problem (even every grave problem) that arises (GS 43). Fourth, they are therefore summoned to prayerfully discern themselves what promotes and what frustrates human dignity. Their individual decisions lead to the formation of their conscience, that most secret core and sanctuary of every person where they are "alone with God, whose voice echoes in his depths" (GS 16; see also 26 and 41). The Catholic tradition has consistently asserted, and the Second Vatican Council reaffirms, that a well-formed conscience is inviolable and is to be followed to live a moral life. The following of one's conscience is at the very core of the moral life.

If every individual "Is bound to follow his conscience faithfully, in order that he may come to God" and "is not to be forced to act in a manner contrary to his conscience" (*Dignitatis Humanae* [DH] 3), it is inevitable that different persons will come to different conclusions about human dignity and the ethical norms that promote it. That reality is the origin of legitimate pluralism in the Church and in the world, which is not to be confused with the relativism that both John Paul II and Benedict XVI excoriate. Relativism leads to conclusions that are false. Perspectivism, i.e., different conclusions derive from different perspectives, leads to conclusions that are true but only partially true. What is required, then, is not wholesale condemnation of differing conscientious judgments but the kind of dialogue much prized by Pope Paul VI. We shall discuss fully the relationship of relativism and perspectivism in chapter 3.

A plurality of views is inevitable when one considers the conjunction of conscience and the four traditional sources of ethics, the so-called Wesleyan Quadrilateral: Scripture, tradition, secular disciplines of knowledge, and human experience. Any given person can select, prioritize, interpret, and integrate these sources in different ways, leading to plural ways of defining human dignity with consequent plural norms for facilitating its attainment. These plural definitions and norms highlight the moral imperative of *Gaudium et Spes* to constantly be attuned to the signs of the times and to dialogue about these plural, partial truths. A woman at a third-story window in a skyscraper sees only what the third-story window allows her to see of the full panorama outside the window. If she were to go up to the twentieth floor or further up to the viewing platform on the roof, she would get an ever fuller view of what lies outside the building. So it is with dialogue about inevitably partial truths regarding human dignity and the norms that promote and do not frustrate its attainment.

Part 2 of *Gaudium et Spes* addresses "Some Questions of Special Urgency" and was shaped by the Zurich text, which had five appendices that were, in fact, five "signs of the time" (GS 4) in the latter half of the twentieth century. These appendices were: The Dignity of the Human Person, the Dignity of Marriage and Family, Culture and Its Promotion, Social and Economic Life (which included discussion of the poor), and the Solidarity between Peoples (which included questions of peace and war). Questions were raised about the authority of those appendices, which were answered in the finally approved *Gaudium et Spes* by being incorporated as five freestanding chapters in its part 2.

The first of those chapters dealt with the dignity of marriage and family. Up to that time, three principles summarized the traditional Catholic teaching on sexuality and marriage. The first was that, to be moral, any sexual act must be within the context of marriage. The second was that every act of sexual intercourse within marriage must be open to the procreation of new life. The third derived from the second, namely, that among the various ends of marriage, procreation was primary. The initial schema on marriage, "Chastity, Marriage, Family, and Virginity," prepared by the theological commission headed by Cardinal Ottaviani, prefect of the Holy Office and staffed largely by theologians from the Holy Office, focused heavily on each of these three principles. The schema, Ottaviani explained, set out "the objective order . . . which God himself willed in instituting marriage and Christ the Lord willed in raising it to the dignity of a sacrament. Only in this way can the modern errors that have spread everywhere be vanquished."[14]

---

[14] *Acta et Documenta Concilio Oecumenico Vaticano II Apparando (Praeparatoria)*, vol. 2, part 3 (Roma: Typis Polyglottis Vaticanis, 1968), 937.

The initial schema was not approved by the Central Coordinating Committee, though some elements of it were later incorporated into the chapter on marriage in *Gaudium et Spes*. Once real debate began, the neo-Augustinian classicists generally opposed the direction of the debate on the contents of the entire document—how it treated the topic of marriage and family was no exception. The neo-Augustinians thought the proposed texts did not state clearly enough what they took to be the unchangeable teaching of the Church and that the historically conscious neo-Thomists wanted to advance the Church's teaching on the basis of largely contemporary developments. It should be noted that the text— either in its developing or final form—made no mention of birth control because of an "elephant in the room": namely, John XXIII's and Paul VI's reservation of a decision on that issue to their Pontifical Birth Control Commission and themselves. This debate will be analyzed in detail in chapter 4 of this book.

In chapter 3, we examine what became part 2, chapter 2 of *Gaudium et Spes*: namely, "The Proper Development of Culture." In examining the document's ideas on culture, chapter 3 offers fundamental methodological consideration for doing Catholic theological ethics in the twenty-first century. The words of *Gaudium et Spes* on culture are perhaps more relevant than ever today, with the impact of globalization that highlights the fundamental interrelationship between human beings socially, politically, economically, and spiritually, as well as the various manifestations of this interrelatedness in and through culture. Humanity "can come to an authentic and full humanity only through culture" (GS 53), and human culture reveals the nature of humanity itself where "new roads to truth are opened" (GS 44). The Church must be in ongoing dialogue with culture to learn from it when it contributes to understanding human dignity and to critique it when it misunderstands this dignity.

We explore in chapter 5 *Gaudium et Spes*'s "Economic and Social Life," which focuses on the foundational call—grounded in Scripture and central to the vocation of every Christ-ian—to seek and promote human dignity and the common good with and for the poor and excluded, a theme that will be revisited in the words of Pope Francis. Historical accounts of Catholic social teaching often begin with Pope Leo XIII's *Rerum Novarum* (Of New Things) and end with Pope John Paul II's celebration of its hundredth anniversary in *Centesimus Annus* (The Hundredth Year) and include *Gaudium et Spes* as an important document in this period. The roots of this teaching, however, extend back to Sacred Scripture, the Old Testament and New Testament, and find a unique and profound expression in the life and words of Jesus. Scripture highlights that the biblical God, and the Christ whom God sent to reveal God's self, is a God of love and justice who in real historical time stands preferentially on the side of the poor and oppressed. All who would be truly Christ-ian and "perfect as your heavenly Father is perfect" (Matt 5:48) have no option but preferentially to do the same. Catholic social teaching, as it has come to be known, is the formulation and articulation of this foundational Gospel imperative, in dialogue with history, culture, and context. It takes on a special urgency in *Gaudium et Spes* and in the twenty-first century. The constitution notes, "If the demands of justice and equity are to be satisfied, vigorous efforts must be made . . . to remove as quickly as possible the immense inequalities which now exist" (GS 66). Pope Francis speaks out of the biblical tradition, the best of the Church tradition, and *Gaudium et Spes*, when he teaches that "alleviating the grave evil of poverty must be at the very heart of the Church's mission. It is neither optional nor secondary."[15]

Gaudium et Spes's chapters 4 and 5, "The Life of the Political Community" and "The Fostering of Peace and the Promotion of a Community of Nations," respectively, are treated in our chapter 6. The first part of the chapter investigates the interrelationship between Church and State and the proper role and function of each in realizing human dignity and the common good. It also investigates the active involvement of the laity and their distinct role and function, guided by conscience, in relation to Church and State. We suggest guidelines to navigate these different relationships in light of both *Gaudium et Spes* and recent Church documents on the political involvement of the lay faithful.

The second part of chapter 6 explores the methodological foundations of the just war tradition in light of the four sources of moral knowledge and traces the historical evolution in the Catholic just war tradition from focusing on just war criteria for when to go to war and how to conduct war to developing a strategy for peacebuilding. The shift from just war to peacebuilding reflects theological developments in response to *Gaudium et Spes*'s call "to undertake an evaluation of war with an entirely new attitude" (GS 80). An especially important evolution in the tradition is recognizing and explicitly articulating the causal relationship between poverty and violence. It is in recognizing this causal relationship that Catholic social teaching has much to offer in building a peaceful world in the twenty-first century by promoting human dignity and the common good through development and confronting poverty and those structures that perpetuate it.

---

[15] See Bishop Robert W. McElroy, "A Church for the Poor," *America* 209, no. 11 (October 21, 2013): 13.

This book celebrates the contributions of *Gaudium et Spes* as a fundamental gift of the Holy Spirit to the Church's evolving self-understanding as a pilgrim people of God. Let us continue as Church to recognize the Holy Spirit working in the Church to reform it and to enable it to more profoundly reflect God's unconditional love for all of humanity. In the words of Pope Francis, the Second Vatican Council "was a beautiful work of the Holy Spirit." Let us continue to reflect on how the Holy Spirit is communicating to us in and through the Second Vatican Council in general, and *Gaudium et Spes* in particular, in the twenty-first century. Let us also heed the warning of Pope Francis on quenching the Holy Spirit and the council's vision:

> We want to tame the Holy Spirit. And that is wrong. Because He is God, and He is the wind that comes and goes and you do not know where. He is the power of God, what gives us consolation and strength to move forward. But move forward! And this bothers you. Comfort is more beautiful.
>
> [It seems] we are all content [in the presence of the Holy Spirit]. It is not true. This temptation is still [present] today. Just one example: we think of the Council. The Council was a beautiful work of the Holy Spirit. Think of Pope John: he seemed a good pastor, and he was obedient to the Holy Spirit, and he did that. But after 50 years, have we done everything that the Holy Spirit said to us in the Council? In the continuity of the growth of the Church which was the Council?
>
> No, we celebrate this anniversary, we make a monument, but that does not bother us. We do not want to change. What is more: there are voices that want to go back. This is called being stubborn, this is called wanting to tame the Holy Spirit, this is called becoming fools and slow of heart.[16]

Let us not attempt to tame the Holy Spirit, but to continue to recognize, embrace, nurture and live the gift of the Holy Spirit and what the Spirit communicated, and continues to communicate, to us in the Second Vatican Council. Let us not attempt to quench that gift out of fear of where it might lead us as Church in the twenty-first century.

---

[16] "Pope Francis Emphasizes the Second Vatican Council Is the Work of the Holy Spirit," http://www.catholicculture.org/news/headlines/index.cfm?storyid=17610, accessed February 7, 2014.

Chapter One

Gaudium et Spes: The History

Historical Context

The great Roman orator Cicero once declared that those who do not understand their history remain children forever. Nineteen hundred years later, at the opening of the Second Vatican Council, one of the theologians who would exert a great influence on the council in general and on *Gaudium et Spes* in particular, the French Dominican Marie-Dominique Chenu, expressed a similar opinion. "Since Christianity draws its reality from history and not from some metaphysics, the theologian must have as his primary concern . . . to know this history and to train himself in it."[1] Chenu was one of several French theologians who popularized the theological movement called *ressourcement*, a return to the biblical and patristic sources. (Their Roman opponents derisively called it "the new theology.") In fact, Pope Pius XII's encyclical *Humani Generis* (1950) proscribed the new theology and all its proponents were removed from their teaching positions, only to see both themselves and their movement restored and become influential at the council.

The "return to the sources" marked a definitive methodological shift in Catholic theology from a primarily classicist to a primarily historically conscious worldview. The classicist worldview approaches reality as static, fixed, necessary, and universal. The method utilized and the norms taught within a classicist worldview are regarded as timeless, universal, and immutable. It was such a face that Catholicism offered to the world prior to the council, and it was such a face that provided a barrier to any real approach to an evolutionary modern world. By

---

[1] Marie-Dominique Chenu, *Une École de théologie: Le Saulchoir* (Paris: Cerf, 1985), 132. All translations from languages other than English throughout this chapter are the authors'.

contrast, the historically conscious worldview approaches reality as dynamic, evolving, changing, and particular. The method utilized and the norms taught within a historically conscious worldview are contingent, particular, and changeable. Joseph Komonchak has introduced a theological way of naming these two sides, namely, *neo-Augustinian* and *neo-Thomist*, respectively.[2] Neo-Augustinians see the world in a negative light; it is so steeped in sin that the best thing for the Church to do is to keep its distance from it and not be influenced by it. Neo-Augustinians are allergic to change. Neo-Thomists see the world, both external and internal, fashioned in history and, therefore, steeped in historicity. The world, again external and internal, is in a permanent state of evolution and change and, therefore, the truths, values, and meanings of the past are not necessarily the truths, values, and meanings of the present. Neo-Thomists are comfortable with change and pluralism.

It is common to describe these two sides as *conservative* and *liberal*, respectively, but we find these designations not only pejorative and false but also unhelpful. We shall describe them throughout as classicist neo-Augustinian and historically conscious neo-Thomist. These categories are not to be understood as so watertight that there can be no overlap between them so that, on a particular issue, a neo-Augustinian might act as a neo-Thomist, and vice versa. Such crossover did, in fact, occur with several prominent theologians who acted as neo-Thomists during the council and, largely disillusioned with what they saw as undue optimism toward the world in *Gaudium et Spes*, acted as neo-Augustinians after the council. The intellectual and theological battle between classicist neo-Augustinians and historically conscious neo-Thomists was an ongoing battle, as we shall see, from the council's very first to very last day.

Underlying the fierce battles over the various council documents was always the question of *change* under its softer Catholic word *development*. Development of doctrine, wrote American Jesuit John Courtney Murray, was "*the* issue under all the issues" at the council.[3] Nowhere (except perhaps the furious battle for a text on a Decree on Religious Freedom in which Murray was such an influential and historically conscious participant) was that more evident than in the long battle, first, to find

---

[2] Joseph A. Komonchak, "Augustine, Aquinas, or the Gospel *sine glossa?*" in *Unfinished Journey: The Church 40 Years after Vatican II; Essays for John Wilkins*, ed. Austin Ivereigh (New York: Continuum, 2005), 102–18.

[3] John Courtney Murray, "This Matter of Religious Freedom," *America* 112 (January 9, 1965): 43, emphasis original.

an accepted text for a document on the Church in the Modern World and then to have the finally accepted text approved. Nothing illustrates historical consciousness and change better than this latter document, with its development from Pius IX's condemnation of "that erroneous opinion . . . called by our predecessor Gregory XVI *madness*, namely, that freedom of conscience and worship is each man's personal right which ought to be proclaimed and asserted in every rightly constituted society"[4] to *Dignitatis Humanae*'s (Declaration on Religious Freedom) unadorned declaration that "This Vatican Synod declares that the human person has a right to religious freedom" (DH 2). We will note similar changes in *Gaudium et Spes* as we go along.

Pope John XXIII celebrated the opening Mass of the council on October 11, 1962, at which he outlined his reasons for summoning a council and his expectations for it. He acknowledged the political and economic difficulties of the times without naming anything specific. They were, however, well known. Europe had not long before been devastated by a war of unparalleled savagery and was still reeling from the discovery of the horrors of "the final solution" to the Jewish community in Nazi Germany. The world was traumatized by the destructive threat of the atom bomb dropped on Hiroshima and Nagasaki and by the multiplication of nuclear weapons that could eliminate all life on earth. The end of World War II had given way to a "cold war" between the Western allies and the Soviet Union which, six years before the opening of the council (1956), had brutally suppressed a popular uprising in Hungary. Shortly after the council opened, that cold war reached its moment of greatest anxiety in a standoff between the Soviet Union and the United States of America, the former seeking to install in Cuba nuclear missiles that could reach the United States, the latter vetoing such a move with a determined blockade.

In addition to living amid the very real threat of nuclear war, the council fathers came together as colonialism was coming to an end. This shift in geopolitical reality had profound political and ecclesiastical implications, as the major industrialized nations withdrew from their African and Asian colonies, leaving behind not only poor and sometimes chaotic nations but also missionary churches deprived of government support. The most notorious of these former colonies was Vietnam, which the

---

[4] Pius IX, *Quanta Cura*, in *The Papal Encyclicals 1740–1878*, ed. Claudia Carlen (Raleigh, NC: McGrath, 1981), 383.

French colonists left in 1954. After the French left, it was divided into a communist North Vietnam and South Vietnam, which in turn led to the Vietnam War, with the United States supporting the South against the North as a way to block the spread of communism. That war (1959–1975) was already well underway when the council opened.

Racism was rampant in the world in the first half of the twentieth century, and by the time of the council, problems related to systemic racial injustice were coming to a boil. Civil rights struggles against racism and political structures based on it were being waged both nonviolently and violently in the United States and in Sub-Saharan Africa.

There was also an important ecclesiastical context to the convening of the council. The First Vatican Council (1870) had been interrupted by the seizure of Rome by Italian troops in 1870, and its work had never been completed. Both Pius XI in the 1920s and Pius XII in the 1950s had considered calling a council to complete the unfinished business of Vatican I, but no council had ever been convoked. When John XXIII convoked a council, there were those, particularly classicist neo-Augustinians in the Roman Curia, who perceived its task as completing Vatican I's unfinished work. But there were also those, particularly among historically conscious neo-Thomist diocesan bishops and theologians in direct touch with the needs of their people, who perceived it as a challenge for reform, development, and change that would better equip the Church to both fulfill its mission of evangelization and assist the world in dealing with its multitude of problems. These two different perceptions coalesced into two different parties at the council. Their differences led to virulent debates in the council from the very first day, and those debates were very much in evidence in the creation of the Pastoral Constitution on the Church in the Modern World. Vatican I's definition of papal primacy and infallibility and Pope Pius X's condemnations of what he called "Modernism," which was essentially the emergence of historical consciousness in theological literature, weighed heavily on the Catholic Church prior to the Vatican Council and would continue to weigh heavily, though not definitively, on many of the discussions about the Church at the council.

In his speech opening the council, *Gaudet Mater Ecclesia*, Pope John acknowledged these problems in "the world," but he chose to place his focus more positively on "the marvelous progress of the discoveries of human genius," distancing himself from "those prophets of gloom, who are always forecasting disaster, as though the end of the world were at hand." Mother Church's role in the world requires her to deal with both right and wrong in the world and in the past she has condemned errors "with the greatest severity." Nowadays, however, she prefers "to make use of the medicine of mercy rather than of severity," showing herself to be "the loving mother of all, benign, patient, full of mercy and goodness toward the brethren who are separated from her." Clarification and penetration of doctrine, the pope said, was to be a prime purpose of the council, but this was to be done "through the methods of research and through the literary forms of modern thought. The substance of the ancient doctrine of the deposit of faith is one thing, and the way it is presented is another."[5]

Pope John's council was not to be a council of condemnation, though the Church was as opposed to error at the council as it was in the past. Instead, it was to be one of rediscovering and updating the essential substance of the Church's life. This call for updating, or in Italian *aggiornamento*, which became a kind of rallying word for the council, was a call to move away from the defensive choices the Church had made since the nineteenth-century days of Pope Pius IX to protect itself from the danger of contamination from the world. It specifically encouraged those who would introduce historical consciousness and a return to the historical sources into the council's discussions. Their efforts would eventually win the day in several important doctrinal debates. The Church, in John XXIII's vision, was part of the world and would share, as *Gaudium et Spes* would later declare, "the joys and the hopes, the griefs and anxieties of the men of this age, especially those who are poor or in any way afflicted" (GS 1).

History of the Text

On January 25, 1959, John XXIII announced he would convoke a council. The council opened on October 11, 1962. In the almost four-year interim between the announcement of the council and its opening, there was a ferment of preparatory activity. First, a letter was sent to all the bishops and pontifical universities of the Catholic world asking them for their suggestions for what should be treated at the council and exhorting them to "complete freedom and honesty."[6] The responses, as one would expect from 2,150 responders, were enormously varied. Many

---

[5] Citations of Pope John's speech are taken from Walter M. Abbott, ed., *The Documents of Vatican II* (New York: America Press, 1966), 710–19.

[6] See John W. O'Malley, "Vatican II: Did Anything Happen?" *Theological Studies* 67, no. 1 (March 2006): 3–33.

called for a clear reaffirmation of the Church's *status quo*; many called for the condemnation of modern evils inside and outside the Church, including a condemnation of atheistic communism; some, mostly from Western countries where the Catholic Church was already losing many members, called for Church reform, arguing that a reformed Church would be better able to confront the contemporary world; a few were truly adventuresome, calling for greater responsibility for laity in the Church and, a very few, mostly from non-Western countries, calling for the abrogation or, at least, modification, of priestly celibacy.

Second, the pope appointed ten commissions to sift these responses and to organize them into thematic documents to be debated and voted on at the council. Sixty seven such documents were prepared, most of them couched in condemnatory language far from the positive and reconciling approach enunciated by John in his opening speech. Though there was no document dealing with the Church in the modern world, there were four dealing with issues that would eventually be incorporated in altered forms into *Gaudium et Spes*: the Moral Order; Chastity, Marriage, Family, and Virginity; The Social Order; and the Community of Nations.

The text on the Moral Order, composed mainly by a subcommission of the Roman theologians Hürth, Gillon, and Liu, was classicist neo-Augustinian in structure, based on the prevailing Catholic teaching of an objective, absolute, and immutable moral order. A fourth, extremely well-respected, historically conscious, neo-Thomist moral theologian, the German Redemptorist Bernard Häring, was explicitly excluded from this small subcommission because the others judged him a disturbing element "foreign" to their work. Häring might have qualified as "theologically foreign" because in 1954 he had published a monumental three-volume work on moral theology, titled *The Law of Christ*, which had drawn both the approbation of many Catholic moral theologians and the negative attention of Roman authorities. This preconciliar disagreement between classicist neo-Augustinians and historically conscious neo-Thomists theologians serves as a paradigm for the disagreements that would occur throughout the length of the council itself.

The preparatory schema on Chastity, Marriage, Family, and Virginity underwent the same debates between the same protagonists. Again the classicist neo-Augustinian side won and the text that was sent to the bishops was a text that was a defense of an objective, absolute, and immutable moral order. Cardinal Ottaviani, the prefect of the Holy Office, who chaired the Doctrinal Commission that approved the final version of the schema, explained that the schema laid out the "objective order . . .

which God willed in instituting marriage and Christ the Lord willed in raising it to the dignity of a sacrament. Only in this way can the modern errors that have spread everywhere be vanquished." The most vicious of those errors are "those theories which subvert the right order of values and make the primary end of marriage inferior to the biological and personal values of the spouses, and proclaim that conjugal love itself is in the objective order the primary end."[7] The debate over the schema, in both the Doctrinal Commission and in the council itself when its content was being incorporated into *Gaudium et Spes*, centered around the questions of the hierarchy of the ends of marriage and birth control, specifically around the relative values of procreation, which the schema insisted was the primary end, and conjugal love, which it insisted was a secondary end. When we reach the final, approved text of *Gaudium et Spes*, we will see that the council fathers settled that debate by teaching that these two ends are both objective and equal.[8] Schemas for the Social Order and the Community of Nations were hurriedly prepared without much discussion, possibly a sign that Ottaviani's Doctrinal Commission did not consider them of much importance.

The decisive moment for Vatican II in general occurred in November, 1962. On November 14, the council took up the discussion of the prepared schema *De Fontibus Revelationis* (On the Sources of Revelation). On the eve of that discussion, November 13, the German Jesuit Otto Semmelroth wrote in his diary: "Tomorrow the discussion of the schema *De Fontibus Revelationis* begins. The battles will be bitter."[9] As an expert on the doctrinal commission, he knew firsthand that the battles over the schemata had already been bitter in that preparatory commission, and the same sides would continue the battles in the council itself. The sides were those that had already emerged during the preparatory phase, the Roman classicist neo-Augustinian theologians who had prepared the schemas for discussion, and the historically conscious neo-Thomist bishops and their theologians who were critical of the prepared schemata. Debate between the two camps quickly emerged during the early stage of the council, but a decisive shift occurred on November 19–20. The

---

[7] *Acta et Documenta Concilio Oecumenico Vaticano II Apparando (Praeparatoria)*, vol. 2, part 3 (Roma: Typis Polyglottis Vaticanis, 1968), 937, 910, n. 16; and 917, n. 50.

[8] Though we will draw attention as needed to these marital debates throughout this essay, we will defer any analysis of them to the specific chapter on marriage later in this book.

[9] Otto Semmelroth, Unpublished *Diary* (Munich: Archiv der Deutschen Gesellschaft).

debate over the prepared schema on the Sources of Revelation and on other documents, including a document on the Church in the modern world as it slowly and painfully came to birth, was a debate between neo-Augustinians and neo-Thomists. On November 19, a question was put to all the council fathers: "should the discussion [of the Sources of Revelation] be interrupted?" An explanation was given that "interrupted" meant "redoing the schema."

The vote, an overwhelming 1,368 for interruption and 822 for continuing the debate, created major confusion and the first crisis in the council, for the regulations required a two-thirds vote (1,473) of the 2,209 votes cast to be binding and for the schema to be returned for redoing. For want of 105 votes, a trifling 4.5 percent of the votes cast, Pope John's council was faced with its first crisis, which he himself moved quickly to resolve. On November 20, he sent a note to the presidents of the council stating that, although the vote did not meet the requirement of the regulations for interruption of the debate, he was yielding to the wishes of the many, withdrawing the schema from discussion, and referring it to a new Mixed Commission to emend it and make it more pastorally suitable.

In December 1962, the Schema on the Church, considered to be the most important document of the council, suffered the same fate. It was criticized as being too clerical, too scholastic, and not sufficiently biblical and pastoral, and the debate on it was interrupted without a vote being taken. The vote of November 19 demonstrated a majority of council fathers were disposed to take the Catholic Church in a new direction. John XXIII's solution to the impending crisis on November 20 opened up the way for a comprehensive revision of the preparatory work. By the closing of the first session on December 8, 1962, all seventy of the prepared schemata had been rejected as inadequate and incapable of being improved to the satisfaction of the majority, and directions had been marked out for a new beginning. Included in that new beginning was a document on the Church in the modern world.

There is some debate as to where, and by whom, *Gaudium et Spes* was conceived. There was no such document among the preparatory schemata, though there were, as already noted, some suggestions scattered throughout several schemata. What is clear is that no council document went through such a slow, tortuous, and complex development as the document on the Church in the modern world, a development highlighted by its original anonymous and merely numerical title, Schema XVII. It could be argued that Schema XVII was conceived in the Secretariat for the Apostolate of the Laity, which called attention to some coincidences in the preparatory schemata "On the Moral Order" and "On the Apostolate of the Laity" and proposed a new schema combining ideas from both, outlining the action of the Church in the modern world. There were two chapters in the schema "On the Moral Order," the coordinating commission was told, that could be reworked as part of a document on the Church in the modern world, and there was a long chapter in the schema "On the Apostolate of the Laity" on the activity of the laity that could be also be reworked as part of the proposed new schema. There was also a remote influence on the schema that is worthy of mention, namely, Pope John XXIII's encyclical *Mater et Magistra* (Mother and Teacher), promulgated in May 1961. *Mater et Magistra* introduced a new method for papal encyclicals, an inductive method that started from concrete current world issues rather than the traditional deductive method that started from abstract theological principles. The schema that would be developed on the Church in the modern world would replicate such an inductive method and echo some of the social and economic issues treated in *Mater et Magistra*.

At the end of November 1962, Pope John asked Cardinal Suenens of Malines, Belgium, to prepare a new program for the council, which was to include a study of the relations between the Church and the modern world. On December 4, 1962, Suenens unveiled a plan to the council that proposed that the doctrine of the Church be considered from two points of view: *ad intra* or internally, which demands a study of the nature of the Church, and *ad extra* or externally, which demands a study of the Church's mission to preach the Gospel to all nations. The *ad intra* study yielded *Lumen Gentium*, the Dogmatic Constitution on the Church. The *ad extra* study gave rise to *Gaudium et Spes*, the Pastoral Constitution on the Church in the Modern World. The *ad extra* study was to include the great issues of the times that John XXIII had labeled the "signs of the times." Those issues included the dignity of the human person and human life, social justice, marriage and family, the plight of the poor worldwide, and questions of war and peace. This proposal met with the approval of the council and it was greeted with such prolonged applause that the president for the day, Cardinal Caggiano of Buenos Aires, had to plead for the applause to end.

Was *Gaudium et Spes*, then, conceived originally by Cardinal Suenens, or was it conceived by the Commission on the Apostolate of the Laity? As we proceed, we hope to show that, whatever its conception, both Suenens and the Commission had important roles to play in its coming to birth. We should add here an important event that occurred in April of 1963 which had an important influence on Schema XVII, namely, the publication of John XXIII's encyclical *Pacem in Terris* (Peace on Earth), an exhortation to peace between all nations based on truth, justice, charity, and freedom. That encyclical aroused great interest in international political circles and among the editors of Schema XVII. It would have a lasting effect on the writing of the schema.

The new coordinating committee appointed by John XXIII met in January of 1963 and, after taking up and modifying Suenens's plan, decided to set up a Mixed Commission to develop a document on the Church in the world of today. This Mixed Commission, which had copresidents in Bishop Guano of Livorno and Archbishop Garrone of Toulouse and drew members from the Commission on the Apostolate of the Laity and the doctrinal commission, met daily in Rome between May 20 and 25, 1963. They settled on a not-very-clear schema of six chapters with essentially two titles, one heading the entire document, "On the Presence and Action of the Church in the Modern World," and one heading the first chapter, "On the Principles and Actions of the Church to Promote the Good of Society." This schema became known as "the Roman Schema." The Mixed Commission agreed to divide its task among six subcommissions which would each study and edit one of the chapters, which were as follows: the Vocation of Humans according to God; the Human Person in Society; Marriage, Family, and the Demographic Problem; on Rightly Promoting the Progress of Culture; the Economic Order and Social Justice; the Community of Nations and Peace. This proposed document of the Mixed Commission, known simply as Schema XVII, thanks to its numerical place in the schemata being reworked for debate at the second session of the council, already contained many ideas that, after a tortuous development, would be finally approved in *Gaudium et Spes*.

One very clear statement that survived was a statement about the immorality of the use of nuclear weapons which so threatened the world in the 1960s. "The use of arms with effects that are incalculable and cannot be rationally tempered by men exceeds just proportion and, therefore, cannot be held to be moral." This judgment turned out to be one of the most controverted in the debates on *Gaudium et Spes* but it did survive in the approved document, albeit somewhat altered (GS 80–81).

Though this Roman Schema XVII, which was largely sociological in nature, would provide the basis for further discussion, it did not receive majority support. It was criticized for lack of cohesion and a clear theological vision of the relationship between the Church and the world, between nature and grace. There continued to be contentious debate on the third chapter on marriage which still asserted that the primary end of marriage was the procreation and education of children. That particular debate would continue until the very last public session of the council on December 7, 1965, when it was settled by the declaration that procreation and the love of the spouses were equal ends. The council's new coordinating commission considered the Roman schema at the beginning of July, rejected it as unsuitable, and requested that Cardinal Suenens of Malines produce a new schema that would be more theological and more clear. He transmitted the task to a group of theologians at the Catholic University of Louvain, situated within his diocese in Belgium, and added to the Louvain group three theologians who had distinguished themselves as theological experts during the first session: the German Jesuit Karl Rahner, the French Dominican Yves Congar, and the Italian editor of the Vatican newspaper, *Osservatore Romano*, Giuseppe Tucci. This group undertook their work under a new pope. John XXIII died on June 3, 1963, and Pope Paul VI was elected on June 21, 1963, immediately proclaiming his intention to continue the council which he wanted, he said, to throw out a bridge to the contemporary world.

Malines and Zurich Schemas

The Malines group took the new pope's intention to heart and produced a document titled "On the Active Presence of the Church in the Building Up of the World." It was divided into three parts: On the Proper Mission of the Church, On Building the World, and On the Service of the Church to the World. Part 1 was addressed exclusively to Christians, parts 2 and 3 to all men and women. Given its place of origin, this document came to be known as "the Malines Schema." Congar, who was probably the best prepared of any for a debate on the presence and action of the Church in the world, since he had published several books on the topic, argued that, to be heard by non-Christians, the schema needed to be presented as a theology of history. Rahner argued to the contrary that such an approach risked undervaluing some important theological problems, particularly those of the relationship between nature and grace and of the presence of sin in the world, on which he had written extensively. It would not do, he urged, to present an overly optimistic picture of "the world." He continued to make the same arguments all through the long gestation of *Gaudium et Spes*, and when the final document was approved and promulgated in 1965, he was still critical of it precisely because he judged that it was overly optimistic toward the world and did not give an in-depth explanation of the relationship between nature and grace and the presence of sin in the world. When the Malines document was shared with the coordinating commission and the bishops in September 1963, it was severely criticized, among other things for being too theological. The coordinating commission distanced itself from both it and from the Roman Schema, and urged the continuation of the search for an adequate Schema XVII.

A German group submitted a proposal suggesting that the ecclesiological structure of the Malines Schema be retained but elaborated with more concrete treatment of the more pressing problems of the modern world. A key theme must continue to be the active presence of the Church in the construction of a better world. A French group submitted a schema under the title "Towards Schema XVII—On the Active Presence of a Servant Church of the Lord among Men of Good Will." This schema had much in common with a "Church of the poor" movement that had emerged at the end of the first session and with the book recently published by Congar under the title *Toward a Poor and Servant Church.*[10] It would have a certain influence as Schema XVII wended its way toward final approval, especially in the consideration of what it called the two great evils of the time, hunger and war. Faced with these evils, the Church absolutely had to place itself at the service of the needs of the world.

At the end of January 1964, the subcommission officially appointed to prepare a new document unveiled a totally new one. It showed traces of the French proposal but had an entirely new structure. It was titled "The Active Participation of the Church in the Construction of the World," and had four chapters: first, an anthropological description of the condition of humankind; second, principles for the presence of the Church in the world; third, the actions of Christians in the world; fourth, the more urgent problems of the modern world. Of note is the opening of this document in which there were echoes of a passage from the council's message to the world in October 1962. "The joys and the sorrows, the hopes and the anxieties of the men of today, especially of the poor and those who suffer, are also the joys and the sorrows, the hopes and anxieties of this Assembly." This opening encapsulated the tone of the entire document and would be retained, lightly edited, to become almost two years later the opening of the finally approved *Gaudium et Spes.* This text was distributed to the members and consultors of the Coordinating

---

[10] Yves Congar, *Pour une église pauvre et servante* (Paris: Cerf, 1963).

Commission in time for a meeting of the Commission in Zurich at the beginning of February 1964. Here the text, introduced and explained by Bernard Häring and the Dominican Raimondo Sigmund, who had been its principal editor, received much criticism. But in the end, it received substantial approval. The criticisms were largely those that Rahner had continued to make, namely, that the text was so pastoral and instructional that it had an insufficient theological foundation, and it was so optimistic about the world that it obscured the reality of evil, sin, injustice, and poverty. Nevertheless the schema, which became known as the Zurich Schema or the Häring Schema, was accepted as a basis for all further discussion of the document on the Church in the modern world.

The Zurich text sought a *via media* between the two extremes of hyper-naturalism and hyper-supernaturalism. The first was rampant in the world of the 1960s, especially in its extreme form of atheism which en-closed men within the material world and taught that there was nothing beyond that world. The second had led over the years to contempt of the world, an attitude that held that any positive valuation of human and worldly realities was a betrayal of the human's eternal vocation. The Zurich text did not use the words *materialism*, *atheism*, or *supernaturalism* so as not to raise barriers to the dialogue it was proposing as a key to the Church's relationship with the modern world. But it did propose a double vocation for humankind. Women and men are called to the king-dom of God, but they are called also to be concerned with worldly affairs in which there are many values open to the kingdom of God: values such as solidarity, justice, love, marriage and family, culture, arts and sciences.

The schema sought both to underline the duty of Christians to be involved in the world and to bring to it Christian principles and explain that this involvement in the world in no way detracted from the vocation to the kingdom of God. The kingdom, in fact, was to be found in the first instance in this world before being found definitively in the next. The schema was now in four chapters: the Integral Vocation of the Human Person, the Church in the Service of God and Humankind, the Conduct of Christians in the World, and the Chief Responsibilities of Christians Today. Attached were five Appendices: the Dignity of the Human Person, the Dignity of Marriage and Family, Culture and its Promotion, Social and Economic Life, and the Solidarity between Peoples, which included questions about war and peace. At the first assembly of the Third Ses-sion of the council on October 1, 1964, Archbishop Marcel Lefebvre, Superior General of the Spiritans, later to lead a schism from the Catholic Church over the council, raised a question about the authority of these

Appendices: were they official or merely private? He was told that they were more than private and that the extent of their authority would be clarified later. They were later clarified by being embraced into *Gaudium et Spes* as its part 2.

The schema was discussed at a plenary meeting of the Mixed Commission in March and again in June 1964. There was continued criticism, especially in the June meeting over what was said about marriage. Cardinal Ottaviani and the Roman Jesuit theologians, Tromp and Hürth, attacked Häring, accusing him of what they called "Häringismus,"[11] something to be understood as just a little short of heresy. Congar noted in his diary that "This is the great concerted offensive: Franic, Lio, Tromp—in short, the Holy Office."[12] The coordinating commission examined the text on June 26 and, because the order for discussion of the schemas to be considered was changed, at this meeting Schema XVII became Schema XIII. So it would remain in the eighteen months until its final approval as *Gaudium et Spes*. In spite of continuing criticism that the schema was too weak and still not sufficiently theological, it eventually made its way to discussion during the council itself in the third session in the fall of 1964.

In this third session, the council fathers had before them a succession of schemas related to the world external to the Church—religious liberty, ecumenism, non-Christian religions, and Judaism—but Schema XIII had raised the most excitement and expectation, for it dealt with questions concretely relating to the women and men of the day. It was in this context that it was introduced for discussion on October 20, 1964, which continued for some three weeks. Ottaviani, president of the Doctrinal Commission, had already sent to the secretariat of the council a memo in which he distanced himself from the schema, asserting that it "had been worked out, prepared, and arranged by the Commission for the Lay Apostolate and the responsibility of the Doctrinal Commission had only been to see that it contained nothing contrary to right doctrine."[13]

There were many contrasting, sometimes contradictory, criticisms of the schema. It was too theological; it was not theological enough; it was too naturalist; it was too supernaturalist. Again Häring was attacked, this

---

[11] See Giovanni Turbanti, *Un concilio per un mondo moderno: La redazione della costitutione pastorale "Gaudium et spes" del Vaticano II* (Bologna: Mulino, 2000), 362.

[12] Yves Congar, *My Journal of the Council* (Collegeville, MN: Liturgical Press, 2012), 552.

[13] *Acta Synodalia Sacrosancti Concilii Vaticani II*, III/5 (Roma: Typis Polyglottis Vaticanis, 1970), 425.

time by Cardinal Heenan of Westminster, who proclaimed (paraphrasing Virgil's "I fear Greeks bearing gifts"), "I fear experts bearing Appendices!" Heenan's concern was largely with the section on marriage, about which he had tussled with Häring in the English press earlier in the spring of the year, though he did say that the schema as a whole was unworthy of an ecumenical council and that the redactional committee had failed everyone. A powerful neo-Augustinian, Cardinal Ruffini of Palermo, agreed, charging that the schema was full of doctrinal errors and recommending that it be rejected and reorganized along the lines of the great social encyclicals of Leo XIII, Pius XII, John XXIII, and Paul VI. Many, especially from the Third World, wanted a greater attention to poverty. Some wanted a greater openness to the contemporary sciences. Bishop Spülbeck of Meissen in Germany declared that, since the Galileo case, the Church had been perceived as inimical to science and should now encourage more science, especially Catholic science. There were continuing tensions between the neo-Augustinians and the neo-Thomists, which the Dutch Dominican Edward Schillebeeckx, later summed up as tensions "between the recognition of truth that is historical and mobile [historical consciousness] and truth that is theoretical and static [classicist consciousness]."[14]

In spite of these criticisms, the text was generally appreciated and passed on as the basis for further discussion. On November 16, 1964, just a week after the debate in the council had ended, the Mixed Commission met to review the bishops' suggestions for improvement and to plan for its task of editing and emending. Häring offered his resignation as chair of the subcommission for the ongoing editing of Schema XIII. Häring had proved too intransigent in his dealings with both the subcommission and Cardinal Ottaviani's Doctrinal Commission, and was replaced by Father Pierre Haubtmann, the National Assistant of French Catholic Action. It was Haubtmann who would organize the transition of Schema XIII into *Gaudium et Spes*.

Ariccia Schema

Haubtmann began his work as chair of the editing subcommission by seeking to enlarge the number of theologians on the commission. He was advised by Bishop Guano, cochair of the subcommission and a

---

[14] Edward Schillebeeckx, "The Third Session of Vatican II," *Documentation Catholique* (Paris), n. 172 A.

consistent proponent of the development of Schema XIII, that he should include the French Jesuit Jean Danielou, Congar, and, given the consistent German opposition to the text, Rahner and Semmelroth. Guano also recommended Pietro Pavan, Professor at the Lateran University in Rome and a respected authority on the social teaching of the Church, who was acknowledged as one of the principal architects of John XXIII's encyclicals, *Mater et Magistra* and *Pacem in Terris*. Häring advised him to also include Joseph Ratzinger (later Pope Benedict XVI), who was the theologian of Cardinal Frings of Cologne and had influence with the German bishops. This core group would work assiduously on emending the text and would eventually bring it to completion. Throughout December 1964 and January 1965, the editing subcommission considered, mostly via an exchange of letters, the text that was discussed in council in 1964, the criticisms of it by the bishops, the many suggestions that came flooding in, and a proposal from a group working on the "signs of the times." This latter proposal would have a significant influence on the first chapter of the text the subcommission put together. This text had four chapters: first, a general introduction; second, a general look at the situation of the modern world; third, a cosmology of man in the universe; fourth, an anthropology of man in society. This text was ready to be presented to a major meeting at Ariccia, southeast of Rome.

The Ariccia meeting took place in the week of January 31 through February 6, 1965, and brought together eighty-seven persons, including thirty-five theologians and seventeen lay experts. Compared to the Zurich meeting of the previous year, where only seventeen persons had been in attendance, Ariccia was a full-scale convention that was to prove decisive for the structure and content of, first, Schema XIII and, eventually, *Gaudium et Spes*. Though there were some doubts when the meeting realized that Haubtmann's text was a substantially reorganized one (not just an edited version of the one discussed in council in 1964), there was still a favorable acceptance of it. After he read it, Congar noted in his diary: "In my view, this text is clearly better than the Zurich-Häring one. It has found the right tone, and that is half the battle. It is a text that the people will be able to read; it brings in doctrine (not enough perhaps and not sufficiently) within the context of human realities. It is more theological."[15] On February 1, on behalf of the Polish bishops, the bishop of Cracow, Karol Wojtyla (later Pope John Paul II), introduced a text to

---

[15] Yves Congar, *My Journal*, February 1, 1965, 710.

replace both the Zurich and the Haubtmann texts, but this text, which included a condemnation of communism, never gained much traction, though Wojtyla himself made a great impression.[16] He was assigned along with Congar, Grillmeier, and Semmelroth to elaborate an as yet unwritten chapter on the salvific meaning of the Church in the modern world, and right up to the end of the council on December 8, 1965, he would keep the issues of communism and atheism alive.

The text approved at Ariccia retained some elements from the Zurich text accepted by the fathers in council in 1964, modified others according to the votes of that debate, and added entirely new elements to enrich the text. Among the elements retained from Zurich was an inductive approach to a Christian anthropology, one constructed from a consideration of what human beings concretely do. This approach brought to light the many problems humans face in the modern world, and consideration of those problems, in turn, brought to light possible solutions to them. Another remnant of Zurich was the five appendices which were redone and inserted into the text as chapters in its second part as "Some Problems of Special Urgency." Thus was Lefebvre's question about the authority of the appendices finally answered. Strongly debated at Ariccia was the question of contraception but, in deference to the pontifical commission which John XXIII had set up and Paul VI had enlarged to study the question, no resolution was offered. The Ariccia text did say that the actions "with which the spouses united themselves intimately are *per se* noble and worthy and, when expressed in a truly human manner, signify and promote reciprocal self-giving." This judgment made its way, lightly edited, into the chapter on marriage in *Gaudium et Spes* (GS 49). When it came to the discussion of the chapter on peace, the participants did not hide the fact that they had diverse and often contradictory advice from the third session of the council, particularly on the question of war. They contented themselves with a condemnation of modern warfare and dropped any judgment of the morality of either the possession or the use of modern arms, particularly nuclear arms. This reticence was replicated in *Gaudium et Spes* (GS 79–80).

The participants left Ariccia still uncertain as to which direction the final schema should take. They were sure that, for all its disorganization

---

[16] Congar notes in his diary on February 2, 1965, that Wojtyla, the future Pope John Paul II, "made a very great impression. His personality is imposing. A power radiates from it, an attraction, a certain prophetic force that is very calm, but incontestable." *My Journal*, 714.

and uncertainty, this schema was the best basis they had for further positive development. Bishop Guano insisted that there were four general perspectives that ought not to be lost: a fundamental optimism founded in belief in and open to the movement of the Holy Spirit; the reality of women and men and their real problems in the world which were leading them away from the Church; the need for the text to be pastoral, and not a treatise on theology; and the issue of the presence of Christians in the world as a leaven or, as *Lumen Gentium* had already said and *Gaudium et Spes* would finally say, as a sacrament (LG 1, 9, 48; GS 42). The final editing of the text was done in Paris by Haubtmann alone, who sent the edited text out chapter by chapter for consideration by the other editors. Congar noted in his diary for February 20 that he ran into Haubtmann in Rome. "I saw Haubtmann. He is redoing the text in French; Philips will put it into Latin . . . Haubtmann is rewriting everything. So, in the main, the time spent at Ariccia and at the Vatican has been largely wasted. It seemed to me (and I told him so) that the drafting team—that is to say, in practice himself—is taking a good deal of liberty with a text that had been discussed and accepted by the subcommission and the commission."[17]

The Mixed Commission, which had originally established the editorial subcommission, considered the Ariccia text at its meeting in Rome at the beginning of April 1965. Due to Haubtmann's sustained personal editing, the text was now so new that no one at the meeting, including those who had been part of the Ariccia consultation, knew it in its entirety. There was great expectation about the schema, not only in the commission, but also in the world outside the council, for Schema XIII would be one of the most important schemas discussed in the fourth session. The major discussion centered on atheism in response to various requests, including one again from Wojtyla, for an explicit condemnation of Marxism and communism. The discussion of the second part, the original Zurich appendices, was constrained by a request from Pope Paul VI that the commission not discuss the topic of birth control, an issue which he had restricted to his pontifical commission. There were criticisms about the overevaluation of spousal love in marriage, about the nonprioritization of procreation among the ends of marriage, that the schema should speak more of forging peace rather than condemning war, and that the notion of culture was exclusively limited to Western culture.

---

[17] Congar, *My Journal*, February 20, 1965, 729.

On May 11, the schema was presented to the coordinating commission by Cardinal Suenens. That Commission's remit was only to consider whether the schema should be sent to the fathers for discussion at the council's fourth session, but there was some discussion about its title, whether it merited the title of *Constitution* since this suggested a doctrinal clarity and authority that the present text did not have. That debate was unresolved and the schema was again accepted and forwarded to Pope Paul VI, who would have the final decision on its suitability to be sent to the council for debate. Paul decided on May 28 that the text could be sent to the fathers. Four years of work on a text on the Church in the modern world was almost at an end. There remained only the debate in council, which began on September 21, 1965, and the final editing which followed the further suggestions of the fathers.

Before we consider the final conciliar debate on Schema XIII, we should mention Paul VI's consistent support for a document on the Church in the modern world. He never interfered directly, as he did in November 1963 with *Lumen Gentium*, though late in November 1965, when the subcommission was doing its final editing on Schema XIII, he did submit some suggestions that he later clarified were to be treated as a bishop's suggestions and not papal orders, but he was always supportive. In his homily at the Mass of his consecration as pope, he declared he wanted the council to be a bridge to the modern world. In his speech opening the second session of the council, he laid out four objectives for the council: a complete and profound doctrine of the Church; a reform of the Church itself; a broadening of ecumenism; and a dialogue between the Church and the world. Dialogue, he argued, is the key for relating to the present age.[18] The following year, his programmatic encyclical, *Ecclesiam Suam*, developed the notion of dialogue between the Church and the modern world. His journey to Israel in January and his meeting with Patriarch Athenagoras of Constantinople concretized the importance of dialogue in his eyes. On February 16, Haubtmann was summoned to an audience with the pope, who insisted that he wanted a pastoral document, one that could be understood in depth, though he commented that we might not always know how to respond to the questions of the modern world. The pope expressed his satisfaction both with the experts who had worked on the text and with the text they had produced, and he used his influence to bring together the critics and the editors of the

---

[18] See *Acta Synodalia*, II/1, 195.

Ariccia document so that they could dialogue about their differences. It is probably too strong to claim that *Gaudium et Spes* would not have happened without Paul VI, but it is not too strong to claim that he was a strong supporter during the several years of its gestation.

Conciliar Discussion of Schema XIII

On his way to Rome for the fourth session of the council, Congar met up with Bishop Elchinger, the auxiliary bishop of Strasbourg, and notes that Elchinger's impressions of the schema he had received were "excessively severe."[19] The reaction of the German bishops, fueled by Rahner's continuing opposition to the edited schema, was also severe. Cardinal Döpfner had asked Rahner to prepare some observations on the schema, and Rahner had prepared a document that repeated the objections he had expressed all along: the text did not have a sufficiently theological basis, it did not take sufficient account of the supernatural elevation of all creation toward union with God or of the theological relationship between the order of creation and the order of redemption, it lacked a profound sense of sin and its effects in the world, and it did not elaborate an adequate Christian anthropology—these were topics Rahner had been writing on for some thirty years. He suggested there were two possible solutions to the schema's problems: first, the council could abstain from voting on it and assign it to a postconciliar commission which could further develop it in a calmer atmosphere; second, the council could vote on the schema and transmit it to the world as an initial step toward a more mature dialogue between the Church and the world.[20] Rahner's objections became the objections of the German episcopate and, right up until *Gaudium et Spes* was approved, they held fast to two points: the text was so imperfect that it was not a good starting point for dialogue between Church and world, and it should be presented as a letter from the Church to the world and not as a constitution.

The extent of the negative reaction to Schema XIII took its editors by surprise. They had worked on the assumption that, in their editing of the document, they were responding to the suggestions of the fathers from the debate in the third session, but the situation had changed. Since that debate, the Dogmatic Constitution on the Church had been promulgated

<hr>

[19] *My Journal*, September 13, 1965.

[20] Karl Rahner, *Anmerkungen zum schema De ecclesia in mundo huius temporis*, 4, in der Fassung vom 28.5.65. See also Turbanti, *Un concilio per un mondo moderno*, 386–90.

at the end of the third session, and many thought that, at least, some of the teaching in *Lumen Gentium* about God's saving interventions in human life should be repeated again in the Pastoral Constitution on the Church in the Modern World. The editors' intent had been to construct an inductive Christian anthropology, to begin with the consideration of natural truths and from there to arrive at supernatural truth to show, in the traditional Catholic formulation, how grace builds on nature. This intent was apparently not well communicated to the bishops and there were many who reproached the text with what they called *naturalism*. Haubtmann insisted on the pastoral style of the text, something entirely new in a conciliar document, and that it should be read as such. It should also be read in *Lumen Gentium*'s preferred model of Church, the people of God, (LG 9–17), rather than in the traditional Vatican I model of Church as hierarchical institution.

There was no great surprise when the Italians, Cardinals Ruffini of Palermo and Siri of Genoa, made the complaint of naturalism. These two had been consistently on the minority, neo-Augustinian side of the council. When two of the leaders of the neo-Thomist majority, however, the German cardinals Döpfner of Munich and Frings of Cologne, speaking for the German-speaking episcopate, made the same complaint, there was serious doubt whether Schema XIII could even survive. Frings, in fact, asked for a radical revision of the text, which would have been very difficult in the few weeks remaining before the end of the council. If that were not possible, the Germans also suggested, then any approved text should not carry the title of *Constitution* but should be simply a *Letter* from the council, which could then be reworked and made more theologically precise after the council.

The text had its supporters too. Cardinal König of Vienna argued that there was no point including in this text what was already taught in *Lumen Gentium*, which Paul VI had declared the master text of Vatican II, in the light of which all of its other texts are to be read. Cardinal Shehan of Baltimore congratulated the Ariccia editors for not having separated the natural and the supernatural orders, for these two orders together make up human life in the world. The outcome of that debate and the final blending of the natural and supernatural can be read in *Gaudium et Spes*, n. 40. "The Church has a saving and an eschatological purpose which can be fully attained only in the future world. But she is already present in this world, and is composed of men [and women], that is, of members of the earthly city who have a call to form the family of God's children during the present history of the human race, and to keep increasing it until the Lord returns." As it pursues "the saving purpose which is proper to it, the Church not only communicates divine life to men [and women] but in some way casts the reflected light of that life over the entire earth." The mission of the Church and *Lumen Gentium*'s teaching that a "secular quality is proper and special to lay persons" (LG 31) were saved. So too was John Paul II's later definition of laity: "disciples and followers of Christ, members of the Church who are present and active in the world's heart so as to *administer temporal realities and order them toward God's reign.*"[21]

A second criticism of the Ariccia text was that it was overly optimistic about the affairs of the world and did not give sufficient place to the notion of sin. It did not highlight two ancient Catholic teachings: first, that sanctification and salvation are always graces from God, though to be saved women and men must cooperate with those gifts;[22] second, that humans and the world in which they live and work out their salvation are both in a *fallen* state. They have need of grace and that ought to be stated. German criticism was again to the fore. On September 21, Cardinal Jaeger of Paderborn declared: "We must avoid all unrealistic optimism that forgets the ambiguities and dangers of progress. The scripture, above all Saint John, witness to the permanent conflict between the reign of Christ and the reign of Satan which continues throughout history and becomes ever more acute with time . . . The schema ought to mention it briefly." Döpfner of Munich followed up the following day: "the consequences of sin are not sufficiently put into evidence."

Though the criticisms that the proposed schema ignored the reality of sin were actually unfounded—for Ariccia's Schema XIII spoke often about sin and its effects in the world—to respond to the criticisms many hasty modifications were made to it. We can read a very clear one in *Gaudium et Spes*'s "Introductory Statement on the Situation of Men in the Modern World." "As a weak and sinful being, he often does what he would not and fails to do what he would [Rom 7:14]. Hence, he suffers from internal divisions, and from these flow so many and such great discords in society" (GS 10). And in the introduction to part 1, "The

---

[21] John Paul II, "Communion, Participation, Evangelization," *Origins* 10 (July, 31, 1980): 135, emphasis added. He repeated this idea of a Church "in the heart of the world" in an address to the bishops of Scotland in October 1992. See "Specialis Filia Romanae Ecclesiae," *Catholic International* 4 (1993): 5.

[22] Henry Denzinger and Adolf Schönmetzer, *Enchiridion Symbolorum* (Herder: Freiburg, 1965), n. 396–7.

Church and Man's Calling" (GS 11), we can read about the goodness of human values which are from God, but "they are often wrenched from their rightful function by the taint [sin] in man's heart, and hence stand in need of purification." If one reads *Gaudium et Spes* carefully, one can have no doubt that the pessimism embedded in the criticism did not carry the day. Ariccia's optimism won out in the end.

Two issues dominated the discussion of Schema XIII in the council itself: the question of a condemnation of atheistic communism and the question of marriage. Communism had been condemned in the schema Wojtyla presented at Ariccia, but that approach had not gained much acceptance. The Ariccia document refrained from explicitly condemning communism because, the editors judged, such a condemnation would end any possibility of dialogue. But Wojtyla and the continuing discussion both inside and outside the council kept the question alive. Some bishops took the political route of gathering petitions for a condemnation, but the Mixed Commission resisted, and eventually, so did the council.

The debate on marriage was extended and sometimes intemperate. Those classicist neo-Augustinians who had written the preparatory document on "Chastity, Marriage, Family, and Virginity," which had been roundly rejected by the coordinating committee prior to the first session, continued to press their case. They were, in general, a group associated with the Holy Office and its president, Cardinal Ottaviani, who when presenting his preparatory schema had explained that it laid out the "objective order . . . which God himself willed in instituting marriage and Christ the Lord willed in raising it to the dignity of a sacrament. Only in this way can the modern errors which have spread everywhere be vanquished."[23] The cornerstone of that document and of the debate in the final session of the council was the teaching on the ends of marriage, whether procreation was, indeed, as had been traditionally taught, the primary end, and the mutual love of the spouses a mere secondary end. The Ariccia document chose a middle course, presenting the two ends as equal. This raised serious opposition from the theologians of the Holy Office, who argued such a position amounted to abandoning the established and immutable teaching of the Church. The finally-approved *Gaudium et Spes* rejected the criticisms of this minority and approved

---

[23] *Acta et Documenta Concilio Oecumenico Vaticano II Apparando (Praeparatoria)*, vol. 2, part 3 (Roma: Typis Polyglottis Vaticanis, 1968), 937.

the Ariccia formulation (GS 48–50). This debate and its outcome will be considered in detail in the essay on marriage later in this book.

The multiple criticisms in council might lead one to conclude that there were serious divisions among the bishops about the teaching of relationship of the Church and the modern world. That conclusion would be misleading, as is demonstrated by the final vote of approval of the document. Some 97 percent (2,309) of the bishops voted to approve it, a thoroughly overwhelming majority. Only 3 percent (75) voted against it. One could argue that the substance of the Ariccia document was always going to be maintained. The criticisms were about individual details and, when these details were modified to meet the desires of the critics, the document emerged substantially intact. The neo-Thomist majority was flexible with respect to the criticisms of the neo-Augustinian minority, and Paul VI was instrumental in both encouraging the editors to continue on their path, and bringing them to compromise with their critics. The outcome was that the document proposed to the bishops in the fourth session of the council, while it may have been disfigured a bit, was not substantially changed. Cardinal Montini had been an early proponent of a document on the Church in the modern world and, as Pope Paul VI, he brought the Ariccia document to fruition as *Gaudium et Spes*.

The Pastoral Constitution on the Church in the Modern World, *Gaudium et Spes*, along with three other documents, including *Dignitatis Humanae* (the Declaration on Religious Freedom), were read in the presence of the pope in the final public session of the council, December 7, 1965. The final editing of the text after the fathers comments on it in assembly was dominated by two factors; time was fast running out and did not allow for starting again from scratch, and the expectation for a document on the Church in the modern world, both inside and outside the council, would be enormously disappointed if no document was produced. The pace of work was so frenetic, indeed, that several of the experts fell ill and had to resign their tasks. The bishops voted on it as reported above. It is of historical interest that the vote on the Declaration on Religious Freedom was along the same lines, only 70 voting against it. After a frenetic, anxious, and tortuous genesis of a document on the Church in the modern world, the voice of the assembly could not have been clearer: it overwhelmingly approved a *Pastoral Constitution*, not a *letter* as had been suggested as a stopgap resort. All that remained was for Pope Paul VI to promulgate it in the established conciliar words. "Each and every single thing written in this Decree has proved pleasing to the Fathers of this holy Council. We, together with these venerable Fathers, and with the apostolic authority entrusted to us by Christ, approve it in the Holy Spirit, recognize it, and order that it be promulgated as synodally approved for the glory of God."[24] The opening sentence of the document, the opening Latin words of which became its title, *Gaudium et Spes*, summed up John XXIII's pastoral vision of, and Paul VI's consistent support for, not only a document on the Church in the modern world, but also for the council itself: "The joys and the hopes, the griefs and the anxieties of the men [and the women] of this age, especially those who are poor or in any way afflicted, these too are the joys and the hopes, the griefs and the anxieties of the followers of Christ" (GS 1).

Conclusion

So what *aggiornamento*, updating, did the Catholic Church achieve with the promulgation of *Gaudium et Spes*? What, if anything, changed in its official teaching? The structure of the final document, perhaps, answers that question better than any other analysis, showing that the greatest change was a more positive judgment of both humans and the world in which they lived. It opens with a detailed analysis never before attempted by any Church document of "The Situation of Men in the Modern World." It proceeds to an analysis of "The Dignity of the Human Person," specifically man and woman as made in God's image. Here, the dignity of men and women, in spite of their acknowledged sinfulness, is proclaimed without reticence. "This Council lays stress on reverence for man [and woman]; everyone must consider his every neighbor without exception as another self, taking into account first of all his life and the means necessary to living it with dignity" (GS 27). The Church acknowledges this dignity and proclaims that it is in the world to promote it. "By virtue of the gospel committed to her, the Church proclaims the rights of man. She acknowledges and greatly esteems the dynamic movements of today by which these rights are everywhere fostered" (GS 41). What the Church specifically brings to men and women to illuminate their world is, as a result of the incarnation, the Gospel of "Christ as the New Man" (GS 22, 45), and by her relationship with Christ, the Church is "a sacramental sign and an instrument of union with God and of the unity of all mankind" (GS 42; see also LG 1, 9, 48).

---

[24] *Acta Synodalia* IV/7, 804.

Both Pope Paul VI and Pope John Paul II would later link this mission of the Church in the world specifically to laity. In 1964, *Lumen Gentium* had taught that "a secular quality is proper and special to laymen" (LG 31). A decade later, Paul VI took up this secular quality, teaching that the Church "has an authentic secular dimension, inherent to her inner nature and mission, which is deeply rooted in the Word incarnate and which is realized in different forms through her members."[25] Both the nature and the mission of the Church, *Gaudium et Spes* taught in 1965, are rooted in the incarnation, that central Christian doctrine which confesses that God became man in Jesus of Nazareth. In the incarnation, Dermot Lane explains, "the gulf between heaven and earth, between God and man, between the supernatural and the natural, between the sacred and the secular . . . has once and for all been overcome so that now we can glimpse heaven on earth, God in man, the supernatural in the natural, the sacred amidst the secular."[26] After, and in the light of, the incarnation, nothing in the world is ever exclusively profane or secular, certainly not humans and the world in which they live their lives and seek their salvation.

John Paul II insists that the secular character of the Church and its members is to be understood in a *theological* sense. "The term *secular* must be understood in the light of the act of God . . . who has handed over the world to women and men so that they may participate in the act of creation, free creation from the influence of sin, and sanctify themselves" (*Christifideles Laici* 15). Service in and for the world, no matter what that service is, is not just *secular* service, in the sense that it falls outside God's plan of salvation. It is also *salvation* service, in the sense that it is for the salvation of the world and the women and men who serve in it. A *theological* characteristic of Christians is that they live in the world, know the world, value the world, and seek to show that God in Christ is incarnated in it. To be secular in this sense is, for Christians, a double badge of honor, for it bespeaks valuation of and commitment to both the world in which they live and the God who seeks to save it.

That, ultimately, is the hard-won message of *Gaudium et Spes*. The divisions and contrasting, sometimes contradictory, positions that emerged during the elaboration of Schema XIII ensured that the reception of *Gaudium et Spes* would be as difficult as its ratification, and that difficulty

---

[25] *Acta Apostolicae Sedis* 64 (1972): 208.
[26] Dermot Lane, *The Reality of Jesus* (New York: Paulist Press, 1975), 137.

perdures. Paul VI's idea of *dialogue*, however, so forcefully expressed in his opening address to the second session of the council and in his encyclical *Ecclesiam Suam*, as well as in *Gaudium et Spes* (GS 44), and which Pope John Paul II would later teach to be "rooted in the nature and dignity of the human person" and to be "an indispensable step along the path toward human self-realization" (*Sollicitudo Rei Socialis* 28), has taken deep enough root to eventually bring to fruition a positive relationship between the Church and the modern world. Nowhere was the power of that notion of dialogue demonstrated so effectively as in the council's discussion of atheism. There were constant demands for its condemnation but, powerfully influenced by John XXIII's opening speech of no condemnation and by Cardinal Šeper, archbishop of Zagreb, who had lived under an atheistic regime and yet made an impassioned plea that atheism not be condemned so that dialogue could continue,[27] the council refrained from condemnation. The cure for atheism, Seper argued, is not condemnation and teaching but the living witness of Christians. It is clear from the preliminary to the final discussions of the document on the Church in the modern world that *Gaudium et Spes* was accepted, not as definitive teaching on the topic, but as an incomplete document that was the beginning of a dialogue.[28] The task of solidifying and developing the dialogical relationship between Church and world mapped out by *Gaudium et Spes* has not been an easy one, but it is one that needs to done if God's plan for the fullness of time, "to unite all things in [Christ], things in heaven and things on earth" (Eph 1:10), is ever to be achieved. How *Gaudium et Spes* contributes to that achievement will be illustrated as this book unfolds.

Questions for Reflection

1. How do you understand the designations *classicist neo-Augustinian* and *historically conscious neo-Thomist*? What differences do they exhibit toward an approach to the relationship between the Church and the world?

2. In your opinion, was the council convoked by Pope John XXIII a continuation of the unfinished First Vatican Council or something

---

[27] *Acta Synodalia*, IV / 2, 435–37.
[28] See Congar, *My Journal*, 779, September 17, 1965.

genuinely new? What difference does the choice make to Church and theology?

3. What was the first moment of crisis of the Second Vatican Council? What effect did its resolution have on the future direction and decisions of the council?

4. What progression do you see in the development of Schema XVII from its original Roman document, through the Malines, Zurich, and Ariccia documents, to the finally approved version of *Gaudium et Spes?*

5. *Lumen Gentium* (LG 31) taught that "a secular quality is proper and special to laymen [and women]" and John Paul II interpreted that secular quality to mean that God "has handed over the world to women and men so that they may participate in the act of creation, free creation from the influence of sin, and sanctify themselves." How do you see Christian women and men exercising their secular quality in the world? How do you see their secular activity as contributing to both their salvation and the salvation of the world?

Chapter Two

The Ecclesiological Focus
of *Gaudium et Spes*

Gaudium et Spes was a complex and untraditional final document for a council of the very traditional Catholic Church. Reviewing the contentious history of the development of this document enables a reader to understand why the application of the document's teaching after fifty years continues to cause both positive and negative responses among Christians and non-Christians alike. This chapter highlights some of the key ecclesiological themes of the document, explores reasons those themes first challenged the Church fifty years ago, and suggests reasons why these same themes operate at the heart of an invitation to continued efforts toward renewal today.

Generally speaking, ecclesiology is the branch of systematic theology that focuses on the theory of what the Church is. This area of study researches how the Church began, how it exists in time, how it relates to Jesus Christ, the Holy Spirit and the fullness of trinitarian life. It asks how the humanity of its members, historically contingent and limited with both sinful and graced reality, factor into its reality. Ecclesiology also ponders questions of purpose or mission; what the Church is for and what it accomplishes in the world; and, finally, ecclesiology deals with the believability or credibility of the Church. In the earliest days after Jesus' ascension and the outpouring of the Spirit, we find the disciples preaching not just what Jesus said and did, but *who* Jesus is and the nature of the relationship of his disciples to him and his lifework. The Scriptures witness that Jesus "spoke with authority," which was convincing. What gives the community of disciples "authority" to speak in his name? What is the nature of that "authority"? How is to be exercised? That question was central for the self-consciously pastoral theologians and bishops at the Second Vatican Council. How to be both understandable and believable was important to Pope John XXIII in his call for the council, as it was to the majority of bishops as they worked their way through many pages of text to speak truth to the modern world with "authority."[1]

Threshold Concept:
The Historical Character of the Church and Its Teaching

Recent scholarship of teaching and learning has identified certain activities of human learning as "threshold concepts."[2] These activities are learned behaviors but so basic to the rest of knowing that they alter the human capacity to see, understand, and know virtually anything else. One of the obvious threshold concepts is the ability to read. Once one acquires the ability to read a language, one can't help reading it when seeing words in that language in print. Thus reading provides a threshold into a whole new way of knowing and of gathering and grasping reality around us. Reading reshapes the meaning of what is known. A similar threshold of knowing is historical consciousness—recognizing that all humans live within structures of culture, language, imagination, etc., that frame, and to some extent limit, the capacity to ask questions, to see responses and certain challenging disjunctions, and so forth.

Since the close of the council, theologians and Church historians have shown that Vatican II addressed and shaped resolutions for ecclesiological questions in much the way the early councils of the Church dealt successively with the great questions of God: the trinitarian life, the two natures of Christ, and the role and work of the Spirit. Trent, Vatican I and Vatican II (the last three of the twenty-one ecumenical councils) all dealt with issues that theologically address the nature of the Church. Vatican II, more than the two previous councils, however, developed both a more dynamic description of the nature of the Church, and a clearer vision about the central mission or purpose of the Church. We could say that on the one hand, the bishops addressed the "Who the Church is and who belongs to the Church" questions primarily for insiders (referred to as *ad intra)*, and then turned and addressed the questions about "*why*

[1] John O'Malley, in his book *What Happened at Vatican II* (Cambridge, MA: Harvard University Press, 2008), 8–12, defines authority and how to exercise it as one of the three underlying themes of the Second Vatican Council. Here we are using the term in its simplest understanding of who speaks the truth believably.

[2] See for example, *Threshold Concepts and Transformational Learning*, ed. Jan H. F. Meyer, Ray Land, and Caroline Baillie (Rotterdam, Netherlands: Sense Publishers, May 2010), for insights into how higher education is considering this concept.

the Church exists at all?" or, more demandingly, "What is the Church for?" The bishop addressed the answers to these questions not only *ad intra,* but also to the rest of the world (*ad extra*). In fact, the Church attempted to clarify more precisely "Who is the Church in relationship to all of humanity?"[3]

It is not as if these questions had never been raised or studied before, but never so systematically, and certainly never in the context of the world of the late twentieth century. However the Church might have answered these and similar questions in past eras, the answers needed to be reconsidered in light of the development of human self-understanding, historical knowledge, scientific advances, and global consciousness that were not available in earlier times. A discussion of the place of Christianity in the context of human culture required a reimagination of the way the Church understood human personhood and the effects of historical placement. Changes in languages, technology, economic forces, and philosophies shape human life; new political systems greatly influence human well-being—these, and other culture-shaping forces, all enter the theological and pastoral ambit of the Church, working to make its message of human flourishing clearer. Anthropological, cultural, social, political, and economic questions are expressed through faith orientation but are also rooted in reason and the historical development of human self-knowing and understanding. Furthermore, many such expressions are, of their nature, temporal rather than eternal realities. Many bishops were therefore reluctant to address these questions in relationship to faith and the mission of the Church. In the centuries preceding the council, theology had depended on neoscholastic philosophy, often couched in ahistorical terms, as a pattern of thought through which one could engage the world of knowing between human reasoning and revealed

---

[3] This language of *ad intra* and *ad extra* was formally presented to the council by Cardinal Suenens in an address to the council fathers on December 4, 1962, in which he outlined a "plan" for the council to address a series of ecclesiological concerns about the interior life of the Church (who and what the Church *is* theologically) and the public purpose or work of the Church in the larger human community. This distinction colored all the work of the council, although the "lines" between *intra* and *extra* are not always clear and distinct—they "bleed" into one another. For a more detailed discussion of this important address to the council fathers and its overall import at the council see Giuseppi Ruggieri, "Beyond an Ecclesiology of Polemics: The Debate on the Church," in *History of Vatican II*, vol. 2, ed. Guiseppe Alberigo and Joseph Komanchak (Maryknoll, NY: Orbis Books/Leuven: Peeters, 1997), 343–44.

truth.[4] The modern world challenged the hegemony of this philosophy and brought forward historical context as a way of understanding how humans think and act. The institutional Church, perforce, had to recognize historical context, that is, cross this troubling threshold of knowing, in order to fully appreciate and articulate its own history, doctrine, and purpose in terms that the people of modernity would understand and be drawn to.

After the French Revolution with its disastrous impact on Catholic life and structures in the late eighteenth and early nineteenth centuries, the European-led Church was resistant to many of the thought constructs of the Enlightenment that undergirded that era, including the concept of historical consciousness, going so far as to actively condemn some "modernist" ideas in the late nineteenth and early twentieth centuries.[5] But by the time of the Second Vatican Council, the practical and political situa-

---

[4] Thomas O'Meara presents an excellent description of the type of nonhistorical thinking based in neo-Thomism, an ahistorical, philosophically based interpretation of the theological texts of Thomas Aquinas: "As the twentieth century progressed, narrow styles of neo-Thomist philosophy sought to be nonmodern and timeless and some identified their neo-Thomism with revelation or with the teaching office of the church. Written in a dead language, an artificial Latin imitating medieval or Baroque styles, it could protect but not vitalize Catholic life. Did its claim of timelessness come true in an unexpected way? The genres of system (*summae*) and open discussion (medieval disputation) were replaced by the seminary textbook and by the defense of artificial and irrelevant propositional theses. From 1878 to 1962 dogma, theology, philosophy, ecclesiology, liturgical rubrics, and canon law melded into a synthesis directed and furthered by the Roman schools and the Vatican. Many aspects of Catholic life were removed from their own age. Whether in Milan, Boston or Nairobi—there was a kind of universal sociology of thinking and pedagogy of communication, one inspired and limited by highly philosophical neoscholasticism. *This philosophy* of Catholic Christianity, uncomplicated in its normal and normative seminary form, *furthered a church which appeared isolated or asleep.*" Thomas O'Meara, *Thomas Aquinas, Theologian* (Notre Dame, IN: University of Notre Dame Press, 1997), 172. Emphasis added.

[5] Roger Aubert wrote, in the introduction to vol. 5 of *The Christian Centuries* series: "It should be remembered that the period running from Pius IX to Pius XII [1848–1958] was probably the one in which confessional barriers were at their most impermeable ever as far as the Roman Catholic Church was concerned." *The Church in a Secularized Society* (New York: Paulist/London: Darton, Longman and Todd, 1978), ix. Thomas O'Meara stated that the scholars of *ressourcement* "developed a critique of a theological and ecclesiastical era designated as the 'Baroque.' That word joined the properly Baroque time to its variation reaching from 1800 to 1960. That 'system' took in absolutely everything. . . . It was anti-Protestant in the style of the seventeenth century, antiliberal in terms of the period after the French Revolution, neoscholastic

tion of the Church and world had dramatically changed. Furthermore, modern theological scholarship had begun a *ressourcement*, a returning to ancient sources that had been discovered and/or translated into living languages that demonstrated that the Church had understood itself and functioned differently in its early history than it had in the Medieval or post-Reformation periods. Bishops came to understand that theological statements and faith action depended on the historical context in which they were expressed, believed, and carried out to make sense. In earlier eras of the Church, this understanding was implicit in the formulation and interpretation of doctrinal statements—even if the process or method was not explicitly defined or even fully understood. Through their work in the council the bishops effectively asserted that historical development of doctrine and praxis is itself a teaching of the Church intimately related to the Mystery of the incarnation (41, 44, and 53).

John Courtney Murray, an American Jesuit who served as a *peritus* (expert) at Vatican II, maintained that the Church's acknowledgment of the historical character and development of doctrine was the issue that underlay every other issue of the council.[6] Human understanding of revealed content needed to develop through experience and reflection. Indeed, this development is the very essence of the Church's confidence in the "Tradition" (with a capital "T"). Yves Congar's landmark book *Tradition and Traditions* (written just before the council), demonstrated that, rightly understood, the Holy Spirit's presence within the Church guaranteed this development as a way to sustain genuine fidelity to the intention of the apostolic teaching from Jesus.[7] Thus the Catholic community did not depend solely on a literal rendering of any text in any language, because all meaning of words was bound or limited by historical and cultural contexts. Careful exegesis was, therefore, essential to the lively expression of faith in different time periods or even different cultures within the same time period. *Dei Verbum* affirmed this concept

and papalist." Thomas O'Meara, "Reflections on Yves Congar and Theology in the United States," *U.S. Catholic Historian* 17, no. 2 (Spring 1999): 97.

[6] O'Malley, *What Happened At Vatican II*, 39. See also 338n52, where O'Malley cites an article in *America* magazine, January 9, 1965, written by Murray, with this statement.

[7] Yves Congar, *Tradition and Traditions: An Historical and a Theological Essay*, trans. Michael Naseby and Thomas Rainborough (London: Burns and Oates, 1966). Originally published as *La Tradition and les traditions. Essai théologique* (Paris: Fayard, 1963). See especially "Part 2: A Theological Essay," 264–70 and 338–48.

in regard to Scripture, and since it also declared that doctrine must be rooted in Scripture, it necessarily applies to all doctrine as well (DV 12 and 24).

The Church's spiritual characteristic of catholicity implies the power of the Spirit to discern various movements within culture to recognize how God is acting within the world. The gift of discernment flows from God's Spirit and requires that the community must trust that the Spirit actively resides in the baptized, the whole people of God, in order to be able to pay attention to "signs of the times," that is, various cultural shifts or historical events/movements. For some Christians, even those in leadership, any change has often been seen as a source of fear and concern—as a work of the dark. In any particular moment the world can appear to be entirely falling apart, or a dark and dangerous place to flee from. Such a stance does not take into account the mystery of the Spirit's indwelling in the Church nor the intrinsic character of the mystery of the incarnation, where it is precisely in and through the operation of human development that God enters and saves. Confidence that the Spirit resides in the community is difficult to sustain in the midst of major crises, however. The patience required to faithfully discern can be in short supply.

One could say that the first half of the twentieth century was such a period. By the early 1960s, much of the world's population was slowly recovering from a long and brutal period of wars, widespread genocide, harsh dictatorships, breakdown of social structures, economic ruin, and dissolution of various political powers. Many parts of the world were still suffering from crippling poverty and a lack of education and human rights. Indeed, the world had so dramatically changed that after his election in 1958, Pope John XXIII made *aggiornamento* (updating)—that is, admitting and engaging some change in order for the faith to be understandable to the human community of the twentieth century—the centerpiece of an ecumenical council's task, because the Church's absence from updating may have contributed to that darkness.[8] Too many of the baptized who

---

[8] In the decade of the 1950s, Yves Congar took up some significant questions that were posed about the state of the world and the fact that Christianity statistically made up at least 25 percent of the world population. In a scathing critique of what he called "hierarchology," Congar had come to the conclusion that the life of the Church was greatly diminished not only by the loss of participation of the laity in the real life of the Church, but also by the loss of their voice in the discernment of ongoing faith development. The long-term effect of this loss reached its climax in the horrors of

were not ordained did not see that they had the ability to respond to the Spirit's gifts of courage, compassion, and counsel—in fact, they had been taught that their only role in the Christian faith was to save their own souls by "paying, praying, and obeying" as the saying went in English.[9]

In no other document of the council is this updating more obvious than in *Gaudium et Spes*. As the last of the four "constitutions" to be written, debated, and promulgated, and as the only constitution that originated within the council itself (the other three were developed from preconciliar drafts), *Gaudium et Spes* is the fruit of four years of growth by the bishops: daily prayer together, the debates on the other documents, experience of the truly global character of the Church in their own membership, trust in one another's faith and good will, growing recognition of the complexity of world culture, economy, and political systems, interaction with eminent Catholic, Protestant, and Orthodox theologians (the latter two participated as invited observers at the council) which caused both a richer historical awareness of why things are the way they are at this time, and a significantly renewed theological awareness of the developing character of doctrine and practice. Pope John XXIII's opening address to the council begged the bishops not to be afraid of the world and of human development. His final encyclical, *Pacem in Terris*, as well as Paul VI's speech on peace at the United Nations (October 4, 1965) further contributed to the development of the method of the text and its anthropological and sociological import. Like no other council document written in the Church's history, *Gaudium et Spes*, in content, form, and style, witnessed to a changed understanding of the Church's purpose that was to have a radical effect on the life of the Church in many parts of the world.

Ecclesiology of Mission

The ecclesiology of *Gaudium et Spes* presumed the already-developed and stated *ad intra* dimensions of ecclesiology described in the other

---

the twentieth century, most notably the massive wars of aggression and the various genocides carried out by historically Christian nations. See Yves Congar, *Lay People in the Church: A Study for a Theology of the Laity* (Westminster, MD: Newman, 1959), 41.

[9] In the introduction to *Lay People in the Church*, Congar recalls a pamphlet written in the early 1920s, in which a lay person queries a priest about the role of the laity. The response—apparently a classic one—was: "He kneels before the altar . . . and he sits below the pulpit," and the author of the pamphlet added "the layman also puts his hand in his purse." Congar cited this to say how distant this attitude was from an authentic biblical appreciation of the role of the baptized. *Lay People in the Church*, xxvii.

documents of Vatican II that were debated in the first three sessions. *Lumen Gentium* (The Dogmatic Constitution on the Church) privileged the biblical analogy of "the People of God" (LG 9ff.) while also drawing on and developing more dynamically the analogies of the Church as "Body of Christ" (LG 7) and "Sacrament of Unity" (LG 1 and 9) from Paul's letters. This latter image is the foundational image of *Sacrosanctum Concilium* (The Constitution on the Sacred Liturgy), which firmly asserts that when the (whole) Church celebrates liturgy it is really Christ who celebrates (SC 7).

Gaudium et Spes, being a constitution on the Church in the modern world and defined as a pastoral constitution, aims at implementing in a practical way the "theory" of the Church's Christic character developed in the earlier documents. Here the focus is on the Church as actor—the Church, who is Christ, fulfilling his mission under the guidance of the Holy Spirit. Various New Testament writers spoke in terms of Jesus' mission—that is, his being sent from the Father to accomplish a task—in various ways: Mark's and Luke's gospels talk about Jesus proclaiming (and effecting) the reign of God. Matthew speaks more of the kingdom of the Heavens, and the kingdom of God in an analogous way. These political images describe a total relationship of all the created order under the governance of God. Paul's theology employs the image of a "new creation" to speak of the task or mission of Jesus—and the new creation is in Christ—but as with the "reign" or "kingdom" image, the new creation is already begun by Christ's death and resurrection in the present order of creation. Virtually all Scripture scholars assert that John certainly alludes to the new creation with the beginning of his prologue, which is a direct allusion to the original creation ("In the Beginning . . ."). But the Johannine writings express more frequently the language of "eternal life"—which is life in Christ. In other words, John too is describing life in this world as "eternal life."

While this language of eternal life has not often been preached or catechized to ordinary Christians in the same categories as the present and active "reign of God," it should be understood in this way as a fuller appreciation of the transformation that Jesus Christ brought about, and that it continues in the life of the Christian Church. The biblical scholarship revival that had begun in the Catholic Church well before the council helped the council fathers begin to appreciate the mission implications of this language—not just the "ontological state" of being in God's life (often described as the "state of grace"). Biblical scholars have explored the links between the language of reign of God, reign of Heaven, new creation, and eternal life to all express this eon of the Church—that is the time between the life, death, resurrection, and ascension of Jesus and his final coming in glory. Congar, among many theologians, described this eon as the "time of Christ" or "the time of the Spirit" or "the already given and the not yet complete"[10]—the reign of God that has begun, the new creation that has been created already, and eternal life as the fullness of life that began and continues "in Christ" through the Church when it is faithful in its mission of proclaiming and baptizing as commanded by Christ before his ascension into heaven (Matt 28). All these biblical analogies imply a call from and empowerment by God requiring human response and cooperation. Baptized Christians have a profound responsibility to be faithful to being what we are (in Christ). The analogies are biblically based, and they share both the horizontal and vertical character of all ecclesial relationships. Thus members of the Church are intimately connected to God and to each other through the variously characterized relationships with Jesus' human and divine reality. Through this transformed life, all Christians are called to cooperate in transforming the present created order into the reign of God/new creation/eternal life.

It follows that since the Church is participative in, and a sacrament of, Christ's mission of proclaiming and effecting the reign of God, the new creation, and eternal life, then the Church has a responsibility to all of humankind—a service to render in God's name through the power of the Holy Spirit and in the manner of Jesus himself. But how is the Church to accomplish the mission in an ever-changing world? If we understand the human condition to be lived in history, the life of the Church in this already-and-not-yet eon is precisely the location for mission. The real and practical character of the mission has to be within the context of a changing and developing human condition. If the Church is to be a servant to the world in carrying out its mission, then the means and the message itself must be carried out in terms the world understands. To do this the mission of the Church must be continually discerned, in every generation and culture, according to *Gaudium et Spes*, by reading the "signs of the times."

A Renewed Understanding of "World"

Before exploring the implications of the biblical phrase "the signs of the times" as the council fathers understood the phrase and applied it in

---

[10] Yves Marie Congar, *Divided Christendom: A Catholic Study of the Problem of Reunion*, trans. M. A. Bousfield (London: The Centenary Press, 1939), 50–51. Originally published as *Chrétiens désunis: Principes d'un oecumenisme catholique* (Paris: Cerf, 1937).

Gaudium et Spes, it is helpful to examine another term employed in the document, namely, *the world*. Irish theologian Enda McDonagh pointed out in an early commentary on *Gaudium et Spes* that the "ambiguity, indeed multiguity of the word caused much difficulty for drafters and debaters."[11] The problem with the term "the world" for Christian theology is rooted in the ambiguity of the Scriptures where the term, on one hand, means the created order that is good (Gen 1) and so loved by God that he sent his only begotten Son (John 3) but, on the other hand, also means the place of danger where disciples of Jesus must be *in*, but not *of* (John 16).

One dominant (but not sole) theme of Christian theology, heavily influenced by Greek philosophies, pushed the latter admonition to a dualistic opposition between world as the locus of the kingdom of evil and the Church as the locus of God's grace. A strong dualism emerged between those who were of "the world" and those who were "of God." The "temporal state" was utterly inferior to the "eternal state." Catholics were often urged to ponder the words of spiritual classics such as the *Imitation of Christ*, which is filled with instructions such as "Forsake this wretched world and your soul shall find rest."[12]

Gaudium et Spes, written out of this spiritual history, but now influenced by the awakened historical consciousness of the bishops, illustrates the bishops' efforts to overcome the dualistic negativity without losing the sense of difference between the created order and the new creation, and without condemning or diminishing the present reality of the earth or the human cultures that inhabit it:

> For the Council yearns to explain to everyone how it conceives of the presence and activity of the Church in *the world* of today. Therefore, the Council focuses its attention on *the world* of men, the whole human family along with the sum of those realities in the midst of which that family lives. It gazes upon that *world* which is the theater of man's history, and carries the marks of his energies, his tragedies, and his triumphs; that *world* which the Christian sees as created and sustained by its Maker's love, fallen, indeed, into the bondage of sin, yet emancipated now by

[11] Enda McDonagh "The Church in the Modern World (*Gaudium et Spes*)" from *Modern Catholicism: Vatican II and After*, ed. Adrian Hastings (Oxford, UK: Oxford University Press, 1990), 102.

[12] Thomas Á Kempis, *Imitation of Christ*, trans. Aloysius Croft and Howard Bolton (Milwaukee: Bruce Publishing Co., 1940), bk. 2, # 1.

Christ. He was crucified and rose again to break the strangle-hold of personified Evil,[13] so that *this world* might be fashioned anew according to God's design and reach its fulfillment. (GS 2, emphasis added)

Most of the references to "the world" in the text will deal with the widely varying cultures, that is, economies, political structures, technology and other forces, that make up the ordinary dimensions of human life in the twentieth century. It is the human person in community, and his or her daily life, that the Church understands itself called to serve through the proclamation of God's reign made present in the Paschal Mystery.

The dualistic opposition to the world, the patronizing diminishment of those who are called to marriage and family life, and the disparagement of those who serve in politics, art, education, technology, etc. (the works of the world), must be set aside as Church leaders seek to understand that God dwells precisely within the world both through the Church and in the creation itself. Service to the world is the mission of God for which Jesus was sent, and for which the Church was called and developed. Ultimately the mission is the priority—rather than saying that the Church *has* a mission, we can say with other theological thinkers that with this document, there is an understanding that the mission has a Church to carry it out. A Church that was called and shaped by the life and teachings of Jesus, formed and propelled through history by the Spirit that was poured out in the blood and water from the side of Christ as he entered death on the cross (John 19:33-34), in the breath of Christ after the resurrection (20:21-22), and in the dramatic enflaming of the Pentecost event seven-times-seven days after the resurrection (Acts 2:1-4).

The Role of the Holy Spirit
in the Church Fulfilling the Mission of God

But how do the members of the Church engage and care for the world without fear of the world's less savory characteristics? Without being subsumed into the darkest aspects of human culture? One of the early criticisms of *Gaudium et Spes* was that it was too optimistic about humans—that the text did not clearly name and condemn the evil in which

---

[13] In the original translation by Abbot: "The Latin text at this point speaks of the power of '*Malignus*,' a biblical usage. The editors of the text indicate the special sense of the term here by capitalizing the initial letter."

humans are capable of engaging. But the document does indeed address that concern, and it is through the Holy Spirit that the Church is made capable of discerning where such evil operates.

Pneumatalogical ecclesiology (the theology of the Spirit of God in the Church) is a relatively new (or a renewed old) subfield of systematic theology in the Latin Rite Church. The dynamic appreciation of the work of the Holy Spirit has from the early Church been a lively topic for theologians of the Eastern Churches, but after the East-West Schism, formalized in the eleventh century, the division of language and culture between the East and the West, exacerbated by Muslim control of some of the lands between the old Roman Empire of Constantinople and the new "Holy Roman Empire," allowed the Latin Church to focus almost entirely on the divine roles of Jesus and the Father. Congar pointed out that from the time of the Protestant Reformation, there is strong evidence to support saying that appreciation for the role and work of the Spirit was largely subsumed or translated into devotion to Mary, devotion to the reserved Eucharist (the Blessed Sacrament), and to the growing development of the doctrine of papal infallibility.[14]

With the exception of a few theologians in the nineteenth century,[15] the active work of the Spirit in guiding the bishops and the whole body of the Church (laity and clergy) was often unexamined, unreflected on, and therefore largely unknown by ordinary Catholics and their clergy in the West from at least the time of the Reformation. This diminishment of a full-blown pneumatology (*realized* belief in the Spirit's mission) powerfully affects the life of the Church. The patristic creeds of the Church express an absolute connection between belief in the Holy Spirit's mission and the characteristic expression of unity, catholicity, apostolicity,

---

[14] Yves Congar, *I Believe in the Holy Spirit*, three-volume work in one volume, trans. David Smith (New York: Crossroad, 1997). Congar is quoting French theologian P. Pare, who had originally written this criticism. Congar finds merit in the criticism and even expands on it with the data he has, but he also wanted to nuance the assertion that the Holy Spirit was "replaced" by these three "sacraments" of the presence of the Spirit. Overall, Congar asserted and defended the Latin Church's theological consciousness of the Spirit—even while he acknowledged the Eastern theologians' criticism that the West had neglected the Spirit—and was often defensive of the ways that Western theology held on to the Tradition.

[15] Theologians concerned with the importance of the living Tradition of faith most notable in the nineteenth century are the theologians of the Tübingen school in Germany, especially Johan Möhler, and, in England, John Henry Newman and William Manning. O'Malley summarized much of this scholarship under his discussion of "development" in chapters 1 and 2 of *What Happened at Vatican II*.

and holiness of the Church. Diminishment of an actualized faith in the Spirit's mission weakens the reception of the Spirit's efficacious presence in and to the Church. In turn, the vitality or efficacy of these dynamics in concrete ecclesial life becomes seriously impaired.

The Church's free and loving exercise of *unity* has been first and most obviously harmed. The fundamental fractures grounded in the schism between the Churches of the East and West, and the further fragmentations caused by the Protestant Reformation within and against the Latin Church are symptomatic. Furthermore, today's Church is constantly imperiled by further schisms as voices of various "parties" refuse to participate in dialogue with anyone 'who speaks in error.' Greater awareness of the Spirit's activity in the ecumenical movement enabled the various leaders of the Christian movement to begin to redress some of these divisions. That they still remain largely unreconciled today indicates that the whole Church must develop clearer perceptions of how the Spirit works in human relationships and risk practicing greater freedom in following the Spirit's creative initiatives toward reconciliation.

The diminishment of realized faith in God's Spirit has limited the ability of the Church to authentically exercise its character of *catholicity*—that ability whereby the apostolic faith in Jesus Christ is distinctly incarnated within diverse cultures, across geography and history—precisely as good news for every human community, redeeming the sinful dimensions of culture and preserving what is truly human and worthy within every community.[16] For too many years, the Church acted suspicious of, and alienated from, the various cultures it was called to express itself within. It suffered the consequence, therefore, of a lessened ability to adapt itself to the needs of non-European civilizations and even from new generations of its own children in Europe and the Americas. Too often in recent centuries, it has less participated in the redemption of cultures than it has in the efforts of suppression and amalgamation into Westernized colonies of the European powers. This has contributed to the fact the Church remains alien to over 75 percent of the peoples of the modern world, a circumstance about which the fathers of the Second Vatican Council addressed concern.[17]

---

[16] Yves Congar, *I Believe in the Holy Spirit,* vol. 2, *He Is Lord and Giver of Life,* 24–38. See also: Yves Congar, *Diversity and Communion,* trans. John Bowden (London: SCM, 1984). Originally published as *Diversité et Communion: Dossier historique et conclusion théologique* (Paris: Cerf, 1982), chaps. 1–3.

[17] *Ad Gentes Divinitus* (Decree on the Church's Missionary Activity), *Vatican Council II: Conciliar and Postconciliar Documents; New Revised Edition,* ed. Austin Flannery (Collegeville, MN: Liturgical Press, 2014), 825–35.

The diminishment of appreciation for the work of the Spirit leads to a decrease in the witness of *holiness*—that is, a nearness to God—which is observable in the widespread virtues, described in the New Testament, of humility, compassion, truth telling, courage, wisdom, generosity, openheartedness, kindness, long-suffering, self-control, etc.[18] The worldwide sexual abuse of children, nearly universal lying and cover-up by many ecclesial authority figures, the corruption of the Vatican bank, "Vati-leaks," and the significant scandals that have ensued from these and other widely reported public corruptions in the Church have caused widespread mistrust in the leadership of the hierarchy, and abandonment of lives of faith by many.

Finally, diminished recognition of the role of the Spirit makes sustaining the apostolic tradition difficult in a time of widespread change in technology, science, general knowledge of the physical universe, or change in the philosophical foundations for human understanding. All of these kinds of change are part of the dramatic shifts in human culture over the last few centuries. Without a constant appreciation of the Holy Spirit's guidance, members of the Church tend to become narrow, tentative, or defensive in efforts to communicate the Gospel. Thus, the apostolic faith is perceived as outdated, meaningless, divisive, and even fundamentalist, rather than a dynamic, catholic force for unity and flourishing in the human family.

Retrieval of a conscious appreciation of the role of the Holy Spirit at the council was the fruit of the various renewal movements that occurred in the Latin Church in the century preceding the council. The Biblical movement, a foundational project that bore fruit in the Encyclical of Pius XII, *Divino Afflante Spiritu* (1943), and in the Constitution on Divine Revelation (*Dei Verbum*) from the council, sourced all the other movements with competent scriptural scholarship. The liturgical movement bore fruit in *Sacrosanctum Concilium* (the Constitution on the Sacred Liturgy), and laid the liturgical, scriptural, and doctrinal foundations for all the other documents through the method of *ressourcement*, which grounded its conclusions. As John O'Malley points out, *ressourcement* "entails a return to the sources with a view not to confirming the present but to making changes in it to conform it to a more authentic or more appropriate past . . . a more profound tradition."[19]

---

[18] See, for example, Gal 5:22-23 or 2 Cor 6:6-7.

[19] O'Malley, *What Happened at Vatican II*, 40. O'Malley goes on to comment that poet Peguy coined the term early in the twentieth century and that Yves Congar gave

The active presence of Eastern Catholic bishops throughout the council, as well as Orthodox observers in its last two years, combined with the scholarly work of the theologians, and the presence of many of them on the working commissions of the council, all contributed to enabling the bishops at Vatican II to move rapidly toward articulating a rich and full consciousness of the activity of the Spirit of God in the Church across the whole theological/catechetical spectrum from the most doctrinal to the most practical.

Not only does the Spirit constitute and enliven the Church, but also, as the work of the four creedal marks, the Spirit enables the Church to be faithful to its mission of proclaiming and carrying out God's reign in human history.

Gaudium et Spes referred to the work of the Holy Spirit nearly forty-five times in its paragraphs and clearly pointed out that through the indwelling and labor of the Spirit of God, the Church will accomplish the mission of God. Examining all of these passages is beyond the scope of this chapter, but this "return" to a strong pneumatological ecclesiology cannot go unappreciated if we are to truly grasp the continuing importance of this document in the Church's life.[20]

Reading the "Signs of the Times": A Biblical Imperative

In his final encyclical, *Pacem in Terris*, Pope John XXIII frequently spoke of the biblical imperative of reading the signs of the times. The phrase comes from parallel passages in Matthew and Luke, where Jesus chides the Pharisees for being able to recognize the weather by natural signs, but not recognizing who he is, and what he is doing by the signs that are

---

it some currency through his work *Tradition and Traditions*. The method was generally associated with a number of theologians who were identified with "la nouvelle théologie." Susan Wood has written extensively on the work of Henri De Lubac and points out that, because there never was any formal "group" or school of *la nouvelle théologie*, different authors, commentators, and critics have identified somewhat different lists. The theologians themselves denied participating in any group or school as such, although they practiced the method of *ressourcement*. See Wood, *Spiritual Exegesis and the Church in the Theology of Henri de Lubac* (Grand Rapids, MI: Eerdmans, Edinburgh: T & T Clark, 1998), 6.

[20] One can read almost any number of part 1of the document and find references to the Holy Spirit, God's Spirit, Christ's Spirit or The Spirit—not to mention the many cases of language such as the Spirit of the Church or spiritual life, which are secondarily referential to the Holy Spirit.

evident in his mission among the people.[21] The bishops chose to follow Pope John's insight, and used this language in *Gaudium et Spes* (GS 3, 4) to address the responsibility of the Church to discover what God is doing in this particular time in human history by discerning the signs in culture around us. With this ecclesial interpretation of biblical imperative, the experience of contemporary societies has become a part of the content of theological thinking and teaching of the Church at both world and local levels. To do this competently, however, requires careful study, in light of biblical witness and prayerful reflection, of what has been thought of as purely secular knowledge: history, sociology, psychology, economics, political science, and the natural sciences of biology, physics, and chemistry, etc. This effort goes beyond the conclusions of the secular subject fields and sees within the human experience the work of God's Spirit or the work of evil.

This practice of discernment is not possible with mere human skills, but requires the constant guidance of the Holy Spirit to recognize the historical dimensions of a situation, the structural elements involved, the ways in which a situation involves various divisions within societies, and the multiple levels of importance within the issues under reflection—and all in light of the mandates of the reign of God made evident in the Scriptures and apostolic tradition.[22] We might take for granted the work of historical and social analysis as a foundation for theology fifty years after *Gaudium et Spes*, but this is the document that made reading the "signs of the times" an essential element of ecclesial mission. To implement that mission well, however, there has to be an appreciation of the active and present work of the Holy Spirit in the Church collectively and within members particularly. This pneumatological dimension of Christian ecclesiology is not always given proper due.

The Pneumatological Ecclesiology of Responding to the Signs of the Times

Early in his pontificate, Pope Francis asserted that we in the Church must be confident that the Holy Spirit guides the Church. In just the first

---

[21] See Matt 16:2-3 and Luke 12:54-56.

[22] John A. Coleman and T. Howland Sanks, *Reading the Signs of the Times: Resources for Social and Cultural Analysis* (New York: Paulist Press, 1993), 5. Sanks and Coleman call attention to the early work of Peter Henriot and Joe Holland, *Social Analysis: Linking Faith and Justice* (Maryknoll, NY: Orbis Books, 1983) in developing a whole area of social and cultural analysis as the basis for theological reflection.

six months of his tenure, he challenged leaders and laity alike to get out into the streets, into the "messiness" of human life, without fear. In the homily of his first Chrism Mass, he called on priests to "take on the smell of the sheep," rather than hiding behind clericalism; he urged youth in Brazil to make noise, demand change and involvement in the world; and to all of the Church he has insisted on the urgency of believing that God's Spirit is with us so we must move beyond worrying about the internal security of the Church and boldly proclaim the Good News of God's love to the world.[23] In all these efforts he is echoing the insights of *Gaudium et Spes*, particularly two sections that describe, briefly but characteristically, the Spirit's role in ecclesial discernment. The first section is in the third paragraph and is part of the introduction:

> Though [humankind] is stricken with wonder at its own discoveries and its power, it often raises anxious questions about the current trend of the world, about the place and role of [the human] in the universe, about the meaning of its individual and collective strivings, and about the ultimate destiny of reality and of humanity. Hence, giving witness and voice to the faith of the whole people of God gathered together by Christ, this council can provide no more eloquent proof of its solidarity with, as well as its respect and love for, the entire human family with which it is bound up, than by engaging with it in conversation about these various problems. The council brings to [humankind] light kindled from the Gospel, and puts at its disposal those saving resources which the Church herself, under the guidance of the Holy Spirit, receives from her Founder. For the human person deserves to be preserved; human society deserves to be renewed. Hence the focal point of our total presentation will be [the human] self, whole and entire, body and soul, heart and conscience, mind and will. (GS 3)

In the Christian tradition the Spirit is understood to bring wisdom, counsel, and knowledge, all of which are at the center of making wise choices, of staying on a discerned course, of cutting through extraneous information and getting to the heart of issues so that judgments or decisions are based on the truth of things rather than on opinion, hearsay, appearances, partial information, and, above all, fear of change. Because

[23] http://www.vatican.va/holy_father/francesco/homilies/2013/index_en.htm, accessed March 31, 2014. These themes have been iterated many times through the daily homilies, Angelus messages, special events homilies, etc.

the Church believes that the Spirit gives to the community of believers these most important gifts, the Church can lead humanity to the reality of situations, discoveries, innovations, or changes if and when the Church is attuned to its own gifts of the Spirit.

Furthermore, the Holy Spirit gives to the Church the gift of courage or fortitude that enables the members to hold fast to true wisdom, to fight for that which is genuine truth, and to remain steadfastly disciplined in testing various opportunities and changes to find the light of wisdom. This gift of fortitude is particularly important in discovering truth, because there are often apparent or implicit dangers in change or newness that can cause organizations to embrace shallow fads too quickly, or worse, to succumb to fear and hide behind the secure, the "old ways" (the ways we have historically understood the topic). To be steadfast in testing the outcomes of change so as to determine if newness is merely fad, or if it represents a new flowering of growth and development, takes real courage.

In receiving the gifts of the Spirit, the Church is subject to the requirement that it operate in the manner of Jesus. Authority figures must not act like worldly authorities, lording it over others or acting in any manner that hints of oppression. All the baptized must listen attentively and critically to those given to them as leaders. The baptized must take responsibility for their life of faith—taking advantage of opportunities given to grow in the life of grace and understanding, and never act in the manner of petulant children who are put upon by the challenges of spiritual maturity.

Asserting the truth as it is understood and known is the whole Church's responsibility—and so is it her responsibility to do so without being insulting or abrasive. This can be especially difficult in modern Western culture, in which the faith community must speak the truth in the face of mockery, rejection, or violence, or in a time when various stratagems of politicians to co-opt some partial aspect of truth without embracing all the implications of it, may make it difficult to teach or preach without being heard as partisan. Humans frequently exhibit offensive behavior when feeling the need to "defend" something, and Christian leaders are certainly human and subject to this kind of weakness. Christians, however, assert that it is the Holy Spirit's work to transform hearts, theirs and others, and it is the work of pastors, theologians, and bishops—in fact of all Christians—to remain patient, just, and merciful, even in the face of seeming threat or apparent failure. Fidelity to truth, while maintaining behavior that is both respectful and compassionate at one and the same time, may seem nearly impossible. But all things are possible with the presence of the Spirit. Congar once said that the face of the Church is meant to be that of a gentle mother, but too often she presents a face that is harsh and forbidding[24]—a theme that Pope Francis has echoed frequently in the first year of his pontificate.[25]

The Church Called to Service to the World

Perhaps no aspect of the ecclesiology of *Gaudium et Spes* is more evident (or more absolute) in its pastoral teaching than the definition of the Church as a servant of humankind. The role of servant flows from Jesus' mission of bringing forth the reign of God on Earth—that is, his mission of salvation. This extended service of the Church (as Jesus' own service) is characterized as evangelizing or proclaiming in word and deed the Good News of God's love. The service is also described as liberating or releasing the world from the forces of destruction that hold humans in various forms of material and spiritual enslavement. Finally, the Church's mission entails witnessing to the unity of humanity in and with the Creator and the created order. In all cases, the bishops saw this as not merely a kind of spiritualized mission, but actual, material, and concrete witness to the liberation of humans from various evils that afflict and enslave, including material poverty, intellectual and spiritual ignorance, physical hunger and various hungers of the human heart, unjust physical imprisonment and imprisonment by various forms of psychological, sociological, or spiritual bondage. The service of the Church is to address, and where possible eliminate, all the elements of human suffering that prevent the reign of God from being realized "on earth as it is in heaven," as we pray at various liturgies during every day.

[24] *Dialogue Between Christians*, trans. Philip Loretz (Westminster, MD: Newman Press, 1966). Originally published as *Chrétiens en dialogue: Contributions catholiques à l'oecuménisme,* Unam Sanctam, no. 50 (Paris: Cerf, 1964), pp. 5–7, n. 5. In this extended footnote, Congar reproduces a text he wrote in his personal journal in mid-September 1930 during a visit to Germany.

[25] See, for example, "A Big Heart Open to God," An Interview with Pope Francis by Antonio Spadara, *America Magazine* 209, no. 8 (September 30, 2013): 6 (section on the Church as a "field hospital"), or *Evangelii Gaudium* (Apostolic Exhortation: The Joy of the Gospel) 46–49. This text is available electronically at: http://www.vatican.va/holy _father/francesco/apost_exhortations/documents/papa-francesco_esortazione -ap_20131124_evangelii-gaudium_en.html, accessed March 31, 2014.

The document states "Now, the gifts of the Spirit are diverse: while He calls some to give clear witness to the desire for a heavenly home and, to keep that desire green among the human family, He summons others to dedicate themselves to the earthly service of [humanity] and to make ready the material of the celestial realm by this ministry of theirs. Yet He frees all of them so that by putting aside love of self and bringing all earthly resources into the service of human life they can devote themselves to that future when humanity itself will become an offering accepted by God (2 Thess 3:6-13; Eph 4:28)" (GS 38). If we listen carefully to the gospels, the message is clear: "I came, not to be served but to serve."[26]

Service of others is not rendered by mere words. Words of truth are made credible by an attitude of humility, solidarity in suffering, and genuine labor on behalf of others and according to their needs, not according to the servant's wishes. Furthermore, service is most fully rendered when both the servants and those who are served are in accord with the outcome. Service rendered on behalf of someone who cannot receive it is wasted. Service must be enculturated, that is, received into the culture it is meant to serve. In order for genuine enculturation to occur, the community of faith is to engage in dialogue as a work of the Spirit.

The Role of Dialogue in Pneumatologically Based Discernment

A key to presenting the compassionate face of truth is relationship with Christ and the Spirit who communicate themselves in the deepest inner life of the human. Sharing that inner wisdom with one another in trust is an essential element of being able to discern whether something comes from God. In *Gaudium et Spes* the bishops assert, for example, that while they must reject the ideology of atheistic Communism "root and branch, the Church sincerely professes that all [persons], believers and unbelievers alike, ought to work for the rightful betterment of this world in which all alike live; such an ideal cannot be realized, however, apart from sincere and prudent dialogue" (GS 21).

The whole Church, clergy and laity, listens carefully to the wisdom and insights given to one another. This mutual listening is at the heart of attending to the Spirit, who guides both Church and world from within the created order. Careful attention to the ideas and conclusions of others,

---

[26] See, for example: Matt 20:28; Mark 10:45; Luke 22:27; John 13:13-14.

whether they are scholars of the topic or simply persons for whom the question is urgent, is a first element. Refusing to race to a judgment of ideological concurrence or avid disagreement is the second component of the practice of dialogue which the document calls for.

Pope Francis has already challenged the entire Catholic Church to exercise this listening to the Spirit by retrieving the image of "the people of God" from *Lumen Gentium* and urging the Church to attend to one another as well as to the world beyond the Church:

> The image of the church I like is that of the holy, faithful people of God. This is the definition I often use, and then there is that image from the Second Vatican Council's "Dogmatic Constitution on the Church" (12). Belonging to a people has a strong theological value. In the history of salvation, God has saved a people. There is no full identity without belonging to a people. No one is saved alone, as an isolated individual, but God attracts us looking at the complex web of relationships that take place in the human community. God enters into this dynamic, this participation in the web of human relationships.

"The people itself constitutes a subject," he continued in the interview:

> And the Church is the people of God on the journey through history, with joys and sorrows. Thinking with the Church, therefore, is my way of being a part of this people. And all the faithful, considered as a whole, are infallible in matters of belief, and the people display this *infallibilitas in credendo,* this infallibility in believing, through a supernatural sense of the faith of all the people walking together. This is what I understand today as the 'thinking with the church' of which St. Ignatius [of Loyola] speaks. *When the dialogue among the people and the bishops and the pope goes down this road and is genuine, then it is assisted by the Holy Spirit.*[27]

Gaudium et Spes identifies the work of dialogue as the means for discovering how service might be most effectively rendered. John O'Malley points out that "Dialogue manifests a radical shift from the prophetic I-say-unto-you style that earlier prevailed and indicates something other than unilateral decision making."[28] Understanding the characteristics

---

[27] Pope Francis, "A Big Heart Open to God." Emphasis added.
[28] O'Malley, *What Happened at Vatican II*, 50.

of dialogue has become something of a theological discipline in its own right since the council. By the very meaning of the word, any practice of unilateral speech or action is impossible. Dialogue means the engaged speaking/listening of two (at least) social realities—individual persons, small or large groups, or even nations. Where there are two talking who want to understand each other, there also has to be the same two listening. Dialogue is as much about humble listening—with an open heart—to the voice, experience, wisdom of the other as it is about sharing one's own voice. It is about respecting the other, and trusting that the other is making an effort to speak the truth, just as one is attempting to speak the truth as one knows it.

Theologically, the practice of dialogue is an ordinary route to really hearing the Spirit of God. The whole practice of prayer presumes the practice of humans speaking with and listening to God. In human-to-human relationships God also operates. Through the voice of the other, and also in the revelations of one's own voice, the Spirit is disclosed to those with ears to hear.

The act of open and humble listening presumes that the other has a contribution to make that is valuable and necessary; it demonstrates that the other is important, lovable, worth one's time and emotional energy. Genuine and open sharing of one's own heart presumes that the other wants to receive what one offers. Quoting *Ut Unum Sint* 29, an encyclical letter of Pope John Paul II, Archbishop John Quinn, has written: "Dialogue is not conflict, an effort to prove oneself right and the other wrong. It is not carried out in hostility or hauteur: 'It is necessary to pass from antagonism and conflict to a situation where each party recognizes the other as a partner . . . and any display of mutual opposition must disappear.'"[29]

Dialogue with other Christians in an effort to restore unity in the Christian Church; dialogue with members of other world religions to discover how the Spirit is working in the world beyond the boundaries of the Christian community to bring unity, world peace, and economic flourishing to the whole human family; dialogue with nonbelievers both to open their hearts to the voice of God's Spirit operating in their lives and to discover the ways that believers have failed to communicate that truth; dialogue with families to discover how the Church might more

[29] John R. Quinn, *The Reform of the Papacy: The Costly Call to Christian Unity* (New York: Crossroad, 1999), 21.

fully serve and support the important work of bringing new human persons to lives of love and hope; all these and more are articulated challenges of *Gaudium et Spes* and are just the beginning of the ways that the document challenges the leaders of the Church and all its members to engage in the basic work of announcing the Good News of God's saving love.

The witness of life lived authentically through the graciousness of God's Spirit is the most effective means of concretely proclaiming the truth of God's reign and the gift of eternal life. The tedious, generous, demanding work of dialogue is part of this personal and institutional witness that God's Spirit dwells in the Church, giving her authority to teach in God's name, because she acts in the manner of God's Son.

The Ecclesiology of a Poor Church in Service to the World

In the final section of this short ecclesiological review of *Gaudium et Spes*, it is important to consider the ecclesiological implications of a poor Church at the service of the poor. Service in union with Jesus' mission and empowered by Christ's Spirit has to be rendered in accord with the manner of the One in whose name it is given—that is, with the generosity of a God who humbled the Divine Self to become human among the ranks of the poorest citizens of a conquered and oppressed nation. The Church challenges us to ponder this truth through the Scriptures and prayers of the Christmas Octave liturgies. The writings and practices of theologians, pastors, and saints remind us of the "poverty of God." St. Ignatius of Loyola invites those who undertake the Spiritual Exercises to deeply contemplate this truth in the exercises beginning the second week. Solidarity with the least, the most impoverished, those who are suffering, marginalized, or despised, is at the heart of Christian witness. *Gaudium et Spes* virtually shouts this "fundamental option for the poor" in its opening sentence: "The joys and the hopes, the griefs and the anxieties of the [men and women] of this age, *especially those who are poor or in any way afflicted,* these are the joys and hopes, the griefs and anxieties of the followers of Christ" (GS 1).

The practice of voluntary poverty or simplicity in a world where wealth is often worshipped—even at the expense of the lives and well-being of other humans and the cost of creation itself—was a central concern to many of the bishops at the council. It has remained a challenge from the margins of the Church for the last fifty years, particularly from liberation theologians and the new eco-conscious theologians. The consideration of the service of the world's impoverished peoples is taken up in another chapter in this book, but here we ask the question, what does it mean to have an ecclesiology of a "poor Church at the service of the poor"? We might easily conjecture why sociologically or politically it is important to be with those we seek to serve, but is there a theological imperative in being poor—and if so, what does that mean or look like?

Through the centuries of the Christian tradition, numerous tracts, books, essays, homilies, and meditations have been written on poverty as a necessary condition for a genuinely transfigurative relationship with God. Jesus is witnessed in the synoptic gospels as asserting definitively to the rich young man: "You are lacking in one thing. Go, sell what you have, and give to the poor and you will have treasure in heaven, then come and follow me" (Mark 10:21).

When the young man sadly leaves, Jesus turns to the disciples and says "How hard it is for those who have wealth to enter the Kingdom of God" (Mark 10:23).[30] One of the evangelical counsels all Christians must attend to, not just those in the vowed life, is poverty. Most saints identify it as an essential trait of the Christian life. Whole treatises have been written to interpret the meaning of poverty since there is also a powerful theological argument that any kind of enforced poverty is morally wrong. Anthropologically, it is useful to look at the human state at both birth and death to grasp something of the essential character of the poverty of being human. We come into the world naked and helpless and leave the world leaving behind even that naked body. Theologically, we ponder the state of God's entry into and exit from the human life by stopping at the manger and at the cross. Even more radically, we can meditate on God's *request*—not command—of Mary, a simple, powerless, girl-child of the Hebrews, to become her human child. Thus God demonstrates his own humble poverty in human terms—the poverty that lies at the heart of complete vulnerability otherwise associated with freely-given love. In case we miss the point, we follow the God-man and his parents into an undocumented sojourn as refugees from political persecution in a foreign country where they are utterly dependent on the kindness of strangers to survive. We then walk with the Son of Man who "has no place to lay his head," we go with him to a tortured death brought about by the most powerful nation on earth, a nation terrified of his freedom in that poverty.

---

[30] See also parallel texts for this whole account: Matt 19:16-30; Luke 18:18-30.

It does not take an extended, close reading of the Christian theological tradition to discover text after text considering poverty as a necessary spiritual state for a real relationship with God. But does this poverty apply only to the individual members of the Church? Is the Church institutionally called to this actual poverty as well, and not just the poverty of Spirit, in order to fulfill its mission of proclaiming the reign of God? How is it that a condition could be only identified in the members and not in the whole social structure binding the members? The Church asserts that corporately it is a sacrament of life with God on earth. To function in this role with authority the community and its leaders cannot just talk about its call but must participate in the poverty of God as a way of life. It is impossible for active members, much less official leaders of the Christian Church to have the authority of the proclamation of the Gospel unless they do without the comforts and controlling power afforded by material wealth. This is true of the community together as well as the individual members, for the danger of material wealth lies in the way it enslaves its possessor. It is not that poverty itself is a virtue but that poverty as a chosen state brings the freedom that is inherent in God's divine nature. For the Church to participate actively in that nature, it must be granted the grace of poverty that brings such freedom.

Approximately forty of the bishops of the Second Vatican Council addressed this question personally by signing a document called the "Pact of the Catacombs" at the Catacombs of Domitilla shortly before the council ended in 1965. This pact was a thirteen-point affirmation that said in part:

> We [the signers below] will seek to live according to the ordinary manner of our people, regarding habitation, food, means of transport, and all which springs from this (Cf. Matt 5:3; 6:33s; 8:20). We definitively renounce the appearance and reality of riches, especially regarding to our manner of dress (rich material, loud colors) and symbols made of precious materials especially neither gold nor silver. (They should in reality be evangelical signs. Cf. Mark 6:9; Matt 10:9; Acts 3:6). We will not possess real estate, goods, bank accounts, etc. in our own names; if it should be necessary to have them, we will place everything in the name of the diocese, or of charitable and social works (Cf. Matt 6:19-21; Luke 12:33).[31]

---

[31] The text of the pact has been challenging to track down in English. It was available to the historians at the Bologna School as they were working on the five-volume

This concept of institutional poverty has been explored by various religious communities through the centuries, most notably by Francis of Assisi and Ignatius Loyola. In both cases, these leaders foresaw institutional investment in property as dangerous for the actual poverty of members. Few in religious life today, especially in Western congregations, would disagree with their concern. But how does the faith community, or an institutional structure of it, practice poverty, or at least simplicity, in a world where wealth is seen as essential for fulfilling the mission of the Church? The easiest way out of the dilemma is simply to ignore it. If one pursues the Christian life in prayer and commitment, however, or if the large worldwide communion of the Church wants to be credible in proclaiming the Gospel, the issue can't simply be ignored. The authority of the Church to speak the truth in love requires it to practice what it preaches, institutionally as well as member-by-member.

Gustavo Gutiérrez has written frequently and passionately about the gospel passages wherein Jesus asserts that the "last will be first." Gutierrez insists that for the Church to be a sacrament of God's kingdom, it must be faithful to Jesus' mandate that his followers not be trapped in the idolatry of money that is so much a part of modern cultures, but must be a practical witness to a God who hears the cries of the poor and chose to be poor with the poor.

> The church, which is the community of Christ's disciples, is a sign of the kingdom to the extent that it allows its historical activity to be judged by the kingdom. This judgment is not rendered only at the end of history. It begins now. . . . The criteria of God's judgment are provided by the nature of the kingdom, which is a kingdom of peace, love, and justice. . . . Like each individual, the church as a whole is judged by its relation to Christ. And it is works of justice, solidarity and love that give content to this relation.[32]

Ignatius of Loyola placed poverty, and the freedom it brings, at the center of the Spiritual Exercises. He insisted that those who respond to the call of Jesus to undertake the mission of their baptismal vocation

---

history of the council, which refers to it in several places. But it was not published in the English edition. Some months ago it was translated and posted online at: http://www.monasterodibose.it/content/view/5197/122/lang,en/, accessed November 9, 2013.

[32] Gustavo Gutiérrez, *The God of Life* (Maryknoll, NY: Orbis Books, 1991), 107.

will be confronted by two standards, one of which must be rejected: The Standard of Christ and the Standard of Evil. In Ignatius's experience, the ability to engage true discernment of the "signs of the times" in one's own life or corporately for the Church and world is given through grace of this meditation on the two standards.[33] In speaking about this meditation in his popular English-language commentary on the Spiritual Exercises, Dean Brackley said,

> The meaning [in this meditation] of "riches, honors, and pride" and "poverty, insults, and humility" determines what it means to be received under the standard of Christ, or to be "placed with his Son." This is the heart of Ignatian spirituality. My insistence on the concrete and social meaning of the key terms in the Two Standards is not, however, motivated by "Ignatian fundamentalism." The point is rather that Ignatius is faithfully and creatively communicating the gospel message, the good news, for today: To be placed with the Son is to be placed where he said he would be found: among the hungry, the naked, the sick, and the imprisoned (Matt 25:31-46). It is to opt for the poor. Only in this way will "thy Kingdom come."[34]

Lest anyone think this applies only to those called to religious vocations, however, Brackley concludes,

> The Two Standards speak to our society, and to my middle-class 'tribe' in particular. While the gospels say a great deal about rich and poor, which were the most important social classes in Jesus' day, they say little directly about those in between. The Two Standards' inspired interpretation of the gospel message throws a bright light over the rocky moral terrain of today's large middle classes. . . . Christ calls us to humility and solidarity via a double freedom, the readiness to renounce everything, and even to embrace material poverty, and freedom from the fear of rejection to which members of the lonely middle-class crowd are so vulnerable.[35]

In a recent lecture at Creighton University, historical theologian Massimo Faggioli stated that Pope Francis, though early in his historic

---

[33] See 136–48 in any standard translation of the *Spiritual Exercises of Saint Ignatius*.

[34] Dean Brackley, *The Call to Discernment in Troubled Times* (New York: Crossroad, 2004), 87–88.

[35] Ibid., 89.

pontificate, is notable for his practical implementation of the teachings of Vatican II without a great deal of discussion about the theory of the teachings.[36] In no area is this more evident, perhaps, than the practical way he challenges the whole Church to become a poor Church, while at the same time addressing the needs of the poor, implementing the missionary ecclesiology of *Gaudium et Spes*.

In his first major official document, an Apostolic Exhortation on the "new evangelization," Francis wrote:

> I claim only to consider briefly, and from a pastoral perspec-
> tive, certain factors which can restrain or weaken the impulse of
> missionary renewal in the Church, either because they threaten
> the life and dignity of God's people or because they affect those
> who are directly involved in the Church's institutions and in her
> work of evangelization . . . [in the current economic situation of
> the global economy]. . . . The thirst for power and possessions
> knows no limits. In this system, which tends to devour every-
> thing which stands in the way of increased profits, whatever is
> fragile, like the environment, is defenseless before the interests of
> a deified market, which becomes the only rule. . . . One cause of
> this situation is found in our relationship with money, since we
> calmly accept its dominion over ourselves and our societies. . . .
> We have created new idols. The worship of the ancient golden
> calf (cf. Exod 32:1-35) has returned in a new and ruthless guise
> in the idolatry of money and the dictatorship of an impersonal
> economy lacking a truly human purpose.[37]

The effectiveness of Francis's personal efforts to practice what he preaches, the same Spirit-energy that drove the bishops who signed the Pact of the Catacombs decades ago, is attested in the secular weekly journal *Time*, which selected Pope Francis as "Person of the Year" in late December 2013 and stated as a rationale for the choice: "But what makes this Pope so important is the speed with which he has captured

---

[36] Massimo Faggioli spoke at a conference celebrating the fifty-year legacy of Vatican II on November 7, 2013. A video of the presentation is available at http://www.youtube.com/watch?v=CWohIgtkH2k&feature=youtu.be, accessed December 10, 2013.

[37] Pope Francis, *Evangelii Gaudium*, November, 2013, n. 52–54. Text available at http://www.vatican.va/holy_father/francesco/apost_exhortations/documents/papa-francesco_esortazione-ap_20131124_evangelii-gaudium_en.html, accessed November 27, 2013.

the imaginations of millions who had given up on hoping for the Church at all. People weary of the endless parsing of sexual ethics, the buck-passing and infighting over lines of authority when all the while (to borrow from Milton), 'the hungry Sheep look up, and are not fed.' In a matter of months, Francis has elevated the healing mission of the Church—the Church as servant and comforter of hurting people in an often harsh world—above the doctrinal police work so important to his recent predecessors."[38]

Conclusion

The ecclesiological themes of *Gaudium et Spes* focus on the reality of the Mission of God having an effective Church to carry it out. But unless the Church takes seriously the demand that every baptized person takes up the mission of proclaiming and realizing the Reign of God on earth, as it is in heaven, the Church fails in ways small and large to accomplish the task which is its *raison d'etre*. The Church teaches in *Gaudium et Spes* that it exists because God has a task for the whole community in Jesus' name and manner. Through the power of the Spirit of God within the whole People of God in every generation that task can be carried out, by discernment of the signs of the times and a willing witness to gospel virtues and values.

The implementation of these themes was begun, as any good historian of the last fifty years can attest, through starts and stops. Great successes, and some remarkable failures, at living up to the hope and vision of the text are the record for making this teaching real and concrete. *Gaudium et Spes* has been received, in whole or in part, in some areas of the world Church more successfully than others. We can point to, but not elaborate on here, the development of Liberation Theology in Latin America, the developments toward enculturation of the Church in Africa and Eastern Asia, the dynamic practices of dialogue with other world religions in the large populations of Eastern Asia, and the inspiring documents on nuclear weapons and poverty in the United States during the 1980s. Various scandals and crises throughout the world illustrate the checkered reception by bishops every bit as much as by the laity.

The document asserts, and Pope Francis has reaffirmed, that a hope for the future of humanity, in some sense, lies in Church members' actively

---

[38] Howard Chua-Eoan and Elizabeth Dias, "Pope Francis, The People's Pope," *Time Magazine* (December 11, 2013).

believing that God's Spirit is breathed into every single Christian at baptism and remains within each and all who choose any measure of fidelity to God. The Spirit remains, operating within, in every genuinely Christlike endeavor, personal and corporate, making discernment of the signs of the times possible and action to accompany that discernment fruitful. That same Spirit shapes a Church willing to practice poverty—both spiritual and actual—into a people genuinely free to live and act on God's behalf as a sacramental proclamation of God's eternal compassion.

Questions for Reflection

1. Why is the mission or task of the Church significant for better understanding the Church's nature?

2. How is thinking about historical consciousness as a way of crossing a threshold of knowing helpful for understanding how whole generations might not have thought a particular way? How does this kind of knowing change the way we view what other generations thought or did?

3. How do you understand the Holy Spirit working in your own life? In the life of the Church? Does it matter if the Holy Spirit operates in the Church?

4. What are some "signs of the times" in the circumstances of your life? How do you recognize God's activity in various things that happen in your community or in your world?

5. What does the evangelical counsel of poverty (or the Gospel call to poverty) mean for you if you are religiously vowed? If you are baptized laity? If you are ordained clergy? What would you say poverty means in your own life? Does Pope Francis's call to poverty make you uncomfortable?

6. How will the reign of God "judge" the Church if the Church is unfaithful to her mission?

Chapter Three

Gaudium et Spes: Perspectivism, Conscience, and Ethical Method

Gaudium et Spes marks a historical and radical development in the Catholic Church's openness to, and commitment to dialogue with, the modern world. With this openness and commitment comes a profound methodological development in how the Church reflects on its relationship to the modern world and the moral implications of this relationship for specific ethical issues such as marriage, social justice, and peace and war. Reading the "signs of the times" not only challenges the Church to discern God's presence in the earthly city and to engage in dialogue with the modern world to more deeply understand that presence, but it also invites the Church to systematically reflect on those challenges in light of the Gospel and human experience. This chapter, which is divided into four sections, focuses on the methodological implications of this relationship for addressing contemporary ethical issues. Section 1 briefly summarizes part 1 of *Gaudium et Spes*. Section 2 explores a specific "sign of the times" in the twenty-first century, a "dictatorship of relativism" that denies objective truth and that Pope Benedict labels the "gravest problem of our time."[1] It proposes perspectivism as an epistemology that responds to this problem. Section 3 investigates the Second Vatican Council's treatment of the nature and authority of a well-formed conscience, which accounts for plural objectivist perspectives. Section 4, drawing from *Gaudium et Spes*'s unique methodological insights, proposes components of an ethical method for the formation of conscience to respond to *Gaudium et Spes*'s invitation for all people "to search for truth" and to seek "genuine solution[s] to the numerous problems which arise in the life of individuals and from social relationships" (GS 16) in the twenty-first century.

---

[1] Cardinal Joseph Ratzinger, "Christ, Faith and the Challenge of Cultures," http://www.ewtn.com/library/CURIA/RATZHONG.HTM, accessed March 31, 2014.

I. *Gaudium et Spes*

Gaudium et Spes is divided into two main parts. Part 1 focuses on "The Church and Man's Calling." Part 2 focuses on "Some Problems of Special Urgency," where specific issues of social life are addressed. In this chapter, we focus on part 1; in chapters 4, 5, and 6, we focus on part 2: Marriage and Family Life, Social and Economic Life, and Political Life, Peace and War, respectively.

The preface (1–3) to *Gaudium et Spes* is a prophetic call for solidarity between the Church and the whole human family: "The joys and the hopes, the griefs and the anxieties of the men of this age, especially those who are poor or in any way afflicted, these too are the joys and hopes, the griefs and anxieties of the followers of Christ" (1). The message of *Gaudium et Spes* is intended for "the whole of humanity" (2) and has a solitary goal of service to humankind "to carry forward the work of Christ under the lead of the befriending Spirit" (3). The introductory statement (4–10) indicates that to carry out this goal, the Church must scrutinize "the signs of the times" and interpret them "in light of the gospel" (4). This focus on the signs of the times emphasizes an inductive method to analysis and evaluation of challenges confronting individuals and society, beginning with the particularities of those challenges to find fully human solutions. This is an important methodological development that we discuss below.

Scrutinizing the "signs of the times" fifty years after *Gaudium et Spes* was written indicates similar social and cultural changes that present opportunities and challenges. Opportunities include advances in the sciences that bring human beings "hope of improved self-knowledge" (5), promote "socialization" and socioeconomic development that can foster greater stability and liberty (6), and provide critical tools for a more mature faith for believers (7). Challenges include fragmentation of knowledge and its impact on human development, which require "new efforts of analysis and synthesis" (5, 8) that will illustrate and correct the lack of truly personal and equitable socioeconomic development promoting "appropriate personal development and truly personal relationships ('personalization')" (6, 8), and the lack of an appreciation for accepted values that may lead to moral upheaval, abandonment of religion, and nihilism (7, 10). To realize the opportunities and overcome the challenges, the council speaks to all people "to illuminate the mystery of man and to cooperate in finding the solution to the outstanding problems of our time" (10), "solutions which are fully human" (11). These introductory paragraphs highlight the opportunities and challenges facing the Church in the modern world. The people of God (and indeed, all people of good will) can further realize the opportunities and overcome the challenges by discerning authentic signs of human development and working together to realize human dignity and to solve the problems that frustrate that dignity. Part 1 is divided into four sections—the dignity of the human person, the human community, human activity in the world, and the Church's role in the modern world—and indicates ethical methodological criteria to realize these goals.

There are five foundational themes in *Gaudium et Spes* that are central for exploring ethical method and moral theology. First, *Gaudium et Spes* is fundamentally committed to discerning what constitutes the truly human (26, 49, 50, 60, 73, 74), fully human (11), and human dignity (19, 27, 39, 51, 66, 73). This commitment indicates an objectivist metaethic that realizes that what is good or right can be defined universally in terms of human dignity or some similar cognate. What is good or right facilitates human dignity; what is bad or wrong frustrates human dignity. Of course, this begs the question of theological anthropology, or how we define human dignity and formulate and justify norms that facilitate, and do not frustrate, attaining human dignity.

Second, *Gaudium et Spes* gives a clear indication of how to define human dignity. In its section on marriage and the family, it notes: "the moral aspect of any procedure [to harmonize conjugal love with the responsible transmission of life] . . . must be determined by objective standards, based on the nature of the human person and his acts" (51). The official commentary on *Gaudium et Spes* explains that this principle is applicable not only to marriage and sexuality but also to the entire realm of human activity and is formulated as a general principle: "human activity must be judged insofar as it refers to the human person integrally and adequately considered."[2] In our terms, it must facilitate and not frustrate the attainment of human dignity. Drawing from *Gaudium et Spes*, Louis Janssens specifies the commentary's personalist principle and constructs a theological anthropology explaining the various dimensions of the human person. The human person is: a subject (not an object); in corporeality (corporeal and spiritual are integrated); in relationship to the material world, to others, to social groups, and, we add, to self; created in

[2] *Schema constitutionis pastoralis de ecclesia in mundo huius temporis: Textus recognitus et relationes*, pars 11 (Vatican City: Vatican Press, 1965), 9.

the image and likeness of God; a historical being; and is fundamentally unique but equal to all other persons.[3]

What is good or right facilitates these dimensions of the human person; what is bad or wrong frustrates these dimensions of the human person. Moral challenges arise when human acts facilitate some and frustrate other dimensions of the human person. For example, we can travel to a theological conference to discuss important issues surrounding climate change and possible theological and scientific responses to it. In one sense, this facilitates the human person and our relationships with neighbor (colleagues), the impact we can have on social groups (inform Congress and religious groups), and perhaps can have an overall positive impact on our relationship with the material world (environment). However, the material resources that we use to travel to the conference, by car or plane, and the personal services provided by those people in hotels and restaurants that are not paid a just and living wage, have a negative impact on the material world and human relationships and take us away from family or loved ones. Such is the moral complexity of human acts.

Third, the complexity of human acts and their positive and negative impact on the dimensions that make up the human person integrally and adequately considered challenge humans to discern those acts which, considered in their entirety, facilitate and do not frustrate human dignity. Those acts that facilitate human dignity are good; those acts that frustrate human dignity are bad. This discernment process recognizes the complexity of human acts and the responsibility humans have to be active participants in the search for ethical truth. "Let the layman not imagine that his pastors are always such experts, that to every problem which arises, however complicated, they can readily give him a concrete solution. . . . Rather . . . let the layman take on his own distinctive role" (43).

Fourth, humans participate in this process by forming and following their consciences, a fundamental human right and responsibility. "Conscience is the most secret core and sanctuary of a man. There he is alone with God, whose voice echoes in his depths" (16). To obey conscience is at the core of human dignity.

Fifth, *Gaudium et Spes* provides methodological criteria for searching for answers to complex questions that guide in the formation of

---

[3] Louis Janssens, "Artificial Insemination: Ethical Considerations," *Louvain Studies* 8, no. 1 (1980): 3–29.

conscience and enable the Church and the modern world to dialogue in this search for truth. This search is not without risk, and it is to what Popes John Paul II and Benedict XVI perceive as a fundamental risk to this project that we now turn.

II. Relativism vs. Perspectivism

In an attempt to read "the signs of the times," John Paul II and Benedict XVI have raised concerns over relativism, which denies the existence of an objective order or universal truth and fundamentally threatens humans' search for truth. In his homily at the opening of the 2005 papal conclave, Cardinal Joseph Ratzinger spoke of the "dictatorship of relativism" which "does not recognize anything as definitive and whose ultimate standard consists solely of one's own ego and desires."[4] In this chapter, we are specifically concerned with moral relativism, which denies the existence of universal, objective, valid-for-all-circumstances ethical truth. Such truth is necessary, the magisterium argues, as the foundation for absolute norms which assert that certain acts (contraceptive and homosexual acts, for example), are intrinsically evil and can never be morally justified regardless of motive, context, or circumstance. Concern about relativism is undoubtedly warranted in the twenty-first century, but the magisterium fails to discern the difference between *relativism*, which rejects all objective ethical truth, and *perspectivism*, which acknowledges that there is objective ethical truth, albeit partial. It also fails to discern legitimate theological pluralism, which the International Theological Commission's recent document, "Theology Today" (TT),[5] advances as an essential criterion of Catholic theology. We consider relativism and perspectivism in turn in more detail.

A. *The Magisterium on Relativism*

In modern times, moral relativism has been the subject of much magisterial concern. Pope Pius XII condemned "situation ethics" which, he

---

[4] Joseph Ratzinger, "Cappella Papale," Mass "Pro Eligendo Romano Pontifice," Homily of His Eminence Cardinal Joseph Ratzinger of the College of Cardinals, Monday 18 April 2005, http://www.vatican.va/gpII/documents/homily-pro-eligendo-pontifice_20050418_en.html, accessed March 31, 2014.

[5] International Theological Commission, "Theology Today: Perspectives, Principles and Criteria," http://www.vatican.va/roman_curia/congregations/cfaith/cti_documents/rc_cti_doc_20111129_teologia-oggi_en.html, accessed March 31, 2014.

believed, is a form of relativism that denies universal ethical truth.[6] Pope
Paul VI warned of moral relativism that claims that "some things are
permitted which the Church had previously declared intrinsically evil,"
and that this vision "clearly endangers the Church's entire doctrinal
heritage."[7] *Gaudium et Spes* asserts the need for "objective norms" to guide
the formation of conscience. In *Veritatis Splendor* (The Splendor of Truth),
John Paul II warned of the dangers of relativism which detaches human
freedom from any objective or universal foundation and proposes certain
methods "for discovering the moral norm" which reject absolute and immutable norms and precepts taught by the magisterium. Some Catholic
ethicists complain that in *Veritatis Splendor*, John Paul falsely accused
them of "canonizing relativism."[8] In both a 1993 speech to the presidents
of the Asian bishops' conferences[9] and a 1996 speech to the presidents of
the doctrinal commissions of the bishops' conferences of Latin America,[10]
Cardinal Ratzinger warned of the dangers of a relativism that denies the
existence of objective truth, calling it "the gravest problem of our time."[11]
This concern with relativism and its impact, especially in the area of morality, was a central concern of his pontificate as Benedict XVI.

These and other magisterial statements not only fail to distinguish
between relativism and legitimate theological disagreement on objectivist claims to ethical truth, but also mistakenly conflate such legitimate
disagreement and relativism. Philosophical ethics can aid in distinguish-
ing between the two.

[6] See Pius XII, "Allocution to the Federation mondiale des jeunesses feminines
Catholiques [World Federation of Catholic Female Youth]," *Acta Apostolicae Sedis*
34 (January 18, 1952): 413–19; Radio Message about the Christian conscience, *AAS*
34 (March 23, 1952): 270–78; and Instruction of the Holy Office, February 2, 1956,
in *Enchiridion Symbolorum*, ed. Henry Denzinger and Adolf Schönmetzer, 33rd ed.
(Rome: Herder, 1965), no. 3918.
[7] Paul VI, "Address to Members of the Congregation of the Most Holy Redeemer,"
AAS 59 (1967): 962.
[8] Maura Anne Ryan, "'Then Who Can Be Saved?': Ethics and Ecclesiology in
Veritatis Splendor," in *Veritatis Splendor: American Responses*, ed. Michael E. Allsopp
and John J. O'Keefe (Kansas City, MO: Sheed and Ward, 1995), 11.
[9] Cardinal Joseph Ratzinger, "Christ, Faith and the Challenge of Cultures," http://
www.ewtn.com/library/CURIA/RATZHONG.HTM, accessed April 5, 2014.
[10] Cardinal Joseph Ratzinger, "Relativism: The Central Problem for the Faith Today,"
http://www.ewtn.com/library/CURIA/RATZRELA.HTM, accessed April 5, 2014.
[11] Ratzinger, "Christ, Faith and the Challenge of Cultures."

B. Metaethical Relativism

The Second Vatican Council's documents *Gaudium et Spes* (GS 44, 57) and *Optatam Totius* (The Decree on Priestly Formation 15), and more recently "Theology Today" (64–66), highlight the essential importance of philosophy for doing theology. Philosophical ethical theory distinguishes three levels of ethical discourse, namely: moral judgments, normative ethics, and metaethics.[12] These distinctions shed light on understanding claims that a particular moral position is an expression of relativism. As persons endowed with reason and the ability to choose, humans make moral judgments on the basis of what they believe is right, obligatory, or good. This is the realm of daily moral decision making. These daily moral decisions serve as the source for both normative ethics and metaethics. It is the obligation of all rational human beings to make moral judgments in light of what they think is right or wrong. It is the task of theological ethicists to critically reflect on, analyze, and develop these moral judgments into a comprehensive, systematic, rational ethical theory. The synopsis and synthesis of daily moral judgments into an ethical theory is the area of normative ethics and metaethics. Normative ethics formulates and justifies norms, rules, or laws that prescribe right actions and good motives and proscribe wrong actions and bad motives. Metaethics, which literally means above or beyond ethics, is the foundation of all normative ethics and daily morality. It asks two foundational questions. First, do moral terms like *good* and *right* have any meaning; second, if they do have meaning, how is that meaning justified?

Modern metaethical inquiry emerged in the early part of the twentieth century with G.E. Moore's seminal work, *Principia Ethica*.[13] Since then, various metaethical theories on the meaning of moral terms have been developed. Nihilism claims that moral facts, moral truths, and moral knowledge do not exist and that, therefore, ethics is a meaningless discipline.[14] Emotivism asserts that moral terms are defined by individual emotions and desires; for emotivism, there is no objective or universal

[12] See Henry J. McCloskey, *Meta-Ethics and Normative Ethics* (The Hague: Martinus Nijhoff, 1969), 7; and John D. Arras, Bonnie Steinbock, and Alex John London, "Moral Reasoning in the Medical Context," in *Ethical Issues in Modern Medicine*, ed. John D. Arras and Bonnie Steinbock, 5th ed. (London: Mayfield, 1999), 1–40.

[13] George E. Moore, *Principia Ethica* (Cambridge, UK: Cambridge University Press, 1903, repr. 1968).

[14] Gilbert Harman, *The Nature of Morality: An Introduction to Ethics* (New York: Oxford University Press, 1977), 11.

truth since emotions are relative to each individual.[15] Relativism claims there are no universal truths; moral terms and moral truth are defined either socially or individually. Social or cultural relativism claims that moral judgments are nothing more than descriptions of customs or practices of a society or culture.[16] Personal relativism or subjectivism claims that moral judgments are nothing more than judgments about one's personal emotions or feelings.[17] This latter is the type of relativism castigated in Ratzinger's claim that relativism's "ultimate goal consists solely of one's own ego and desires." Both social and personal relativism deny that the good can be defined universally and, therefore, they assert that there is no objective basis on which to justify claims to universal truth and absolute norms or intrinsically immoral acts.

Objectivist metaethical theories claim both that moral terms do have meaning and that their meaning can be justified.[18] In Catholic theological ethics, the moral terms *good* and *right* are defined in relation to *human dignity*, *human fulfillment*, *human flourishing*, or some cognate formulation. What is good or right facilitates human dignity and flourishing; what is evil or wrong frustrates human dignity and flourishing. Virtually every Catholic theological ethicist espouses an objectivist metaethic and defines the good or right on the basis of what facilitates human dignity. There are among them, however, a variety of theological anthropologies and understandings of human dignity, and this variety explains the different formulations and justifications of norms facilitating or frustrating human dignity.

C. Gaudium et Spes: *Pluralist Objectivist Perspectives*

Whereas recent magisterial statements on relativism, such as *Veritatis Splendor*, seem to identify moral perspectives that disagree with its absolute proscriptive norms, especially in sexual and biomedical ethics,

---

[15] For a discussion of emotivism, see Charles L. Stevenson, *Ethics and Language* (New Haven, CT: Yale University Press, 1944).

[16] Robert M. Veatch, "Does Ethics Have an Empirical Basis," *Hastings Center Studies* 1 (1973): 52–53. See also, David F. Kelly, *Contemporary Catholic Health Care Ethics* (Washington, DC: Georgetown University Press, 2004), chap. 9.

[17] Veatch, "Does Ethics," 55.

[18] William K. Frankena, *Ethics*, 2nd ed. (Englewood Cliffs, NJ: Prentice Hall, 1973), 97–102. Veatch distinguishes between four types of absolutist theories, Supernatural, Rationalist, Intuitionist, and Empirical. Catholic natural law is considered an empirical absolutist theory. See Kelly, *Contemporary Catholic*, 81–85.

as relativist, *Gaudium et Spes* seems to account for pluralist objectivist perspectives; that is, while recognizing the existence of objective norms and universal values, there may be multiple perspectives when formulating, justifying, and applying those norms and values. The methodology which it proposes accounts for those multiple perspectives.

Gaudium et Spes is not preoccupied with situation ethics or relativism, as were previous and subsequent magisterial statements. This is a significant point given the focus of *Gaudium et Spes* and the ethical challenges—and the proposed responses to those challenges—contained in it. It is significant that the council fathers did not make situation ethics or relativism a central focus of a constitution specifically addressing Catholic moral theology, anthropology, and methodology. In fact, the section on conscience references Pius XII's document that includes a statement on situation ethics. However, *Gaudium et Spes* does not cite this reference to warn of the threat of situation ethics to the formation of conscience, as one might expect. Rather, it notes that "Conscience is the most secret core and sanctuary of a man. There he is alone with God, Whose voice echoes in his depths." The emphasis is on the sanctity of conscience and the place where we encounter God's voice in our lives. "For man has in his heart a law written by God. To obey it is the very dignity of man; according to it he will be judged" (GS 16).

While *Gaudium et Spes* is not preoccupied with situation ethics or relativism, it does emphasize the importance of an objective moral order and objective norms within this order. In its discussion on conscience, *Gaudium et Spes* notes that a right conscience must "strive to be guided by the objective norms of morality" (GS 16). There is an objective moral order and objective norms exist within that order. *Gaudium et Spes* espouses an objectivist metaethic. Nevertheless, the objectivism that *Gaudium et Spes* espouses more closely reflects a historically conscious neo-Thomist perspective, which sees the world, both external and internal, fashioned in history and, therefore, recognizes development and pluralism, rather than a classicist neo-Augustinian perspective, which sees the world as static and complete and resists change and denies pluralism.[19] The neo-Thomist perspective, reflected in *Gaudium et Spes* and "Theology Today" and espoused by the vast majority of Catholic ethicists, recognizes plural definitions of human dignity and the corresponding norms that facilitate

[19] Joseph A. Komonchak, "Augustine, Aquinas, or the Gospel *sine glossa?*" in *Unfinished Journey: The Church 40 Years after Vatican II; Essays for John Wilkins*, ed. Austin Ivereigh (New York: Continuum, 2005), 102–18.

its attainment; the neo-Augustinian perspective, reflected in *Veritatis Splendor* and espoused by John Paul II, Benedict XVI, and a minority of Catholic ethicists, recognizes a single definition of human dignity and the absolute proscriptive norms taught by the magisterium that facilitate its attainment. Historical evolution in Catholic teaching on issues such as usury, slavery, and religious freedom justifies a neo-Thomist perspective over a neo-Augustinian perspective. As Bernard Lonergan notes, Vatican II was an "acknowledgement of history."[20] Historicity and a neo-Thomist perspective shaped the council and methodologically informed its documents. It is no surprise that historicity and its methodological, anthropological, and moral implications would be a central consideration of *Gaudium et Spes* and shape its understanding of an objective moral order.

While *Gaudium et Spes* recognizes an objective moral order and objective norms within this order, those objective norms do not always supply us with the answers to many moral questions that confront human beings. *Gaudium et Spes* explains, "In fidelity to conscience, Christians are joined with the rest of men in the search for truth, and for the genuine solution to the numerous problems which arise in the life of individuals and from social relationships" (GS 16). Elsewhere, *Gaudium et Spes* cautions that laypeople should not imagine their pastors have all the answers to complex moral problems and empowers them to seek solutions through a well-formed conscience (GS 43). This seems to indicate that, at times, in the search for truth and in fidelity to conscience, there may be plural definitions of human dignity and the formulation and justification of norms that facilitate its attainment.

For example, whereas the magisterium teaches the objective norm prohibiting artificial contraception within a marital relationship, claiming that it frustrates human dignity and is, therefore, intrinsically immoral, social scientific data clearly show that the vast majority of Catholic couples approve of artificial contraception and, by implication, do not accept either that it frustrates human dignity or that it is intrinsically immoral.[21] Reflecting on the reasoned and conscientious experience of

---

[20] See J. Martin O'Hara, ed., *Curiosity at the Center of One's Life: Statements and Questions of R. Eric O'Connor* (Montreal: Thomas More Institute, 1984), 427.

[21] Studies in the United States indicate 75–85 percent of American Catholics, who consider themselves good Catholics, approve a form of contraception forbidden by the Church. See William V. D'Antonio, *et al.*, *Laity, American and Catholic: Transforming the Church* (Kansas City: Sheed and Ward, 1996), 131; James D. Davidson, et al., *The*

these married Catholic couples, we could formulate an alternative objective norm to the magisterium's as follows. Whether or not artificial contraception facilitates or frustrates human dignity depends on the reasons for choosing or not choosing it and on how it impacts one's relationships with oneself, one's spouse, and one's God. The difference between the magisterium's formulation and justification of an objective norm that facilitates human dignity and alternative formulations and justifications may or may not indicate metaethical relativism, but whether they do or not can be determined only by careful, case by case analysis of the corresponding definition of human dignity and the formulation and justification of objective norms.

If there is difference of opinion about specific objective norms that facilitate or frustrate human dignity, this does not *eo ipso* indicate a relativistic metaethical theory. To prove relativism it is not sufficient simply to demonstrate that basic moral judgments or objective norms are different. One also needs to demonstrate that these moral judgments or objective norms "would still be different even if they were fully enlightened, conceptually clear, shared the same factual beliefs, and were taking the same point of view."[22] Such a standard is high and, for this reason, William Frankena believes metaethical relativism has not been proven. The fact that people disagree with the magisterium on basic moral judgments or objective norms, such as the absolute norm forbidding contraception, in and of itself proves nothing. It may be that people deny the existence of universals, in which case they are certainly relativists. It may also be that they have a different objective definition of human dignity and the objective norms that facilitate or frustrate it, in which case they would be not relativists but objectivists.

Objectivism does not *per se* eliminate difference in either definitions of human dignity or in the formulation and justification of objective norms that facilitate its attainment, as the magisterium's documented evolution in its own moral teachings related to slavery, usury, religious

---

Search for Common Ground: What Unites and Divides Catholic Americans (Huntington, IN: Our Sunday Visitor, 1997), 131. For a similar situation in England, see Michael Hornsby-Smith, *Roman Catholicism in England: Customary Catholicism and Transformation of Religious Authority* (Cambridge, UK: Cambridge University Press, 1991), 177. A 2010 survey of English Catholics reveals that "just 4 per cent of Catholics believe the use of artificial contraception is wrong" (Christopher Lamb, "Few Now View Contraception as Immoral," *The Tablet* [18 September 2010]: 45).

[22] Frankena, *Ethics*, 110.

freedom, and torture well illustrate.[23] These are clear examples of the
magisterium's evolution of its understanding of human dignity, frequently assisted by the scholarly contributions of theologians and the
lived experience of laypeople and accompanied by a corresponding
evolution in the formulation and justification of objective norms. Catholic
ethicists and laypeople can espouse and defend metaethical objectivism
and still disagree on the objective definition of human dignity and the
objective norms that facilitate or frustrate its attainment. What accounts
for this variability is the second question of metaethics, namely, the epistemic justification of the definition of ethical terms. Bernard Lonergan
proposes *perspectivism* as a theory that justifies truth claims and contrasts
it with relativism.

D. Perspectivism or Relativism?

Lonergan's theory of perspectivism, in which different definitions
derive from different perspectives, adequately accounts for the different
definitions of human dignity and the norms that facilitate or frustrate
its attainment, and addresses magisterial charges of relativism aimed
at those who disagree with some of its absolute norms. Writing on the
nature of historical knowledge, Lonergan notes the following: "Where
relativism has lost hope about the attainment of truth, perspectivism
stresses the complexity of what the historian is writing about and, as
well, the specific difference of historical from mathematical, scientific
and philosophic knowledge."[24] Relativism concludes to the falsity of a
judgment; perspectivism concludes to its *partial* truth.

Lonergan offers three factors that give rise to perspectivism in human
knowledge, including moral knowledge. First, human knowers are finite,
the information available to them at any given time is as yet incomplete,
and they cannot attend to or master all the data available to them. Second,
the knowers are selective, given their different socializations, personal
experiences, and ranges of data offered to them. Third, knowers are individually different, and we can expect them to have different interpretations of the data available to them. The theologian-knower trained in the

[23] See John T. Noonan, "Development in Moral Doctrine," *Theological Studies* 54,
no. 4 (December 1993): 662–77; and Bernard Hoose, *Received Wisdom? Reviewing the
Role of Tradition in Christian Ethics* (London: Geoffrey Chapman, 1994).

[24] Bernard J. F. Lonergan, *Method in Theology* (New York: Herder and Herder,
1972), 217.

philosophy of Plato and Augustine for instance, will attend to different data, achieve different understanding, make different judgments, and act on different decisions from the theologian-knower trained in the philosophy of Aristotle and Aquinas, for instance. Augustine and Aquinas produce different theologies, both of which are necessarily partial and incomplete explanations of a very complex theological reality. They are like two viewers at fourth-story and thirteenth-story windows of the Empire State Building; each gets a different, but no less partial, view of all that lies outside the window. We could expect that if they ascended to a higher story they would get a different, but still partial, view again.

Every human judgment of truth, including every judgment of ethical truth, is a limited judgment and decision based on limited data and understanding. "So far from resting on knowledge of the universe, [a judgment] is to the effect that, no matter what the rest of the universe may prove to be, at least *this* is so."[25] It is precisely the necessarily limited nature of human sensations, understandings, judgments, and knowledge that leads to perspectivism, not as to a source of falsity but as to a source of partial truth. Though he said it on the basis of God's incomprehensibility, Augustine's restating of earlier Greek theologians is à propos and accurate here: "*Si comprehendis non est Deus,*" if you have understood, what you have understood is not God.[26] Aquinas agrees: "Now we cannot know what God is, but only what God is not; we must, therefore, consider the ways in which God does not exist rather than the ways in which God does."[27]

No single objectivist definition of human dignity comprehensively captures the full truth of human dignity. Perspectivism, however, accounts for the plurality of partial truths embedded in various definitions. It is a theory of knowledge that presents human persons as they exist, that selects those dimensions of the human person that are deemed most important for defining human dignity, that interprets and prioritizes those dimensions if and when they conflict, and that formulates and justifies norms that facilitate, and do not frustrate, the attainment of human dignity. The only way for humans to achieve knowledge that is

[25] Bernard J. F. Lonergan, *Insight: A Study of Human Understanding* (London: Longmans, 1957), 344, emphasis added. See also *Method in Theology*, 217–19.

[26] *Sermo* 52, 16, *PL* 38, 360; and "Theology Today" no. 97. For a detailed analysis, see Victor White, *God the Unknown* (New York: Harper, 1956); and William Hill, *Knowing the Unknown God* (New York: Philosophical Library, 1971).

[27] *ST*, I, III, preface.

universal is via perspectives that are particular.[28] It is focus on different particular perspectives that leads to different and partially true definitions of human dignity, and the formulation of different objective norms that facilitate or frustrate its attainment.

In summary, there is broad metaethical agreement within Catholic theological ethics. First, it accepts some version of metaethical objectivism; there *are* objective definitions of human dignity. Second, it defines the ethical terms *good* and *right* in relation to some objective definition of human dignity or some cognate formulation. Third, given different perspectives, it can and sometimes does disagree on both the specific definition of human dignity and the formulation and justification of objective norms that facilitate or frustrate its attainment. Fourth, Lonergan's theory of perspectivism, which recognizes the inherent limitations of human knowledge, helps to account for the different definitions of human dignity and the different formulations and justifications of objective norms that facilitate or frustrate its attainment. Fifth, the variability that arises from perspectivism is an essential part of an objectivism that recognizes universals; the good is *objectively* defined as human dignity. Different objective definitions of human dignity are not *eo ipso* a form of relativism that denies universals. Lonergan's perspectivism and its recognition of partial truths are substantiated anthropologically and theologically in *Gaudium et Spes* and other Vatican II documents on the dignity and authority of a well-formed conscience.

III. Conscience and Ethical Method: Objective Perspectivism

The concern with a "dictatorship of relativism" has impacted the magisterium's perspective on the nature and authority of conscience since Vatican II. According to the *Catechism*, "Conscience is a judgment of reason whereby the human person recognizes the moral quality of a concrete act that he is going to perform, is in the process of performing, or has already completed."[29] The Catholic tradition affirms the authority of conscience as the "proximate norm of morality" (VS 59–60); one has a moral obligation to follow one's well-formed conscience in moral mat-

---

[28] Bryan Massingale, "Beyond Revisionism: A Younger Moralist Looks at Charles E. Curran," in *A Call to Fidelity: On the Moral Theology of Charles E. Curran*, ed. James J. Walter, Timothy O'Connell, and Thomas A. Shannon (Washington, DC: Georgetown University Press, 2002), 258.

[29] CCC, no. 1778.

ters. A well-formed conscience must be informed by objective truth as this is reflected in divine law (VS 60).[30] Humans know divine law through a variety of sources including reason, the Word of God, gifts of the Holy Spirit, the witness of respected others, and "the authoritative teaching of the Church."[31] *Veritatis Splendor* and other magisterial documents label as relativism perspectives that disagree with its definition of human dignity and the absolute norms that it claims facilitate attaining human dignity. As we have seen with perspectivism, however, objectivism recognizes plural perspectives on the definition of human dignity and the formulation and justification of norms that facilitate its attainment. How does the epistemic insight of perspectivism impact a Catholic understanding of the authority of a well-formed conscience, especially in cases where there is disagreement between a well-formed conscience and the objective norms taught by the magisterium? In this section, we explore the nature and authority of conscience as developed in *Gaudium et Spes* and other Vatican II documents and the logical implications of perspectivism on the formation of conscience. In the final section, drawing from *Gaudium et Spes* as "a manifesto for contemporary moral theology,"[32] we propose dimensions of an ethical method for the individual and communal formation of conscience to explore the complex issues of our day.

A. Vatican II on the Nature and Authority of Conscience

The following are texts from *Gaudium et Spes* and *Dignitatis Humanae* on the nature and authority of conscience:

> For man has in his heart a law written by God; to obey it is the very dignity of man; according to it he will be judged. Conscience is the most secret core and sanctuary of a man. There he is alone with God, Whose voice echoes in his depths. (GS 16)

> There must be made available to all men everything necessary for leading a life truly human, such as . . . the right . . . to activity in accord with the upright norm of one's own conscience. (GS 26)

> For this Gospel has a sacred reverence for the dignity of conscience and its freedom of choice. (GS 41)

[30] Ibid.

[31] Ibid., nos. 1783, 1785.

[32] Joseph A. Selling, "*Gaudium et Spes*: A Manifesto for Contemporary Moral Theology," in *Vatican II and its Legacy*, ed. Leo Kenis and Matthew Lamberigts (Leuven, Belgium: Peeters Press, 2003), 145–61.

> A person must not be forced to act contrary to his conscience. Nor
> must he be prevented from acting according to his conscience,
> especially in religious matters. (DH 3)

Several points are evident from the above quotes on the nature and
authority of conscience. First, conscience is sacred; it is a gift from God.
Second, it is an intrinsic part of the human person. Third, following one's
conscience on moral and religious matters facilitates human dignity;
violating one's conscience on moral and religious matters frustrates
human dignity. Fourth, one must never be forced to act against one's
conscience; such force is a fundamental violation of conscience and of
human dignity. Fifth, the authority granted to conscience presumes
that one's conscience is well formed. In his *Veritatis Splendor*, John Paul
II warned of the dangers of relativism which detaches human freedom
from any objective or universal foundation and proposes certain methods
"for discovering the moral norm" which reject absolute and immutable
norms and precepts taught by the magisterium (VS 75). The presumption seems to be that if one rejects absolute norms and precepts taught
by the magisterium, one is a relativist.

A central question for the authority of conscience hinges on whether
or not conscience is well formed. Before addressing this question, however, we must make an important distinction between the adjectives
"absolute" (or nonabsolute) and "infallible" (or noninfallible) that classify objective norms. When using the adjective "absolute" to classify a
norm, it designates the status of a norm with regard to moral decision
making and asserts that no conceivable situation provides exceptions
to that norm. That is, according to this classification, the norm (e.g.,
do not murder) applies to all situations and in all cases. When using
the adjective "infallible" to classify a norm, it designates the status of a
norm with regard to its relationship to truth and the ecclesial authority
that makes a judgment on the permanent and enduring quality of that
truth. An infallible norm would be a norm determined as such by the
ordinary or extraordinary magisterium whose truth is essential to one's
faith. An objective norm may be absolute but not necessarily infallible.

Though in theory a norm could be infallible, according to Rahner,
"apart from wholly universal moral norms of an abstract kind [e.g., "do
good and avoid evil"], . . . there are hardly any particular or individual
norms of Christian morality which could be proclaimed by the ordinary
or extraordinary teaching authority of the Church in such a way that
they could be unequivocally and certainly declared to have the force of

dogmas."[33] Curran goes further, "there has never been an infallible teaching on a specific moral norm based on natural law and never can be."[34] Canon law states that "No doctrine is understood to be infallibly defined unless it is clearly established as such."[35] While some theologians have attempted to argue that the magisterium has taught infallible moral norms (e.g., the norm prohibiting contraception),[36] since there is considerable theological debate about whether or not it has taught such norms, the criterion of "clearly established" has not been met. Though it seems reasonable to conclude that the magisterium has not taught infallible objective norms, it has taught many absolute norms. History demonstrates that many of these absolute norms have changed and evolved. For example, the Ecumenical Councils, Lateran II (1139), Lateran III (1179), and Vienne (1311), all taught that taking interest on a loan, then called usury, was absolutely immoral and a mortal sin. That remained the solemn teaching of the Church until the mid-1500s when, in the context of the rise of banks, it began to change. Today, none of the Christian Churches hesitates to seek the best interest rates for its money. The absolute norms that the magisterium is most concerned with, norms addressing issues of human sexuality and biomedical ethical issues, for example, qualify as absolute, noninfallible norms. How should such norms inform conscience?

B. Vatican II on the Relationship between Conscience and Noninfallible Magisterial Teaching

While the authority of a well-formed conscience is clearly affirmed in *Gaudium et Spes*, *Dignitatis Humanae*, and the universal Catholic tradition,

---

[33] Karl Rahner, "Basic Observations on the Subject of Changeable and Unchangeable Factors in the Church," in *Theological Investigations*, vol. 14 (New York: Seabury Press, 1976), 14.

[34] Charles Curran, *The Catholic Moral Tradition Today: A Synthesis* (Washington, DC: Georgetown University Press, 1999), 224.

[35] James Coriden, et al., eds., *The Code of Canon Law: A Text and Commentary* (New York: Paulist Press, 1985), c. 749, no. 3.

36 Germain Grisez and John Ford, for example, claim that the magisterium's teaching against artificial contraception is infallible. See "Contraception and the Infallibility of the Ordinary Magisterium," *Theological Studies* 39, no. 2 (June 1978): 258–312; and Grisez, "Infallibility and Specific Moral Norms: A Review Discussion," *Thomist* 49, no. 2 (April 1985): 248–87; and, "*Quaestio Disputata*: The Ordinary Magisterium's Infallibility: A Reply to Some New Arguments," *Theological Studies* 55, no. 4 (December 1994): 737–38.

there still remains the question of how a conscience is to be well formed to warrant such authority. *The Code of Canon Law*, using the language of *Lumen Gentium*, n. 25, provides guidelines to respond to this question: "A religious respect (*religiosum obsequium*) of intellect and will, even if not the assent of faith, is to be paid to the teaching which the Supreme Pontiff or the college of bishops enunciate on faith or morals when they exercise the authentic magisterium even if they do not intend to proclaim it with a definitive act; therefore the Christian faithful are to take care to avoid whatever is not in harmony with that teaching."[37] A crucial question for interpreting this passage rests on the meaning of the Latin term *obsequium*. What does it mean for the faithful to give *obsequium* to noninfallible magisterial moral teachings in the formation of conscience?

The late Richard McCormick and many other theologians endorse renowned ecclesiologist Francis Sullivan's understanding of *obsequium*, though not necessarily his literal interpretation of the term. Sullivan argues that, in Latin, the term must be interpreted as submission; many theologians interpret it as respect.[38] Regardless of which interpretation one espouses, however, it "should not be translated simply as 'assent.'"[39] This is so because assent implies an either/or proposition; either one assents to the proposition or one does not. Respect, however, denotes an attitude, which entails "a basic respect for the authority of the magisterium, and an openness to its teaching."[40]

Concretely, what this means for Catholics and the formation of conscience is that there is a presumption of truth in favor of magisterial teachings, and that Catholics should strive to convince themselves of the truth of a particular teaching. This requires that they know and understand those teachings, the theology, science, and experience supporting them, and the values which the teachings express and are trying to promote and protect. This process should be followed in a spirit of prayer and discernment, seeking to know and deepen their understanding of divine law. When the faithful fulfill these requirements, however, if they

---

[37] James Coriden, et al., eds., *The Code of Canon Law*, c. 752.

[38] It is of acute interest that the Canon Law Society of America's official translation of and commentary on the revised Code of Canon Law translates *debito obsequio* as "due respect" (Canon 218) and *obsequium religiosum* as "religious respect" (Canons 752 and 753).

[39] Francis Sullivan, *Creative Fidelity: Weighing and Interpreting Documents of the Magisterium* (Mahwah, NJ: Paulist Press, 1996), 23.

[40] Ibid., 24.

conclude that they cannot intellectually assent to a particular teaching, they can faithfully dissent from this teaching while, at the same time, respecting the teaching authority of the magisterium. In this process, they have fulfilled their obligation of *obsequium* toward magisterial teaching and their obligation to form their consciences. In this process of formation, people may come to a definition of human dignity and formulate and justify norms for its attainment that differ from the magisterium's definition of human dignity and the norms that facilitate its attainment. Perspectivism and the authority of a well-formed conscience account for these plural definitions and the formulation and justification of norms.

This conclusion is affirmed in *Dignitatis Humanae* and by theologian Joseph Ratzinger. *Dignitatis Humanae* asserts, "In the formation of their consciences, the Christian faithful *ought carefully attend to* the sacred and certain doctrine of the church" (DH 14). A proposed emendation to the text reads as follows: "ought to form their consciences according to the teaching of the church." The theological commission overseeing this text declared that the proposed emendation "seems excessively restrictive. The obligation binding on the faithful is sufficiently expressed in the text as it stands."[41] According to Sullivan, if Catholics "carefully attend to" noninfallible magisterial teaching in the formation of conscience but, "despite serious and sustained effort," they are "unable to 'form their consciences according to it,'" there is no moral fault or "lack of religious submission to the teaching authority of the Church."[42]

In his commentary on *Gaudium et Spes*, n. 16, Joseph Ratzinger asserts, "Over the Pope as the expression of the binding claim of ecclesiastical authority there still stands one's own conscience, which must be obeyed before all else, if necessary even against the requirement of ecclesiastical authority. Conscience confronts [the individual] with a supreme and ultimate tribunal, and one which in the last resort is beyond the claim of external social groups, even of the official church."[43] In his role as theologian, head of the Congregation for the Doctrine of the Faith, and pope, he never distanced himself from this statement, since it encapsulates well the traditional teaching of the Catholic Church on the authority of conscience.

---

[41] *Acta Synodalia Concilii. Vat. II*, IV/6, 769.

[42] Sullivan, *Magisterium*, 169 70.

[43] Joseph Ratzinger, "The Dignity of the Human Person," in *Commentary on the Documents of Vatican II*, vol. 5, ed. Herbert Vorgrimler (New York: Herder and Herder, 1969), 134.

Though Philip Wogaman formulated the concept of "methodological presumption" in another context, this concept provides insight on how to navigate the relationship between the formation of a well-formed conscience and respect for noninfallible magisterial teaching:

> It is the method of arriving at a judgment despite uncertainties by making an initial presumption of the superiority of one set of conclusions and then testing that presumption by examining contradictory evidence. If, after examining the contradictory evidence, substantial doubt or uncertainty remains we decide the matter on the basis of the initial presumption.[44]

The "presumption" that Wogaman discusses is a reasonable articulation of *obsequium religiosum* and the presumption of truth that Catholics, in the formation of conscience, extend to the magisterium and the noninfallible norms that it teaches. It is an affirmation of those norms when, after examining contradictory evidence through the process of the formation of conscience, "substantial doubt or uncertainty remains" regarding that evidence. If, however, substantial doubt or uncertainty does not remain and the contradictory evidence is credible and compelling, then one has a moral obligation, in fidelity to conscience, to make a judgment that more adequately coincides with that evidence. A central component of that judgment requires a method for collecting, analyzing, and evaluating evidence that either confirms or challenges a presumptive norm.

IV. Perspectivism, Conscience, and Ethical Method

Perspectivism is an epistemological theory that recognizes objectivism and objective norms of morality and accounts for plural definitions of human dignity and the formulation and justification of norms that facilitate attaining human dignity. *Gaudium et Spes* and other documents from Vatican II on the nature and authority of a well-formed conscience account for objectivist perspectives that recognize the presumptive truth of the objective norms that the magisterium teaches, but also recognize legitimate disagreement with those teachings based on theological and scientific evidence that supports different definitions of human dignity and the norms that facilitate its attainment. Combined, perspectivism and Vatican II's discussions on the nature and authority of conscience

[44] J. Philip Wogaman, *A Christian Method of Moral Judgment* (Philadelphia: Westminster Press, 1976), 164.

provide a coherent response to "the signs of the times" and the magisterium's concerns about relativism. Relativism concludes to the falsity of a judgment of ethical truth; perspectivism concludes to its partial truth. They also provide a foundation for *Gaudium et Spes*'s call for laypeople to take an active role in the search for solutions to urgent ethical issues confronting humanity. Perspectivism and the authority of conscience invite further reflection on an ethical method for collecting, analyzing, and evaluating evidence to account for plural objectivist perspectives and to guide the formation of conscience to address these issues. We draw from the insights of *Gaudium et Spes*, as "a manifesto for moral theology," to propose components of an ethical method to guide individuals and community in the discernment of ethical truth.

A. Ethical Method

Bernard Lonergan defines method as "a normative pattern of recurrent and related operations yielding cumulative and progressive results."[45] Operations comprise such processes as gathering evidence; understanding, marshaling, and weighing the evidence; making judgments and evaluating their truth; and deciding to act. To construct a normative pattern, ethical method must account for both epistemic claims about how we know ethical truth and normative claims about the content of that truth. *Catholic ethical method is a theological method that proposes both an epistemology for reaching ethical truth and a normative pattern for reaching a definition of human dignity and formulating and justifying norms for its attainment*, all this within the Catholic tradition. We have already defined perspectivism as an epistemology for reaching ethical truth and the nature and authority of conscience that provides anthropological and theological justification for pluralist objectivist perspectives. Here, drawing from *Gaudium et Spes*, we explore components of a normative pattern to define human dignity and formulate and justify norms for its attainment, which aids in the formation of conscience to address urgent contemporary ethical problems confronting human beings.

B. Gaudium et Spes and Ethical Method

Gaudium et Spes n. 46, which serves as a transition from part 1 (the message the council fathers believed the people of God needed to pass

---

[45] Lonergan, *Method in Theology*, 4.

on to the world) to part 2 (the urgent needs facing the present age), states the following:

> This council has set forth the dignity of the human person and the work which men have been destined to undertake throughout the world both as individuals and as members of society. There are a number of particularly urgent needs characterizing the present age, needs which go to the roots of the human race. To a consideration of these *in the light of the Gospel and of human experience*, the council would now direct the attention of all. (GS 46)

Joseph Selling notes that this paragraph "stands as a milestone in the evolution of Roman Catholic moral theology."[46] It does so because it initiates a monumental methodological shift in Catholic moral theology, grounded in the Gospel *and* human experience, to guide a response to these urgent needs. Catholic moral theology is grounded in the natural law tradition. Aquinas describes natural law as "participation of the eternal law in the rational creature."[47] We know natural law through right reason (*recta ratio*). Prior to Vatican II, the emphasis on the knowledge of natural law and its contents was through rational reflection on creation and human nature. Reason, however, was often defined narrowly in terms of the created, biological order. Human nature, especially in relation to human sexuality, was defined in terms of this biological order, and norms were formulated that either facilitated or frustrated attaining this biological definition of human nature. In *Gaudium et Spes*, there is a revision of this reductionist definition of reason, focusing on the dignity of the human person and, with that revision, a methodological revolution in how to discern ethical truth. In fact, the revision is more of a return to Aquinas's holistic understanding of *recta ratio* which includes the intellectual, affective, relational, spiritual dimensions (though he was not always consistent in how he formulated and applied specific norms of natural law based on this understanding).

It is significant that paragraph 46 of *Gaudium et Spes* focuses on "human experience" as an essential source of moral knowledge to address urgent ethical issues. Human experience more adequately reflects Aquinas's *recta ratio* and encompasses the totality of the human inclination to want to know and understand the entirety of reality in the process of discern-

---

[46] Selling, "*Gaudium et Spes*," 151.
[47] Aquinas, *ST*, I–II, q. 91, a. 2.

ing truth.[48] This entirety includes a comprehensive understanding of reality including observation, research, intuition, common and aesthetic sense, and a comprehensive understanding of the dignity of the human person spiritually, relationally, psychologically, emotionally, physically, as well as intellectually.[49] Since these understandings are always finite and limited, since we are finite and limited human knowers, there will be pluralistic and partial definitions of comprehensive reality and human dignity. Perspectivism accounts for these pluralistic and partial perspectives; a well-formed conscience gives them moral authority; and *Gaudium et Spes* provides methodological components to guide in their ongoing comprehension.

Francis Sullivan summarizes well the relationship between conscience and knowledge of natural law in relation to specific moral issues and the process or method for arriving at this knowledge:

(a) The moral problems facing [hu]mankind today tend to be particularly complex;

(b) while the Gospel sheds light on these problems, it does not provide their solution;

(c) an indispensable role in the process of finding answers to concrete moral problems is played by human intelligence, reflecting on human experience;

(d) Christians share this arduous search along with all other [humans] of good will.[50]

Gaudium et Spes supports this arduous search (GS 43; also 33). And, "In fidelity to conscience, Christians are joined with the rest of men in the search for truth, and for the genuine solution to the numerous problems which arise in the life of individuals and from social relationships" (GS 16).

Recounting a conversation with Pope John XXIII, Roger Schutz remembers "very incredible, even downright heretical" things Pope John XXIII said to him, such as: "the Catholic Church does not possess the whole truth; we should search together."[51] This statement reflects well

---

[48] Richard M. Gula, *Reason Informed by Faith: Foundations of Catholic Morality* (Mahwah, NJ: Paulist Press, 1989), 224.

[49] Selling, "*Gaudium et Spes*," 151.

[50] Sullivan, *Magisterium*, 151.

[51] Yves Congar, *My Journal of the Council* (Collegeville, MN: Liturgical Press, 2012), 7.

both the spirit and content of *Gaudium et Spes*. It is "thanks to the *experience* of past ages, the progress of the *sciences*, and the treasures hidden in the various forms of *human culture*," *Gaudium et Spes* notes, that "the nature of man himself is more clearly revealed and *new roads to truth are opened*" (GS 44, emphasis added). These three sources of moral knowledge, experience, science, and human culture, combined with the Gospel, which includes tradition, indicate methodological components to facilitate a perspectivist, ongoing and evolving understanding of human dignity and the norms that facilitate its attainment. *Gaudium et Spes* provides revolutionary methodological developments that serve as a "manifesto for Catholic moral theology" to aid all people of good will in the search for truth. To those methodological developments we now turn.

C. Method and Sources of Moral Knowledge

As noted earlier, perspectivism is an epistemology that accounts for plural definitions of human dignity and the formulation and justification of norms for its attainment. A well-formed conscience gives moral authority to those definitions; ethical method provides a justification for them by proposing sources of evidence and a normative pattern for the selection, interpretation, prioritization, and integration of evidence to define human dignity and to formulate and justify norms to facilitate its attainment. By common theological and ecumenical agreement, this evidence is mined from what is often referred to as the Wesleyan Quadrilateral, four established sources of moral knowledge: namely, Scripture, tradition, secular disciplines of knowledge,[52] and human experience. Vatican II called for the renewal of Catholic theological ethics. We use the Wesleyan Quadrilateral to respond to this call and to propose a Catholic ethical methodological schema for the twenty-first century. We employ the Quadrilateral for four reasons. First, it includes the sources of moral knowledge we judge essential for doing Christian ethics, sources highlighted in various ways throughout Christian tradition, especially in *Gaudium et Spes* and the documents of Vatican II. Second, these four sources are essential to any Catholic ethical method, though particular

---

[52] Traditionally this source is referred to as "reason." However, we concur with Margaret Farley that every source of moral knowledge relies on reason, and "secular discipline" indicates disciplines distinct from, and not dependent on, revelation. See Farley, *Just Love: A Framework for Christian Sexual Ethics* (New York: Continuum, 2008), 188–89.

methods select, interpret, prioritize, and integrate the sources each in its own way. Third, there is a growing appreciation for, and specific reference to, these sources in the Catholic ethical literature from divergent normative perspectives,[53] though there remains the need for methodological discussion to investigate how the sources are to be selected, interpreted, prioritized, and integrated. This discussion will clarify the sources and their use and account for pluralist perspectives. Fourth, use of these four sources may encourage ecumenical and interreligious methodological considerations that should inform Catholic ethics and aid in the formation of a well-formed conscience.[54]

1. Scripture

The Second Vatican Council's *Optatam Totius* (Decree on Priestly Formation) prescribes that the scientific exposition of moral theology "should be more thoroughly nourished by scriptural teaching" (OT 16) since Scripture is the "very soul of sacred theology" (DV 24). Consequently, any Catholic ethical method must integrate Scripture and demonstrate how Scripture functions in its method. Given that Catholic ethical method is traditionally grounded in the natural law tradition, the role and function of Scripture in method requires serious investigation, especially given the use of Scripture in the manuals of moral theology since the Council of Trent. We ask whether Catholic ethical method has moved beyond the manuals' tendency to use Scripture merely as a source of proof texts and affirmation of ethical assertions that were deduced largely from natural law. Has Catholic ethical method moved, that is, from *eisegesis* to *exegesis*? In formulating ethical assertions, does it truly take into consideration revelation and its expression through Scripture, as this is articulated through the work of biblical scholars under the guidance of the magisterium? What is the role and function of Scripture in different ethical methods? The answers to these questions will reflect

---

[53] Lisa Sowle Cahill, *Between the Sexes: Foundations for a Christian Ethics of Sexuality* (Cincinnati, OH: Fortress Press, 1985), 4–7; Curran, *The Catholic Moral Tradition Today*, 47–55; Farley, *Just Love*, 182–96; James T. Bretzke, *A Morally Complex World: Engaging Contemporary Moral Theology* (Collegeville, MN: Liturgical Press, 2004), 9–41; and Todd A. Salzman, *What Are They Saying about Roman Catholic Ethical Method?* (Mahwah, NJ: Paulist Press, 2003).

[54] See James Gustafson, "Charles Curran: Ecumenical Moral Theologian Par Excellence," in *A Call to Fidelity*, 211–34.

the extent to which Catholic ethical method has taken seriously the call to renew moral theology through the incorporation of Scripture and will also shed light on the use of Scripture in ethical method.

Utilizing Scripture in ethical method, one must bear in mind the following two points. First, when investigating the methodological role of Scripture in a particular method, it is important to recognize that contemporary readers of Scripture bring certain perspectives, preunderstandings, and unacknowledged presuppositions to the text. A crucial part of a methodological investigation of Catholic ethics is to bring these presuppositions to the fore in order to comprehend more fully a particular method.[55] The second point to note is that the attempt to incorporate Scripture into an ethical method is akin to rationally, systematically, and coherently integrating the full mystery of the divine reality to which Scripture attests. As both Augustine and Aquinas remind us, this cannot be comprehensively and definitively done. *"Si comprehendis non est Deus,"* if you understand, it is not God, Augustine judges.[56] "Now we cannot know what God is but only what God is not," agrees Aquinas.[57] Sacred Scripture, a collection of diverse books from diverse times and cultures, seeks to reveal the holy mystery of God, but this mystery is so incomprehensibly rich that it can never be grasped in a single system or perspective. We must, like Augustine and Aquinas, embrace humility and approach Scripture and its use within Christian ethics with great care and trepidation.

The fullness of revelation, Christians believe, is not contained in a book or in a canon of books. It is in a person, the person of Jesus the Christ, who even after his incarnational revelation remains a mystery. *"Si intelligis non est Deus."* The project of developing an ethical method and seeking answers to complex ethical questions, however, cannot be content to live with mystery and, as a result, there is a fundamental tension between the truths contained in Scripture and how we use Scripture

---

[55] Thomas Ogletree, *The Use of Bible in Christian Ethics: A Constructive Essay* (Philadelphia: Fortress Press, 1983), 15–45. See also, William C. Spohn, *Go and Do Likewise: Jesus and Ethics* (New York: Continuum, 2007); Daniel J. Harrington and James F. Keenan, *Jesus and Virtue Ethics: Building Bridges between New Testament Studies and Moral Theology* (Lanham, MD: Sheed & Ward, 2002); and *id., Paul and Virtue Ethics: Building Bridges between New Testament Studies and Moral Theology* (Lanham, MD: Rowman & Littlefield, 2010).

[56] Augustine, *Sermo* 52, c. 6, 16, PL 38, 360.

[57] Aquinas, *ST*, I, 3, Preface.

and its truths in Christian ethics. Christian ethics will never contain the fullness of revelation, though it can reflect certain dimensions or parts of that revelation that, while no doubt important and foundational, do not tell the whole story. The use of Scripture in Christian ethics is impacted by perspectivism. The viewers at the fourth-story, thirteenth-story, and viewing-platform-story windows of the Empire State Building each get a different, but no less partial, view. The richness of Scripture defies complete comprehension as well, though there are methodological guidelines from magisterial documents for establishing parameters for what constitute authentic interpretations of Scripture.

In his important encyclical *Divino Afflante Spiritu*, Pope Pius XII laid the foundation for the methodological integration of Scripture into ethical method by endorsing the historical-critical method for interpretation. This method was reaffirmed by *Dei Verbum* at Vatican II, which prescribes that scriptural texts be read in the "literary forms" of the writer's "time and culture" (DV 12).[58] The Pontifical Biblical Commission's 1994 document, *The Interpretation of the Bible in the Church*, insists that "Holy scripture, in as much as it is 'the word of God in human language,' has been composed by human authors in all its various parts and in all the sources that lie behind them. Because of this, its proper understanding not only admits the use of [the historical-critical] method but actually requires it."[59] The commission acknowledges the historicity of the biblical texts, insisting that "religious texts are bound in reciprocal relationship to the societies in which they originate. . . . Consequently, the scientific study of the Bible requires as exact a knowledge as possible of the social conditions distinctive of the various milieus in which the traditions recorded in the Bible took shape."[60] The Catholic approach to reading biblical texts is clear: an historical-critical methodology is required for their correct interpretation.

Of particular relevance to this essay is the Commission's application of its principles for biblical exegesis to Catholic theological ethics. Though the Bible is God's word to the Church, "this does not mean that God has given the historical conditioning of the message a value which is absolute. It is open both to interpretation and being brought up to date." It follows, therefore, that it is not sufficient for moral judgment that the

---

[58] Pius XII, *Divino Afflante Spiritu*, *AAS* 35 (1943): 297–325.

[59] Pontifical Biblical Commission, "Interpretation of the Bible in the Church," *Origins* 23, no. 29 (January 6, 1994): 500.

[60] Ibid., 506.

Scripture "should indicate a certain moral position [e.g., the practices of polygamy, slavery, or divorce, or the 'prohibition' of homosexual acts] for this position to continue to have validity. One has to undertake a process of understanding and interpreting the text in its sociohistorical contexts and of discerning its contemporary relevance in the light of the progress in moral understanding and sensitivity that has occurred over the years."[61] It is for these reasons that Joseph Fuchs can assert correctly that what Augustine, Jerome, Aquinas, and Trent said about morality cannot exclusively control what moral theologians say today.[62] One must read, interpret, and apply Scripture according to the "signs of the times," in dialogue with other sources of moral knowledge such as human experience and the sciences, all in a particular historical-cultural context.

Scriptural and traditional doctrinal formulations are the result of reflexive, critical, human construal[63] and have to be, therefore, as historically conditioned as their construers themselves. It cannot be otherwise. If God is to be really revealed to historical women and men, there is no alternative but for the revelation to be mediated in their sociohistorical symbols. If the foundational revelation that occurred in the person of Jesus the Christ is to be expressed in human language, oral or written, as it is in scriptural, doctrinal, and theological formulations, there is no alternative but for the expression to be in a language that is historically mediated. There is no transhistorical, transcultural language valid for all times and for all peoples. Since the scriptural rule of faith and the theological writings derived from it are historically and culturally conditioned, they will require translation, interpretation, and cultural application to truly disclose God in every succeeding and different historical and cultural situation. Since the translators, interpreters, and inculturators may stand in different sociohistorical contexts and perspectives, their interpretations of the ancient tradition will almost certainly derive from and issue in a "plurality of theologies" (TT 5) which, in their turn, will almost certainly lead to theological debate. That debate will be profitably

---

[61] Ibid., 519.

[62] Joseph Fuchs, *Moral Demands and Personal Obligations* (Washington, DC: Georgetown University Press, 1993), 36.

[63] We mean by this word "to interpret," "to place a certain meaning on." We use it here to insinuate two connected meanings: first, the character of the theologian as construction worker within the Church; second, the character of theology as social construction, both that theology which preceded writings that came to be called Scripture as well as that theology which succeeded them.

resolved only by theologians, the faithful, all people of good will, and the hierarchical magisterium in respectful dialogue.

Discovering what Scripture says about morality, therefore, is never as straightforward as simply reading a text. The reader must get behind the text to understand how the Church and its theologians interpret Scripture and apply it to contemporary ethical issues. The Second Vatican Council issued instruction on how the Scriptures of both Testaments are to be read.

"Those who search out the intentions of the sacred writers," it teaches, "must, among other things have regard for 'literary forms.' For truth is proposed and expressed in a variety of ways, depending on whether a text is history of one kind or another, or whether its form is that of prophecy, poetry, or some other type of speech. The interpreter must investigate what meaning the sacred writer *intended to express and actually expressed* in particular circumstances as he used contemporary literary forms in accordance with the situation of his own time and culture" (DV 12; emphasis added).

It is never enough simply to read the text to find out what it says about morality. Its original sociohistorical context must first be clarified and then the text can be translated, interpreted, and applied in a contemporary context.

2. Tradition

The second source of moral knowledge is tradition, and it is intrinsically related to the first source, Scripture. Scripture and tradition, indeed, are but one source of divine revelation, since the New Testament is itself the tradition of the early Christian community. Scripture was written in a particular time and place for a particular people and may be said to be secondary revelation as the early Christian community's written interpretations of the primary revelation, namely, God's self-communication in the person of Jesus the Christ. The word *tradition* is used with two meanings. It can mean the handing on of the Church's continuing, Spirit-guided interpretation of the primary revelation in Jesus, and the secondary revelation in Scripture. It can also mean the content of what is handed on. The living tradition of the Catholic Church is precisely that, a living, evolving, and changing tradition. There are certainly fundamental truths of the Christian tradition at the heart of Christian identity—Trinity and incarnation, for example—but our *understanding* of these truths evolves and develops in light of contemporary advances in history, culture, reason, knowledge, and experience. This evolution takes place not only in dogmatic truths but also in Christian ethics and praxis which also evolve and develop in light of advances in moral questions and challenges. Under the guidance of the Holy Spirit, tradition interprets and applies the primary revelation in Jesus and the secondary revelation in Scripture in ever new and contextually appropriate ways.

It is customary to use the word *tradition* with two different spellings. Tradition with an uppercase "T" denotes the infrastructure and process for handing on Catholic faith and morals and *tradition* with a lowercase "t" denotes the content of faith and morals that is handed on.[64] A fundamental difference between ethical methods derives from a different interpretation of the role, function, and authority of both Tradition and tradition. For Tradition, the question of authority within the Church and the ecclesiology the view of authority reflects is central. For tradition, "the hermeneutic problem is to discern the difference between continuing a content that expresses divine revelation and a teaching that merely reflects the sociological and cultural circumstances of a particular time and place."[65] Since the impact of Tradition and tradition on theological ethics is extensive and warrants far greater treatment than we can provide here, we narrow our investigation of that impact to what Sandra Schneiders presents as three meanings of tradition: foundational gift, content, and mode.[66]

---

[64] See P.C. Rodger and Lucas Vischer, eds., *The Fourth World Conference on Faith and Order: Montreal, 1963, Faith and Order Papers, No. 42* (London: SCM, 1964), nos. 38–63, 66–106. It should be noted that the distinction made in this document differs fundamentally from that posited within Catholic theological discourse. In that discourse, Tradition refers not simply to the process and structure but also to the content, whereas traditions refer to particular determinations of the Tradition, which may be permanent in certain contexts, but are not necessarily enduringly normative. See Yves Congar, *Tradition and Traditions*, trans. Michael Naseby and Thomas Rainborough (New York: The Macmillan Company, 1967). Even within this discourse, however, there is fluidity in interpreting these two terms. For instance, while the International Theological Commission published a document titled "The Interpretation of Dogmas," and uses the terms Tradition and tradition throughout the text, it provides no explanation of the terms (see "De interpretatione dogmatum," *Gregorianum* 72 [1991]: 5–37). "Theology Today," no. 31, notes, "*traditions* must always be open to critique."

[65] Curran, *Catholic Moral Tradition Today*, 53.

[66] Sandra Schneiders, *The Revelatory Text: Interpreting the New Testament as Sacred Scripture* (San Francisco: HarperSanFrancisco, 1991; Collegeville, MN Liturgical Press, 1999), 71–81.

Foundational gift is the unfolding experience of the Church throughout history under the guidance of "the Holy Spirit who is the presence of the risen Jesus making the Church the Body of Christ."[67] All Catholic ethical methods recognize and accept tradition as foundational gift, but they can fundamentally disagree on who in the Body of Christ is *gifted* to discern ethical truth and the criteria for determining that *giftedness*, often referred to as charism.[68] Richard McCormick invites attention to the fact that there are unresolved theological tensions in the documents of the Second Vatican Council,[69] tensions which are evident in different passages within the same document describing who are the gifted for discerning ethical truth. *Lumen Gentium*, for instance, notes the following: "Bishops who teach in communion with the Roman Pontiff are to be revered by all as witnesses of divine and Catholic truth; the faithful, for their part, are obliged to submit to their bishops' decision, made in the name of Christ, in matters of faith and morals, and to adhere to it with a ready and respectful allegiance of mind" (LG 25; Flannery). In this passage, those who are gifted to teach are bishops in communion with the pope; the faithful are gifted to adhere to episcopal teaching. Elsewhere, *Lumen Gentium* also teaches that the entire people of God, bishops and laity alike, are gifted to discern both dogmatic and moral truth. "The body of the faithful as a whole, anointed as they are by the Holy One, cannot err in matters of belief. This characteristic is shown in the supernatural appreciation of the faith (*sensus fidei*) of the *whole* people, when, 'from the bishops to the last of the faithful' they manifest a universal consent in matters of faith and morals" (LG 12, emphasis added; Flannery). This gifting of the "whole people" is further affirmed in *Gaudium et Spes* and other Vatican II documents on the nature and authority of conscience, as we have seen.

Discerning who are gifted in the Church has implications for Schneiders's second meaning of tradition, namely, *content*. Content "is the sum total of appropriated and transmitted Christian experience, out of which Christians throughout history select the material for renewed syntheses of

---

[67] Ibid., 72.

[68] See Todd A. Salzman and Michael G. Lawler, "Theologians and the Magisterium: A Proposal for a Complementarity of Charisms through Dialogue," *Horizons* 36, no. 1 (Spring 2009): 7–31.

[69] Richard A. McCormick, *The Critical Calling: Reflections on Moral Dilemmas Since Vatican II* (Washington, DC: Georgetown University Press, 1989), 103.

faith."[70] The content of tradition is drawn from Scripture, church fathers, councils, encyclicals, and official teachings of the magisterium, the ongoing theological reflection within the Church in dialogue with culture, science, experience, and the *sensus fidei*, "the instinctive capacity of the whole Church to recognize the infallibility of the Spirit's truth."[71] The content from these sources must be critically selected and interpreted for its ongoing truth and usefulness for the moral life of the Church, using the same historical-critical method that is used for interpreting Scripture. If found not useful for advancing Catholic moral life, traditional content may be renewed, as was the traditional content related to the denial of a human right to religious freedom, or it may be discarded, as was the traditional content related to the morality of slavery.

One aspect of traditional content that the Second Vatican Council emphasized is an ongoing challenge for Catholic ethical method, namely, a fuller integration of and dialogue with other theological disciplines. In the history of moral theology, the integrated and holistic approach to theology of scholastic theologians such as Thomas Aquinas was abandoned in the aftermath of the Council of Trent. Moral theology became a distinct and separate theological discipline, more closely aligned with Canon Law than with the other three sources of ethics, namely Scripture, secular disciplines of knowledge, and human experience. The Second Vatican Council called for the scientific exploration of moral theology and the integration of moral theology with other theological disciplines. The integration of biblical, dogmatic, contextual, and comparative theology is an ongoing endeavor fully affirmed by "Theology Today." "Dialogue and interdisciplinary collaboration [between various forms of theology] are indispensable means of ensuring and expressing the unity of theology." This integrative approach to theology "serves to indicate a common search for truth, common service of the body of Christ and common devotion to the one God" (TT 80).

Judging who are the gifted in the people of God, who has the authority to discern and transmit the content of ethical truth, and the type of content that is transmitted, are all intrinsically and methodologically linked to Schneiders's third meaning of Tradition, namely, *mode*, "by which that content is made available to successive generations of believers, the way in which the traditioning of the faith is carried on throughout

---

[70] Schneiders, *The Revelatory Text*, 72.

[71] John E. Thiel, *Senses of Tradition: Continuity and Development in the Catholic Faith* (New York: Oxford University Press, 2000), 47.

history."[72] Mode is congruous with Tradition, the infrastructure and process for handing on lived faith. The point is frequently made that how one understands the role of the teaching authority within the Church is intimately linked with one's ecclesiology, or how one understands the nature of Church.[73] One's ecclesiology is central to how one understands Tradition as mode and the role and function of the magisterium in relation to the rest of the people of God, theologians and faithful.

Since the Second Vatican Council, theologians have generally adhered to one of two fundamentally different ecclesiological models. The model that originated in the Middle Ages and predominated up until the council is a hierarchical model, according to which the content of revelation and tradition flows downward from the magisterium to theologians and faithful. The role and function of theologians in this model is to make clear to the faithful the teaching of the magisterium, but not to question or challenge that teaching.[74] *Sensus fidelium* and *experientia fidelium* are sources of moral knowledge, but it is the responsibility of the magisterium to determine how those sources are to be interpreted and incorporated into its teaching. In cases where there is a disparity between *sensus et experientia fidelium* and magisterial teaching, as in the norms prohibiting contraception and homosexual activity, the magisterium gives the definitive interpretation of the meaning of human experience for the definition of human dignity and the formulation and justification of norms that facilitate or frustrate its attainment.

According to the hierarchical model, the magisterium is the final authority for interpreting, formulating, and dispensing ethical truth. Theologians help to explain and disseminate that truth to the faithful, but they are not to question or challenge authoritative, noninfallible teachings where the magisterium has deliberately stated an opinion about a controverted matter, even if their scholarship challenges it. This model is reflected in the Congregation for the Doctrine of the Faith's "Notification" on Margaret Farley's book, *Just Love*. It notes the following in its conclusion: "the Congregation wishes to encourage theologians to pursue

---

[72] Schneiders, *The Revelatory Text*, 72.

[73] See, for example, McCormick, *The Critical Calling*, 19–21, 34–45, 54–55, 163–69; and, "Some Early Reactions to *Veritatis Splendor*," in *Readings in Moral Theology No. 10: John Paul II and Moral Theology*, ed. Charles E. Curran and Richard A. McCormick (New York: Paulist Press, 1998), 28–30.

[74] This model is clearly reflected in Pius XII's *Humani Generis* (see, for example, Denzinger, nos. 2313–14) and more recently in the CDF's *Donum Veritatis*.

the task of studying and teaching moral theology in full concord with the principles of Catholic doctrine."[75] If we think of this ecclesiological model as a pyramid, the magisterium is at the pinnacle of the pyramid and is the hermeneutical key for selecting and interpreting all other sources of moral knowledge.

The Second Vatican Council introduced a renewed model of Church and, by implication, a renewed model of moral epistemology, namely, a people of God or communion model.[76] In this model, moral knowledge is discerned through the people of God in its totality—magisterium, theologians, and faithful alike. There is a trialogue among these three groups guided by the Holy Spirit, with Scripture, tradition, secular disciplines of knowledge, and human experience at the very center of the trialogue. It is this ongoing trialogue, conducted in charity, which moves the pilgrim Church forward in history toward a fuller knowledge, understanding, and appreciation of God's self-communication to humanity. The magisterium maintains authority in this model, and there is a presumption of the truth of its teaching, but its authority is qualified by its role as learner as well as teacher. The faithful in general and theologians in particular can facilitate, contribute to, and sometimes even challenge noninfallible magisterial teachings in this learning-teaching process. Yves Congar, the greatest Catholic ecclesiologist of the twentieth century, points out that obedience to Church authority is required when the Church is conceived on the hierarchical model and dialogue and consensus are required when it is conceived on the communion model. He adds the historical note that "it is certain that this second conception was the one that prevailed effectively during the first thousand years of Christianity, whereas the other one dominated in the West between the eleventh-century reformation and Vatican II."[77]

---

[75] "CDF Publishes Notification on Book 'Just Love,'" http://www.news.va/en/news/cdf-publishes-notification-on-book-just-love, accessed April 6, 2014.

[76] For the explanation of church as communion, see Jerome Hamer, *The Church Is a Communion* (New York: Sheed and Ward, 1965); Gustave Martelet, *Les idees maitresses de Vatican II* (Paris: Desclee, 1966); J. M. R. Tillard, *Church of Churches: The Ecclesiology of Church as Communion* (Collegeville, MN: Liturgical Press, 1992); Michael G. Lawler and Thomas J. Shanahan, *Church: A Spirited Communion* (Collegeville, MN: Liturgical Press, 1995).

[77] Yves Congar, "Reception as an Ecclesiological Reality," in *Election and Consensus in the Church*, *Concilium* 77, ed. Giuseppe Alberigo and Anton Weiler (New York: Herder and Herder, 1972), 62.

Virtually all Catholic theologians accept the first meaning of tradition as gift. They are fundamentally divided, however, on both what content from tradition is selected as normative and the mode for its selection, interpretation, and application. Some ethical methods, for instance, posit the magisterium as the definitive mode for the selection, interpretation, and application of the content of tradition to ethical issues. Others, while respecting the role, function, and authority of the magisterium to operate in this capacity, recognize other modes, such as the *sensus fidelium*, that may disagree with the magisterium's selection, interpretation, and application of content. Resolving such disagreements requires deliberation and "dialogue in charity," guided by the Holy Spirit. Similar methods used for the selection, interpretation, and application of Scripture to ethical issues, such as the historical-critical method, are also useful for the selection, interpretation, and application of the content of tradition. The selection, interpretation, and application of the content of tradition and the infrastructure that judges the normativity of that content will differ depending on perspective, ethical method, and the understanding of tradition as foundational gift, content, and mode.

3. Human Experience

We fully agree with Servais Pinckaers that human experience has "a very important function in moral theology."[78] *Gaudium et Spes* emphasizes, and Pope John Paul II fully affirms, the relevance of human experience for theological reflection. Critically and theologically interpreted human experience, of both past and present, helps to construct a definition of human dignity and to formulate and justify norms to facilitate its attainment; experience serves as a window onto the morally normative. To deny the validity and moral relevance of human experience for assisting in the definition of human dignity and the formulation and justification of norms that facilitate its attainment reflects a reductionist methodology where the only legitimate human experience is that which conforms to, and confirms, established norms. It was such a methodology, in large part, which allowed the magisterium's approbation of slavery until Pope Leo XIII's rejection of it in 1890 and the denial of religious freedom until the Second Vatican Council's approbation of it

---

[78] Servais Pinckaers, *The Sources of Christian Ethics* (Washington, DC: Catholic University of America Press, 1995), 91.

in 1965. John Noonan comments with respect to the magisterium's late condemnation of slavery: "it was the experience of unfreedom, in the gospel's light, that made the contrary shine clear."[79]

A legitimate question at this point is, whose experience is to be used in the formulation of a definition of human dignity and the formulation and justification of norms that facilitate its attainment? We emphasize again that human experience is only one part of the moral quadrilateral and never a stand-alone source of moral theology. "My experience" alone is never a source at all. Moral authority is ecclesially granted only to "our experience," to *communal* experience, as a source of moral theology, and only in constructive conversation with the three other sources, Scripture, tradition, and reason, as well as with the theological reality called *sensus fidelium*, the sense of the faithful and their lived experience. First, however, we must clarify what we mean by experience.

There is little to be gained from simply encountering the world in which we live; many people have many such encounters and learn little from them. The experience we speak of in this chapter, with Neil Brown, intends "the human capacity to encounter the surrounding world consciously, to observe it, be affected by it, and to learn from it."[80] It is of the essence of such experience that it is never raw, neutral, pure, unadulterated encounter with the world. It is always interpreted, construed, socially constructed by both individuals and communities in specific sociohistorical contexts. It is, therefore, also dialectical, differently construed, perhaps, by "me," by "you," by "us," and by "them," by neo-Thomist and neo-Augustinian theologians, for instance. For genuine human experience as we have defined it, the dialectic is necessarily a "dialectic of reason *and* experience" and never a dialectic controlled by either reason or experience alone. It is also a dialectic that results not in an absolutist moral code but in "various revisable rules."[81] In a Church that is a communion of believers, the resolution of different construals of experience to arrive at ethical truth requires an open, respectful, charitable, and prayerful dialogue, such as that lauded and rhetorically

[79] Noonan, "Development in Moral Doctrine," 674–75.

[80] Neil Brown, "Experience and Development in Catholic Moral Theology," *Pacifica* 14 (October 2001): 300.

[81] Edward Collins Vacek, "Catholic 'Natural Law' and Reproductive Ethics," *Journal of Medicine and Philosophy* 17 (1992): 342–43.

embraced by Pope John Paul II.[82] Charitable dialogue must occur internally, among the communion of believers, some of whom are laity, some of whom are theologians, and some of whom are bishops including the Bishop of Rome,[83] all of whom, if feminist theologians are right, and we believe they are, acquire knowledge through practice or action,[84] that is, through experience, and externally, among all people of good will.

In the formation of conscience, people are tasked to discern what human experience confirms or challenges one's definition of human dignity and, correspondingly, to formulate and justify norms that facilitate its attainment. This process of discernment may lead to a confirmation of the definition of human dignity and a corresponding confirmation of the norms that facilitate its attainment, or it may lead to a transformation of the definition of human dignity and a corresponding transformation of the norms that facilitate its attainment. Knowledge of the experiences of the faithful or *sensus fidelium*, which can be collected and measured by the sciences, is an important source of moral wisdom to facilitate this process of confirmation or transformation of the definition of human dignity and the formulation and justification of norms to facilitate its attainment.

4. Sciences

The sciences aid in reflecting on, analyzing, and evaluating human experience and are essential methodological sources of moral knowledge for a well-formed conscience. Pope John Paul II notes that "the Church values sociological and statistical research when it proves helpful in understanding the historical context in which pastoral action has to be developed and when it leads to a better understanding of the truth" (*Familiaris Consortio* 5). He highlights the need for intense dialogue between science and theology.[85] Theology and science must enter into a "common interactive relationship" whereby, while maintaining its own integrity, each discipline is "open to the discoveries and insights of the other." Physicist Ian Barbour

[82] John Paul II, *Ut Unum Sint*, nos. 28–39. See Salzman and Lawler, "Theologians and the Magisterium."

[83] We shall use this tripartite division of believers throughout for purposes that will become apparent as we proceed.

[84] Richard Bernstein, *Beyond Objectivism and Relativism* (Philadelphia: University of Pennsylvania Press, 1985), 74.

[85] John Paul II, "The Relationship of Science and Theology: A Letter to Jesuit Father George Coyne," in *Origins* 18, no. 23 (November 17, 1988): 375–78.

proposes a fourfold typology of the relationship between theology and science: conflict, independence, dialogue, and integration.[86] Particularly germane to our topic are the dialogue and integration typologies.

The *dialogue* typology explores methodological parallels, content, and boundary questions. Methodological parallels seek out similarities and dissimilarities between the methods of each discipline that may either complement or serve the method of the other. Boundary questions delimit the capabilities of each discipline and stipulate how far each may go in explaining reality. The *integration* typology encompasses natural theology, theology of nature, and a systematic synthesis of science and religion. For natural theology, the world is the point of departure and the goal is to deepen theological understanding by integrating theological insights. For theology of nature, a particular theological tradition is the point of departure and the goal is to seek to integrate scientific insights into that tradition. For systematic synthesis, the point of departure is the methods, knowledge, and language of theology and science and the goal is to integrate the two into a single system.[87]

Barbour's dialogue and integration typologies parallel John Paul II's proposal for a "community of interchange" between theology and science to expand the partial perspectives of each and "form a new unified vision." An important caveat should be heeded, however: theology should not seek to become science and science should not seek to become theology in terms of either method or content. "Unity always presupposes the diversity and the integrity of its elements."[88] Neither science nor theology should become less itself but, rather, more itself in a dynamic interchange. Each discipline retains its own autonomy and language and yet draws knowledge and insight from the other.[89] This knowledge and insight shapes the faithful's perspective in the process of forming their consciences and aids in the search for answers to complex questions.

---

[86] Ian G. Barbour, *Nature, Human Nature, and God* (Minneapolis, MN: Fortress Press, 2002), 1–2.

[87] Ibid. See also, Robert John Russell and Kirk Wegter-McNelly, "Science and Theology: Mutual Interaction," in *Bridging Science and Religion*, ed. Ted Peters and Gaymon Bennett (Minneapolis, MN: Fortress Press, 2003), 19–34.

[88] John Paul II, "The Relationship of Science and Theology," 377.

[89] Ibid. See also Michael J. Buckley, "Religion and Science: Paul Davies and John Paul II," in *Theological Studies* 51, no. 2 (June 1990): 310–24.

5. Culture

Culture provides the context and material for the sociological sciences and the faithful's reflection on sociological contributions. *Gaudium et Spes* notes that "from the beginning of [the Church's] history, she has learned to express the message of Christ with the help of the ideas and terminology of various peoples" (GS 44); that is, through the particularity of various cultural experiences. It is undoubtedly true that the Church is called on occasion to be countercultural, to confront cultural theories and actions that do not lead to human dignity, for example, the rabid individualism rampant in the culture of the United States. It is also undoubtedly true that reflection on cultural experience can lead to insight into ethical truth and facilitate the communication of that truth within the culture and from one culture to another. This second case is especially true when a particular cultural context requires specific norms to address specific moral problems. The pastoral letters of the bishops of the United States on the economy and nuclear war are examples of the dialectic between culture and the development of moral norms. The letters draw on the traditional Catholic principles of justice and fairness to formulate culturally specific norms, but the understanding of justice and fairness they evince is transformed in light of the specific and cultural experiences to which they respond. Culture impacts all dimensions of the human person. Discerning the impact of culture on the definition of human dignity and the formulation and justification of norms to facilitate its attainment is an essential methodological consideration that allows for a plurality of definitions and norms in social ethics and sexual ethics.

6. Contextual Theology

One of the major developments in Catholic ethical method in the late twentieth and early twenty-first centuries, one which flows out of *Gaudium et Spes*'s focus on human experience and culture as essential components for discerning ethical truth, has been the emphasis on doing theological ethics in context. Stephen Bevans defines contextual theology "as a way of doing theology in which one takes into account the spirit and message of the gospel; the tradition of the Christian people; the culture in which one is theologizing; and social change in that culture, whether brought about by western technological process or the grassroots struggle for equality, justice and liberation."[90]

---

[90] Stephen Bevans, *Models of Contextual Theology* (Maryknoll, NY: Orbis Books, 1992), 1.

A strong tendency of theological ethics since the Second Vatican Council, which is reflected in contextual theology, is its focus less on the abstract universality of human nature and shared human experience and more on the concrete particularity of the human person and human experience within particular cultures, societies, and histories. We are in full agreement with Bryan Massingale, "the only way to universal insights is through particular perspectives."[91] Focus on contextual theology and particularity has led to different theological anthropologies and norms that facilitate attaining human dignity. There are particular and different norms that fulfill human dignity in different cultural contexts because there are particular and different theological anthropologies and definitions of human dignity.

V. Conclusion

The methodological contribution of *Gaudium et Spes* and its focus on the gospel and human experience, which includes tradition, the sciences, culture, and contextual theology, provides a revolutionary evolution in Catholic moral theology to aid in reading "the signs of the times" and the formation of a well-formed conscience seeking answers to the complex questions facing human beings. Depending on the perspective of individuals and communities, the selection, prioritization, interpretation, and integration of the various sources of moral knowledge may lead to plural definitions of human dignity and the norms that facilitate its attainment. These plural definitions, again, are not *eo ipso* evidence of relativism. Relativism concludes to the falsity of a judgment; perspectivism concludes to its partial truth. The partial truths inherent in every definition of human dignity and every formulation and justification of norms to realize its attainment highlight the ongoing moral imperative of *Gaudium et Spes* to continually read "the signs of the times," relying on perspectivism, a well-formed conscience, and the ethical methodological criteria articulated in *Gaudium et Spes* and other Vatican II documents as well as the Catholic tradition, to seek answers to the complex moral questions facing humanity. It is to those issues that we now turn.

---

[91] Massingale, "Beyond Revisionism," 258.

Questions for Reflection

1. Explain how *Gaudium et Spes* is "a manifesto for contemporary moral theology."

2. What do you understand by the term "method"? What operations are involved in a theological, ethical method?

3. What do you understand by the term "relativism" and by the term "perspectivism"? What is the essential difference between the two realities?

4. What do you understand by the terms "metaethics," "normative ethics," and "moral judgments." What are the functions in ethics of each of these three realities? What is their relationship of one to the other?

5. What are the role, function, and authority of conscience in moral decision making?

6. How do the selection, interpretation, prioritization, and integration of the sources of moral knowledge impact your definition of human dignity and the formulation and justification of norms that facilitate attaining human dignity?

7. How do experience, the sciences, and "the treasures hidden in the various forms of human culture," reveal new roads to truth? Give examples from your own culture that either facilitate or frustrate attaining human dignity.

Chapter Four

Gaudium et Spes: Marriage

Introduction

Human sexuality and marriage in which it is institutionalized are both sociohistorical realities and are, therefore, subject to historicity. In the council's debate on marriage, Cardinals Ruffini and Ottaviani argued, in the classicist neo-Augustinian mode, that the Church need only repeat the past teachings of Pius XI and Pius XII and certainly should not abandon them. Bishop Staverman of Indonesia responded, in the historically conscious neo-Thomist mode, that like every other historical reality, marriage evolves and that, therefore, the Church could not be content simply to repeat its past teachings. To do so is precisely to cause what was already happening, namely, the Church was losing its pastoral effectiveness and moral voice. It is time, he added, to listen to more lay experts who understand modern marriage better than any bishop or priest. Before we embark on a presentation of *Gaudium et Spes*'s theology of marriage, therefore, it behooves us to look at its past history. We will do that in two stages. First, and briefly, we will consider the pre-Christian history that helped to shape a Western understanding of sexuality and marriage. Secondly, and more extendedly, we will consider their understanding in specifically Catholic history. Before embarking on the history, however, we must first say a word about historicity.

Historicity

Bernard Lonergan lays out "the theoretical premises from which there follows the historicity of human thought and action." They are as follows: "(1) that human concepts, theories, affirmations, courses of action are expressions of human understanding . . . (2) That human understanding develops over time and, as it develops, human concepts, theories, affirmations, courses of action change . . . (3) That such change is cumulative, and (4) that the cumulative changes in one place or time are not to be expected to coincide with those in another."[1] From these premises flows the conclusion that the articulations of the values, norms, and actions of one sociohistorical era are not necessarily those of another era. The world, both the world free of every human intervention and the human world fashioned by socially constructed meanings and values, is in a permanent state of change and evolution. It is essentially for this reason that Joseph Fuchs argues, correctly in our judgment, that anyone wishing to make a value judgment about any human action in the present on the basis of its givenness in the past has, at least, two facts to keep in mind.

First, the past simply did not know the entire reality of the human person from its emergence to its full development in the future or its individual elements from the mysterious powers of the physical universe to the possibilities of human sexuality considered physiologically, psychologically, and sociohistorically. "If one wishes to make an objective moral judgment today," Fuchs points out, "then one cannot take what Augustine or the philosophers of the Middle Ages knew about sexuality as the exclusive basis of a moral reflection."[2] Second, "we never simply 'have' nature or that which is given in nature." We know "nature," rather, "always as something that has already been interpreted in some way."[3] The understanding, interpretation, and judgment of rational persons about *nature* and what it demands is what constitutes *natural law*, never simply the pure givenness of *nature* alone. In the Catholic moral tradition, argument is never from nature alone or reason alone, but always from nature *interpreted by* reason. For the human person subject to historicity, moral decision making and action is always the outcome of a process of interpretation controlled by reason. It is never the outcome of the mere fact of *nature*.

We introduced in the preface and first chapter distinctions between classicist theology and historically conscious theology and between neo-Augustinian and neo-Thomist theology. Those distinctions are very important in this chapter and need to be recalled. In its classicist mode, theology is a static, permanent achievement that anyone can learn; in its empirical mode it is a dynamic, ongoing process requiring a free person who is committed and trained. Classicist theologians see theological

---

[1] Bernard J. F. Lonergan, *Method in Theology* (New York: Herder and Herder, 1972), 325.

[2] Joseph Fuchs, *Moral Demands and Personal Obligations* (Washington, DC: Georgetown University Press, 1993), 36.

[3] Ibid.

norms coming from the magisterium as once and for all definitive; marital norms enunciated in the fifth, thirteenth, or nineteenth centuries continue to apply absolutely in the twenty-first century. Historically conscious theologians see the norms of the past not as facts for uncritical acceptance, but as partial insights providing bases for critical understanding, evaluation, and decision in the present sociohistorical situation. What Augustine and his medieval successors knew about sexuality and marriage cannot be the exclusive basis for a moral judgment about sexuality today.

Sexuality and Sexual Ethics in Ancient Greece and Rome

Though generalizations about ancient Greece and Rome are fraught with difficulties, both because their histories were in general written by elite males to the detriment of women's sexual histories, and because we know today more about Athens and Rome than about any other Greek or Roman city, we can safely say that in both societies sexuality was generally accepted as a natural part of life, and that attitudes toward sex were permissive, especially for men.[4] In both societies, marriage was monogamous and regarded as the foundation of social life, but sexual activity was not restricted to marriage. Judith Hallett demonstrates that, at least among elite men and women, erotic intercourse could be sought with partners other than spouses,[5] and concubinage, male and female prostitution, and male intercourse with slaves were also permitted and

[4] See, for instance, David Cohen, *Law, Sexuality, and Society: The Enforcement of Morality in Ancient Athens* (New York: Cambridge University Press, 1991); Kenneth J. Dover, *Greek Popular Morality in the Time of Plato and Aristotle* (Berkeley, CA: University of California Press, 1974); Michel Foucault, *The History of Sexuality*, 3 vols., especially vols. 2 and 3 (New York: Pantheon Books, 1978–1988); Otto Kiefer, *Sexual Life in Ancient Rome* (New York: AMS Press, 1975); Ross S. Kraemer and Mary Rose D'Angelo, *Women and Christian Origins* (New York: Oxford University Press, 1999); Martha C. Nussbaum and Juha Sihvola, eds., *The Sleep of Reason: Erotic Experience and Sexual Ethics in Ancient Greece and Rome* (Chicago: University of Chicago Press, 2002); Sarah Pomeroy, *Goddesses, Whores, Wives, and Slaves: Women in Classical Antiquity* (New York: Schocken Books, 1975); Aline Rousselle, *On Desire and the Body in Antiquity* (Oxford: Blackwell, 1988); Marilyn B. Skinner, *Sexuality in Greek and Roman Culture* (Oxford: Blackwell, 2005); various entries in Alan Soble, ed., *Sex from Plato to Paglia: A Philosophical Encyclopedia* (Westport, CT: Greenwood, 2006). That not all these sources agree about everything is eloquent testimony to the difficulty inherent in historical interpretation.

[5] Judith P. Hallett, "Women's Lives in the Ancient Mediterranean," in *Women and Christian Origins*, 13–34.

common. Divorce was readily available in Greece and the later Roman Empire, with both societies legislating for the economic situation of divorced women. Abortion and infanticide were commonly accepted forms of birth control. Marriage was not about love, which is not to say that marital love was never present between spouses. Men were expected to marry to produce an heir, but for them the greatest love was to be had in relationship, sexual or otherwise, with other men, for between men there was an equality that a man could never attain with a woman.

Greek and Roman attitudes toward sexuality were fashioned in large part by their great philosophers. The Greek dualism between body and soul, with the body being the inferior component, led to a distrust of sex and the negative categorization of sexual pleasure. Both Plato[6] and Aristotle[7] judged sexual pleasure to be a lower pleasure shared with other animals. Plato urged its transcendence for the sake of the higher pleasures of good, beauty, and truth; Aristotle urged its moderation. It was not, however, Plato or Aristotle that had the greatest influence on the Christian approach to sexuality. It was the Stoics, who considered sexual desire and activity to be irrational and liable to excess. They sought, therefore, to rationally order it by situating it in a larger context of human meaning, and they did this by asking about its purpose or end. That end, they judged, was the procreation of children and, therefore, sexual activity was moral *only* when it was engaged in for the sake of procreation. The later Stoics went further. Not only was sexual activity for procreation but also it was to be limited to marriage; there could be no moral sex outside of marriage. Stoic philosophers both "conjugalized" and "procreationalized" sexual relations.

Sexuality and Sexual Ethics in the Catholic Tradition

In 1968, in his postconciliar encyclical *Humanae Vitae*, Pope Paul VI asserted that in marriage "each and every marriage act must remain open to the transmission of life" (HV 11). In 1976, the Congregation for the Doctrine of the Faith asserted that, to be moral, "any human genital act whatsoever may be placed only within the framework of marriage" (*Persona Humana* [PH] 7). In traditional Catholic sexual morality, therefore, every moral sexual act takes place only within the institution of marriage, and within marriage each and every such act must be open

---

[6] The *Republic* IX, the *Symposium, and the Laws*.
[7] *Nichomachean Ethics*, III.

to procreation. The consonance of that teaching with Stoic philosophy is clear. It would be wholly inaccurate, however, to assume that Greek philosophy is the only root of Catholic sexual and marital teaching. Catholicism's first instinct is to consult not ancient Greek philosophers, but its ancient sacred text, the Bible, believed to be the very word of God. So we begin our analysis of the development of traditional Catholic marital teaching with a brief exploration of, first, the Old and, then, the New Testament. Following the lead of the Second Vatican Council, we then follow the biblical tradition through its subsequent history, in which, under the grace of the Spirit of God, "there is a growth in insight into the realities and words that are being passed on" (DV 8).

Reading Sacred Scripture

The Pontifical Biblical Commission's 1994 document, *The Interpretation of the Bible in the Church*, insists that "Holy scripture, in as much as it is 'the word of God in human language,' has been composed by human authors in all its various parts and in all the sources that lie behind them. Because of this, its proper understanding not only admits the use of [the historical-critical] method but actually requires it."[8] It acknowledges the historicity of the biblical texts, insisting that "religious texts are bound in reciprocal relationship to the societies in which they originate. . . . Consequently, the scientific study of the Bible requires as exact a knowledge as possible of the social conditions distinctive of the various milieus in which the traditions recorded in the Bible took shape."[9] The very nature of the biblical texts requires the use of a historical methodology for their correct interpretation.

Discovering what Scripture says about sexuality and marriage, therefore, is never as straightforward as simply reading a text. The reader must get behind the text to understand how the Church and its theologians construe Scripture and what authority they assign to it. The Second Vatican Council made clear how the Scriptures of both Testaments are to be read. "Those who search out the intentions of the sacred writers," it teaches, "must, among other things have regard for 'literary forms.' For truth is proposed and expressed in a variety of ways, depending on whether a text is history of one kind or another, or whether its form is that

[8] Pontifical Biblical Commission, "Interpretation of the Bible in the Church," *Origins* 23, no. 29 (January 6, 1994): 500.
[9] Ibid., 506.

of prophecy, poetry, or some other type of speech. The interpreter must investigate what meaning the sacred writer *intended to express and actually expressed* in particular circumstances as he used contemporary literary forms in accordance with the situation of his own time and culture" (DV 12; emphasis added). It is never enough simply to read the text to find out what it says about sexual morality. Its original sociohistorical context must first be clarified and then the text can be translated, interpreted, and inculturated in a contemporary context.

The Biblical Teaching

Old Testament teaching on sexuality and marriage must be situated in the context of the ancient Near Eastern cultures with which the biblical peoples had such intimate links. Underlying the themes of sexuality and marriage in the cultures surrounding Israel are the archetypal figures of the god-father and the goddess-mother, the sources of universal life in the divine, the human, and the natural realms. Myths celebrated the marriage, the sexual intercourse, and the fertility of this divine pair, simultaneously divinizing sexuality and legitimating the marriage of every earthly pair. Rituals acted out the myths, establishing a concrete link between the divine and the earthly worlds, enabling men and women to share in both the divine action and the efficacy of that action. This is especially true of sexual rituals, which bless sexual intercourse and ensure that the unfailing divine fertility is shared by a man's plants and animals and wives, all important elements in his struggle for survival in those primitive cultures.

The Hebrew view of sexuality and marriage makes a radical break with this polytheistic perspective.[10] Sexuality is not divinized. There is no god-goddess couple, only Yahweh who is unique (Deut 6:4). In the later Priestly account, God creates merely by uttering a creative word (Gen 1) and, in the earlier Yahwist account, by shaping creation as a

---

[10] There are many good treatments of Jewish approaches to sexuality and sexual ethics, though, as with the Greco-Roman histories we saw, they do not all necessarily agree on everything. We recommend the following: David Biale, *Eros and the Jews: From Biblical Israel to Contemporary America* (New York: Basic Books, 1992); Louis M. Epstein, *Sex, Laws, and Customs in Judaism* (New York: Block, 1948); Michael Kaufman, *Love, Marriage, and Family in Jewish Law and Tradition* (Northvale, NJ: Aronson, 1992); David Novak, *Jewish Social Ethics* (New York: Oxford University Press, 1992); Judith Plaskow, *Standing Again at Sinai: Judaism from a Feminist Perspective* (San Francisco: Harper and Row, 1990).

potter (Gen 2–3). At the apex of Yahweh's creation stands *'adam*, man and woman together: "male and female he created them and he blessed them and named them *'adam*" (Gen 5:2). The fact that Yahweh names male and female together *'adam*, that is, earthlings or humankind, founds the essential equality of man and woman as human beings. They are "bone of my bones and flesh of my flesh" (Gen 2:23), and because they are equal they can marry and become "one body" (Gen 2:24). In marriage, equal man and woman take on the culturally unequal gendered roles of husband and wife,[11] and this provides a foundation for biblical and subsequent patriarchy.

The older Yahwist creation account in Genesis 2–3 situates sexuality in a relational context. "It is not good that the male should be alone," God judges, "I will make a helper fit for him" (2:18). The importance of the helper to the one helped may be gleaned from the fact that twice in the psalms (30:10 and 54:4) God is presented as such a helper of humans. The equality of the partners in this helping relationship is underscored. Male and female are "bone of my bones and flesh of my flesh" (Gen 2:23), they have the same human strengths and weaknesses, and the myth asserts that it is precisely because of their equality that they may marry.

About four hundred years later, the Priestly tradition from Jerusalem has God bless *'adam*, that is, male and female, and enjoin them to be "fruitful and multiply" (1:28). The Priestly myth situates sexuality and marriage in a procreative context. From the beginning of the biblical tradition, therefore, sexuality and marriage are set within two perspectives: in one, the relational, mutual help of the spouses; in the other, their procreative activity together. These two perspectives are ones we found also in the Stoic tradition. They will have convoluted histories in the postbiblical Catholic tradition, and will be a constant source of debate in the genesis of *Gaudium et Spes*.

Another—frequently neglected—Old Testament book, the Song of Songs, is intimately related to any biblical analysis of sexuality and marriage. Any modern man and woman need only listen to the imagery to know what the poetry means. "I am sick with love," the woman exclaims (2:5; 5:8). "Come to me," she cries out in her desire for her lover, "like a gazelle, like a young stag upon the mountains where spices grow" (2:17;

---

[11] For a different interpretation of the creation texts, see Ronald A. Simkins, "Marriage and Gender in the Old Testament," in *Marriage in the Catholic Tradition: Scripture, Tradition, and Experience*, ed. Todd A. Salzman, Thomas A. Kelly, and John J. O'Keefe (New York: Crossroad, 2004), 21–29.

8:14). When he comes and gazes upon her nakedness, he is moved to poetry. "Your rounded thighs are like jewels . . . your vulva is a rounded bowl that never lacks wine. Your belly is a heap of wheat encircled with lilies. Your two breasts are like fawns, twins of a gazelle. . . . You are stately as a palm tree and your breasts are like its clusters. I say I will climb the palm tree and lay hold of its branches" (7:1-8). Her response is direct and far from coy. "I am my beloved's and his desire is for me. Come, my beloved, let us go forth into the fields. . . . There I will give you my love" (7:10-13). No woman or man who has ever been sick with love and desire can doubt the origin of the language or its intent. Karl Barth, who argued that the *Song* was a "second *Magna Carta*" that develops the relationship view hinted at in Genesis 2, notes the equality between the man and the woman in the *Song*. "There is no male dominance, no female subordination, and no stereotyping of either sex."[12] Nor is there any mention of marriage or procreation to justify sexuality. The *Song* is a far cry from the Greek downgrading of sexual desire and pleasure; it is a celebration of human love and of the sexual desire of the lovers. Christian history will seriously patriarchalize the equal sexual relationship between male and female, will institutionalize it within the confines of marriage and procreation, and will follow Plato and Aristotle in their suspicion of sexual pleasure.

Sexuality and marriage play a relatively small role in the Old Testament. Lisa Cahill judges it "striking" that it also "plays a relatively small role in the New Testament."[13] The most extensive New Testament teaching about sexuality is in Paul's first letter to the Corinthians, apparently in response to a question the Corinthians had asked: "Is it better for a man not to touch a woman?" (1 Cor 7:1). Paul's answer, under the mistaken apprehension that the last days have arrived (7:31), is a mixed message. He prefers celibacy over marriage in the situation of the last days, but "because of the temptation to sexual immorality, each man should have his own wife and each woman her own husband" (7:2). It is "better to marry than to be aflame with passion" (7:9). Marriage is good, even for Christians, he seems to say, against the ascetical Encratites and Gnostics who urged celibacy on all Christians, even if only as a safeguard against sexual sins (7:5-9).

[12] Karl Barth, *Church Dogmatics* (Edinburgh: T. and T. Clark, 1958–1961), III, 1, 312.
[13] Lisa Sowle Cahill, *Women and Sexuality* (New York: Paulist Press, 1992), 33.

Much more telling, however, than his grudging affirmation of marriage and sex in the circumstances of his time is Paul's countercultural assertion of equality between husband and wife in marriage. "The husband should give to the wife her conjugal rights, and likewise the wife to her husband. For the wife does not rule over her own body, but the husband does; likewise, the husband does not rule over his own body, but the wife does" (7:3-4). When a Christian man and a Christian woman marry, first-century Paul suggests, the covenant they make with one another is a covenant of equal and intimate partnership, and it embraces their human sexual activity within it. It is a suggestion that the Second Vatican Council will pursue twenty centuries later (GS 48).

In the Old Testament, Hosea presented marriage as a prophetic symbol of the mutually faithful covenant relationship between God and Israel.[14] That approach is continued in the New Testament, with a change of characters, from God-Israel to Christ-Church. Rather than presenting marriage in the then-classical Jewish way as a symbol of the covenant union between Yahweh and Israel, the writer of the letter to the Ephesians presents it as an image of the relationship between the Christ and the new Israel, his Church. This presentation is of central importance to the development of a Christian view of marriage and sexuality and, unfortunately, has been used to sustain such a diminished Christian view that we shall have to consider it here in some detail.

The passage in which the writer offers his view of marriage (Eph 5:21-33) is situated within a larger context (5:21–6:9), which sets forth a list of household duties that exist within a family in his historical time and place. This list is addressed to wives (5:22), husbands (5:25), children (6:1), fathers (6:4), slaves (6:5) and masters (6:9). All that concerns us here is what is said to wives and husbands. There are two similar lists in the New Testament, one in the letter to the Colossians (3:18–4:1), the other in the first letter of Peter (2:13–3:7), but the Ephesians' list opens with a singular injunction: "be subject to one another out of reverence for Christ" (Eph 5:21). This injunction, commentators agree, is an essential element of what follows. Mutual giving way is required of all Christians, even of husbands and wives as they seek holiness together in marriage, and even in spite of traditional patriarchal relationships which permitted husbands to lord it over their wives.

---

[14] See Michael G. Lawler, *Marriage and Sacrament: A Theology of Christian Marriage* (Collegeville, MN: Liturgical Press, 1993), 38–40.

As Christians have all been admonished to give way to one another, there is no surprise in the instruction that a Christian wife is to give way to her husband, "as to the Lord" (5:22). There is a surprise, however, at least for the ingrained male attitude that sees the husband as lord and master of his wife and appeals to Ephesians 5:22-23 to ground and sustain that unchristian attitude, that a husband is to give way to his wife. That follows from the general instruction that Christians are to give way to one another. It follows also from the specific instruction given to husbands. That instruction is not that "the husband is the head of the wife," the way in which the text is frequently cited, but rather that "*in the same way* that the Messiah is the head of the church the husband is the head of the wife." A Christian husband's headship over his wife is to be modeled on and model of Christ's headship over the Church, and the way Christ exercises authority is never in doubt: "The Son of Man came not to be served but to serve, and to give his life as a ransom (redemption) for many" (Mark 10:45).

Diakonia, service, is the Christ way of exercising authority; it was as a servant that "Christ loved the church and gave himself up for her" (Eph 5:25). A Christian husband, therefore, is instructed to be head over his wife by serving, giving way to, and giving himself up for her. Marital authority modeled on that of Christ does not mean control, giving orders, making unreasonable demands, reducing another person to the status of servant or, worse, of slave to one's every whim. It means loving service. The Christian husband-head, as Markus Barth puts it so beautifully, becomes "the first servant of his wife."[15] It is such a husband, and only such a one, that a wife is to hold in awe (v. 33b) as all Christians fear or hold in awe Christ (v. 2lb). There is no reversal of Paul's judgment of equality between spouses in marriage, but rather a confirmation of it from another perspective, that of mutual and equal service, in every part of their life, including the sexual. A husband is further instructed to love his wife, for "he who loves his wife loves himself" (v. 28b; cp. v. 33a). This love is essential to marriage, and the marriage it founds reveals a profound mystery about Christ and Church. The mystery, most scholars agree, is embedded in the text of Genesis 2:24 and cited in 5:31. As the Anchor Bible translation seeks to show, "this [passage] has an eminent secret meaning," which is that it refers to Christ and Christ's Church.

---

[15] Markus Barth, *Ephesians: Translation and Commentary on Chapters Four to Six*, The Anchor Bible (New York: Doubleday, 1974), 618.

The Fathers of the Church

The doctrine about sexuality and marriage in both Old and New Testaments was a Jewish doctrine, developed in the originating Jewish culture of the Christian movement. The developing Christian Church, however, soon moved out of that Jewish culture into a Greco-Roman one in which Greek and Latin fathers of the Church shaped the biblical doctrine about marriage and sexuality within their own cultural contexts and established the Catholic approach to sexuality and marriage. Irenaeus of Lyons has no doubt that marriage is primarily for procreation,[16] and also for a wife to bring help to her husband in the funding of his household, particularly in his sickness and old age.[17] The early Greek Christian understanding of the nature of sexuality resembles that of the Stoic philosophers, represented in a statement from the Christian African Lactantius: "Just as God gave us eyes, not that we might look upon and desire pleasure, but that we might see those actions that pertain to the necessity of life, so also we have received the genital part of the body for no other purpose than the begetting of offspring."[18] By its very nature, therefore, sexual intercourse is for the procreation of children and any intercourse for purposes other than procreation is a violation of nature and, therefore, immoral. It is an argument Latin Church fathers would continue to make into the twenty-first century.

The fifth-century bishop of Hippo, Augustine, sometimes called the father of Christian marriage, was to mold and control the marital doctrine of the Catholic Church down to our own day. His influence is always present in Catholic talk about marriage. Augustine's basic statement about sexuality and marriage is ubiquitous, firm, and clear. Contrary to those Manichee heretics who held that sexuality is evil and who condemn and prohibit marriage and sexual intercourse, he states that sexuality and marriage were created good by a good God and cannot lose that intrinsic goodness.[19] He specifies the good of marriage as threefold, and insists that even after the Fall, the marriages of Christians still contain this threefold good: fidelity, offspring, sacrament.[20] In this triple good Augustine intends the mutual fidelity of the spouses, the procreation of

---

[16] *Adversus Haer.*, 2.23, PG 8, 1086, 1090.

[17] Ibid., 3.12, PG 8, 1184.

[18] Lactantius, *Divinarum Institutionum*, 6.23, PL 6, 718.

[19] Augustine, *De Nupt. Et Concup.*, 2.32.54, PL 44, 468–69; also *De Bono Coniugali*, PL 40, 374–96.

[20] *De Gen. ad Litt.*, 9.7.12, PL 34, 397; also *De Bono Coniugali*, 24, 32, PL 40, 394.

children, and indissolubility. Procreation has priority because "from this derives the propagation of the human race in which a living community is a great good."[21] Alongside the tradition of the threefold good of marriage, Augustine advances another good, that of friendship between the sexes. In *The Good of Marriage*, after asserting that marriage is good, he gives an interesting explication of why it is good. "It does not seem to me to be good only because of the procreation of children, but also because of the natural companionship between the sexes. Otherwise, we could not speak of marriage in the case of old people, especially if they had either lost their children or had begotten none at all."[22] Augustine's basic position can be stated unequivocally, and there can be no doubt about it: sexual intercourse between a husband and a wife is created good by God. The condition under which it is good is the classic Stoic condition we have already seen in the Alexandrians, namely, when it is for the begetting of a child. Any other use, even between the spouses in marriage, is at least venially sinful.[23]

Scholastic Doctrine

Augustine's teaching controlled the approach to sexuality and marriage in the Catholic Church until the thirteenth century, when the scholastic theologians made some significant alterations to it. Thomas Aquinas took over Augustine's three goods of marriage and transformed them into three ends of marriage. "Marriage," he argues, "has as its principal end the procreation and education of offspring . . . and so offspring are said to be a good of marriage." It has also "a secondary end in man alone, the sharing of tasks which are necessary in life, and from this point of view husband and wife owe each other faithfulness, which is one of the goods of marriage." There is another end in believers, "the meaning of Christ and Church, and so a good of marriage is called sacrament. The first end is found in marriage in so far as man is animal, the second in so far as he is man, the third in so far as he is believer."[24] The terminology, *primary end - secondary end,* came to dominate discussion of the ends of marriage in Roman Catholic manuals for the next seven hundred years, but we should note that it is a curious argument, for it makes the claim

---

[21] *De Bono Coniugali*, 9, 9, PL 40, 380.

[22] Ibid, PL 40, 375.

[23] Ibid., 6, 6, PL 40, 377–78 and 10, 11, PL 40, 381.

[24] Aquinas, *S.T.*, III (Suppl.), 65, 1, c.

that the primary end of specifically *human* marriage is dictated not by man's specifically *human* nature but by his generically *animal* nature. It was precisely this curious argument that would be challenged at the Second Vatican Council, leading to a more personalist approach to both sexual activity and marriage.

The Modern Period

When Cardinal Gasparri first codified Catholic law in the 1917 Code of Canon Law, the section on marriage officially codified the claim of the primacy of procreation over every other end of marriage. Up until 1917, that was a *theological* notion, not an official *magisterial* teaching. Urban Navarette, indeed, argues that, in the documents of the magisterium and in the corpus of Canon Law itself, "we find hardly anything about the ends of marriage precisely as goals until the formulation of Canon 1013, 1."[25] He further points out that a preliminary version of Canon 1013 indicated no hierarchy of ends and concludes that the 1917 Code of Canon Law is the first official document of the Catholic Church to embrace the terminology *primary end - secondary end*.

December 1930 was a pivotal moment in the development of the Catholic doctrine of sexuality and marriage. At that time, Pope Pius XI, in response to the Anglican Lambeth Conference's approval of artificial contraception as a moral action in certain situations, published an important encyclical on marriage titled *Casti Connubii*. In it, predictably, he insisted on everything in Gasparri's *Code* but, unpredictably, he did more. He retrieved and gave a prominent place to a long-ignored item from the *Catechism of the Council of Trent*, marriage as a union of conjugal love and intimacy. By emphasizing the essential place of mutual love in a marriage, Pius placed the Catholic view of marriage on the track to a more personalist definition. Marital love, Pius teaches, does not consist "in pleasing words only, but in the deep attachment of the heart [will] which is expressed in action, since love is proved by deeds." So important is the mutual love and interior formation of the spouses, he continues, that "it can, in a very real sense, as the Roman Catechism teaches, be said to be the *chief reason and purpose of marriage*, if marriage be looked at not in the restricted sense as instituted for the proper conception and education of the child, but more widely as the blending of life as a

[25] Urban Navarrette, "Structura Iuridica Matrimonii Secundum Concilium Vaticanum II," *Periodica* 56 (1967): 366.

whole and the mutual interchange and sharing thereof."[26] In these wise words, Pius directs us to see that there is more to marriage than can be contained in the cold, legal categories of the *Code of Canon Law*. European thinkers were poised to point in the same direction, most influentially two Germans, Dietrich Von Hildebrand and Heribert Doms.

In the opening paragraph of his 1939 work *Marriage*, Dietrich Von Hildebrand states the problem precisely. The modern age, he suggests, after the horrors of World War I, is guilty of a terrible anti-personalism, "a progressive blindness toward the nature and dignity of the spiritual person." This anti-personalism expresses itself in all kinds of materialism, the most dangerous of which is Aquinas's biological materialism which considers man as a more highly developed animal. "Human life is considered exclusively from a biological point of view and biological principles are the measure by which all human activities are judged."[27] In contrast to this biological approach, Von Hildebrand introduced a radical innovation in thinking about marriage, claiming Pius XI and *Casti Connubii* in support of his central thesis that marriage is for the building up of loving communion between the spouses. Conjugal love, he claims, is the primary meaning and ultimate end of marriage.

In marriage, Von Hildebrand argued, the spouses enter an interpersonal relationship, in which they confront one another as I and Thou, as Ego and Other, and "give birth to a mysterious fusion of their souls."[28] This fusion of their innermost personal beings, not merely the fusion of their physical bodies, is what the oft-quoted "one body" of Genesis intends. It is this interpersonal fusion which is the primary meaning of the spouses' mutual love and of their sexual intercourse which is the symbol of that love, and intercourse achieves its end when it expresses and leads to interpersonal union. Heribert Doms agreed with Von Hildebrand in that what is natural or unnatural for human animals is not to be decided on the basis of what is natural or unnatural for nonhuman animals. Human sexuality is essentially the capacity and the desire to fuse not merely one's body, but one's very self with another person. Sexuality drives a human to make a gift of herself or himself (not just of her or his body) to another, in order to create a communion of persons and of lives which fulfills them both.

---

[26] Gerald C. Tracy, ed., *Five Great Encyclicals* (New York: Paulist Press, 1939), 83.

[27] Dietrich Von Hildebrand, *Marriage* (London: Longmans, 1939), v.

[28] Ibid., 4 and vi.

The primary end of sexual intercourse in this perspective is the loving communion between the spouses, a communion which is both signified and enhanced, or "made," in intercourse. Popular language is correct: in their sexual intercourse spouses "make love." This primary end is achieved in every act of intercourse in which the spouses actually enter into intimate communion. Even in childless marriages, marriage and intercourse achieve their primary end in the marital communion of the spouses, their *two-in-oneness*, as Doms would have it. He summarizes his case in a clear statement. "The immediate purpose of marriage is the realization of its meaning, the conjugal two-in-oneness. . . . This two-in-oneness of husband and wife is a living reality, and the immediate object of the marriage ceremony and their legal union." The union of the spouses tends naturally to the birth and nurture of new persons, their children, who focus the fulfillment of their parents, both as individuals and as a two-in-oneness. "Society is more interested in the child than in the natural fulfillment of the parents, and it is this which gives the child primacy among the natural results of marriage."[29] Since Doms wrote, social scientific data demonstrate that the well-being of the child is a function of the well-being of its parents,[30] suggesting that the relationship between the spouses is the primary natural result of marriage since all other relationships in the family depend on it.

The Catholic Church's immediate reaction to these new ideas, as has been so often the case in theological history, was a blanket condemnation, which made no effort to sift truth from error. In 1944, the Holy Office condemned "the opinion of some more recent authors, who either deny that the primary end of marriage is the generation and nurture of children, or teach that the secondary ends are not essentially subordinate to the primary end, but are equally primary and independent."[31] In 1951, as the opinions of Von Hildebrand and Doms persisted and attracted more adherents, Pope Pius XII felt obliged to intervene again. The truth is, he taught, that "marriage, as a natural institution in virtue of the will

---

[29] Heribert Doms, *The Meaning of Marriage*, trans. George Sayer (London: Sheed and Ward, 1939), 94–95.

[30] See, for example, Sara S. McLanahan and Gary Sandefur, *Growing Up with a Single Parent: What Hurts, What Helps* (Cambridge, MA: Harvard University Press, 1994); Paul R. Amato and Alan Booth, *A Generation at Risk: Growing Up in an Era of Family Upheaval* (Cambridge, MA: Harvard University Press, 1997); Judith Wallerstein, Julia Lewis, and Sandra Blakeslee, *The Unexpected Legacy of Divorce* (New York: Hyperion, 2000).

[31] *Acta Apostolicae Sedis* 36 (1944): 103.

of the creator, does not have as a primary and intimate end the personal perfection of the spouses, but the procreation and nurture of new life. The other ends, in as much as they are intended by nature, are not on the same level as the primary end, and still less are they superior to it, but they are essentially subordinate to it."[32] This approach was seriously altered by *Gaudium et Spes*.

Second Vatican Council and *Gaudium et Spes*

Three principles summarize the traditional Catholic teaching on sexuality and marriage prior to the Second Vatican Council. The first is that, to be moral, any sexual act must be within the context of marriage. This principle was rearticulated after the council by the Congregation for the Doctrine of the Faith (CDF): "Any human genital act whatsoever may be placed only within the framework of marriage" (PH 7). The second is that every act of sexual intercourse within marriage must be open to the procreation of new life. This principle was reaffirmed by Pope Paul VI in 1968 in his encyclical *Humanae Vitae:* "Each and every marriage act must remain open to the transmission of life" (HV 11). A third principle derives from the second, namely, that among the various ends of marriage, procreation is primary. This principle was articulated by Pope Pius XII in 1951: "marriage, as a natural institution in virtue of the will of the creator," he taught, "does not have as a primary and intimate end the natural perfection of the spouses, but the procreation of new life. The other ends, in as much as they are intended by nature, are not on the same level as the primary end, and still less are they superior to it, but they are essentially subordinate to it."[33] The schema prepared in preparation for the council, "Chastity, Marriage, Family, and Virginity," focused heavily on each of these three principles.

The schema was prepared by the theological commission headed by Cardinal Ottaviani, prefect of the Holy Office, and it was staffed largely by theologians from the Holy Office. Its remit was to prepare a schema which set forth the Catholic doctrine on marriage as articulated by recent popes and to oppose the spreading errors that challenged this position.[34] In his presentation of the schema, Ottaviani explained that it set out "the

---

[32] Ibid., 43 (1951): 848–49.

[33] Ibid.

[34] *Acta et Documenta Concilio Oecumenico Vaticano II Apparando. Series Secunda (Praeparatoria)* (Roma: Typis Polyglottis Vaticanis, 1969), 2/1, 408–9.

objective order . . . which God himself willed in instituting marriage and Christ the Lord willed in raising it to the dignity of a sacrament. Only in this way can the modern errors that have spread everywhere be vanquished."[35] Among these errors are those of Von Hildebrand and Doms "which subvert the right order of values and make the primary end of marriage [that is, procreation] inferior to the biological and personal values of the spouses, and proclaim that conjugal love itself is in the objective order the primary end."[36] This schema, whose primary concern was to defend an objective moral order in marriage against the perceived dangerous effects of personalism, never made it out of the Central Coordinating Committee, though some elements of it were later incorporated into the chapter on marriage in *Gaudium et Spes*. The debate on the schema and on the later chapter on marriage centered on both the hierarchy of the ends of marriage and, intimately related to the proposed primary end of procreation, contraception. The "objective order" set forth in the theological commission's prepared schema was consistently defended vigorously by the classicist neo-Augustinians and the "new morality"[37] personalist position was consistently defended by the historically conscious neo-Thomists.

The debate surfaced first in the discussions of Schema XVII in preparation for what we called in chapter 1 the Roman Schema and the Malines Schema, both of which, remember, were rejected as unsuitable. It continued to boil in the Mixed Commission, which had been set up to prepare a schema on the Church in the modern world. In this commission's discussion of the Zurich schema on June 6, 1964, at which Ottaviani presided, it boiled over as theologians associated with the Holy Office attacked Häring on marriage and specifically on the hierarchy of its ends. Congar made a lengthy comment in his diary about that meeting. "Franic [a leading classicist neo-Augustinian]," he wrote, "opposed Häring, who seemed to want to have the council canonize his position, according to which love is the essential element of marriage . . . Ottaviani had Tromp read out some replies of the Holy Office approved by Pius XII. This is the great concerted offensive: Franic, Lio, Tromp—in short, the Holy Office."[38] Franic also said the entire schema, not only the

---

[35] Ibid., 2/3, 937.

[36] Ibid., 910, n. 16 and 917, note 50.

[37] This phrase had been coined by Pius XII in 1952 in echo of the "new theology" he had rejected in 1950 in his encyclical *Humani Generis*.

[38] Yves Congar, *My Journal of the Council* (Collegeville, MN: Liturgical Press, 2012), 552.

section on marriage, was "Häringian" and "should be more Catholic." Notwithstanding the disagreements on the schema in general and on its section on marriage in particular, it was passed on for consideration to the coordinating commission which changed its place on the council's agenda and renamed it Schema XIII.

The direction of the debate on marriage at the Second Vatican Council may be summed up in the words of Cardinal Alfrink: "Conjugal love," he argued, "is an element of marriage itself and not just a result of marriage. . . . Conjugal love belongs to marriage, at least if marriage be not considered as merely a juridical contract."[39] Much of the debate was opposed to the juridical way of looking at marriage and marital love as exemplified by Gasparri's *Code* and Ottaviani's Holy Office. Alfrink, a biblical scholar, pointed out that "the Hebrew verb *dabaq*, in Greek *kollao*, does suggest physical, bodily, sexual union, but it suggests, above all, spiritual union which exists in conjugal love. Sacred Scripture itself insinuates this when it compares conjugal union to the union between parents and children which is spiritual and presupposes love."[40] This, he continued, is the way modern women and men think, more spiritually, more humanly, and indeed more biblically and theologically. Cardinal Döpfner agreed. "It is not enough to propose conjugal love as a virtue, or as an extraneous subjective end of marriage, and to exclude it from the very structure of marriage itself." The battle lines were already clearly drawn in the preparatory commission: either Gasparri's juridical approach to marriage or a renewed interpersonal approach in which conjugal love is of the essence of marriage. The latter approach began to win in the commission[41] and won, finally, in the council itself.

Gaudium et Spes, into which a section on marriage was inserted in its preliminary stage, describes marriage as a "communion of love" (GS 47), an "intimate partnership of conjugal life and love" (GS 48). The position of the majority of the council fathers could not have been clearer. In the face of strident demands to relegate the conjugal love of the spouses to its customary secondary place in marriage, they declared conjugal love to be of the very essence of marriage, a clear rejection of an exclusively juridical approach. There was another explicit rejection of Gasparri. Marriage, the council declared, is founded in a "conjugal covenant of irrevocable

[39] *Acta et Documenta Concilio Vaticano Secondo Apparando. Series II (Paeparatoria),* 2, 3, 961.

[40] Ibid.

[41] Ibid., 952.

personal consent" (GS 48). Gasparri's word *contract* is replaced by the biblical word *covenant*, which has the same juridical outcomes as contract but also situates marriage in a biblical-theological and *interpersonal* context rather than in an exclusively *juridical* one. The council declared that the spouses "mutually gift and accept one another" (GS 48), rejecting the *Code*'s material biological notion that they gift merely the right to the use of one another's bodies. In their mutual personal covenanting and gifting, a man and a woman create an interpersonal communion of love which is permanent and is to last for the whole of life.

The council also taught that "by its very nature the institution of *marriage* and *married love* is ordered to the procreation and education of children, and it is in them that it finds its crowning glory" (GS 48). We have added emphasis to this citation to underscore not only the teaching of the council, but also of the entire Catholic tradition prior to Paul VI's *Humanae Vitae*, namely, that *marriage*, not *each and every marriage act* as Paul VI taught, is to be open to the procreation of children (HV 11). Once procreation has been mentioned, one would expect a recitation of the hierarchical ends of marriage, but again, despite insistent voices to the contrary, the council fathers rejected the primary end–secondary end dichotomy. To make sure that its rejection was understood, the preparatory commission was careful to explain that the text just cited "does not suggest [a hierarchy of ends] in any way."[42] Marriage and sexual love "are by their very nature ordained to the generation and education of children," but that "does not make the other ends of marriage of less account," and marriage "is not instituted solely for procreation" (GS 50). The intense debate which took place both in the preparatory commission and in the council itself makes it impossible to claim the refusal to speak of a hierarchy of ends in marriage was the result of oversight or, as some classicist neo-Augustinians have argued, a mere avoidance of the primary–secondary terminology, leaving the concept in place.[43] It was the result of a deliberated, intentional, and explicit choice of the Catholic Church meeting in council.

Any doubt was definitively removed in 1983 by the appearance of the revised Code of Canon Law, frequently called the last council document. "The *matrimonial covenant*, by which a man and a woman establish between

---

[42] See Herbert Vorgrimler, ed., *Commentary on the Documents of Vatican II*, vol. 5 (New York: Herder and Herder, 1969), 234.

[43] See Germain Grisez, *The Way of the Lord Jesus, Volume 2: Living a Christian Life* (Quincy, IL: Franciscan Herald Press, 1993), 565, n. 35.

themselves a partnership of the whole of life, is by its nature ordered towards the good of the spouses and the procreation and education of offspring" (Can 1055, 1). Notice three things: first, it is the *matrimonial covenant* and not *each and every act of intercourse* that is ordered toward procreation; second, there is no specification of either of these ends being primary or secondary; third, as in *Gaudium et Spes*, the good of the spouses or *conjugal love* is discussed before procreation and education of children or the biological fruitfulness of marriage. The Catholic Church changed its canon law to be in line with its renewed theology of marriage, moving beyond the narrow legal essence to embrace in the very essence of marriage the mutual love and communion of the spouses. Toward the end of the twentieth century, the Church had come a long way from the negative approach to sexuality and marriage bequeathed to it in a long tradition going back to the struggles of the Church fathers against dualistic Gnostics and Manicheans. It would be naive, and a complete ignorance of past conciliar history, to assume that the debate ended with the council.

Papal Birth Control Commission

The debate on what was, first, an appendix to the Zurich document and, then, a chapter in Schema XIII on marriage and the family centered on the Church's teaching on marriage in general and on two specific issues within that teaching, namely, the ends of marriage and birth control. The debate, as we have several times pointed out, opposed neo-Augustinian classicists, who thought the proposed texts did not state clearly enough what they took to be the teaching of the Church, and historically conscious neo-Thomists, who wanted to advance the Church's teaching on the basis of contemporary scientific gynecological developments. When Archbishop Dearden of Detroit introduced the Mixed Commission's approved text (essentially the Zurich text discussed in chapter 1) for council debate in November 1964, he emphasized that the text was not intended to be a full exposition of the Catholic doctrine of marriage but, rather, a pastoral synthesis of that teaching to assist Christians to understand the dignity of their marriage and to live it in holiness. He specifically pointed out that the text made no mention of birth control because the pope "very wisely" had reserved a decision on that to himself. That instruction notwithstanding, the debate in council concentrated on the ends of marriage and birth control.

The neo-Augustinian leaders, Cardinals Ottaviani, Ruffini, and Browne (former Master General of the Dominicans) argued that the text gave too much weight to the consciences of spouses in deciding the number of their children. This contradicted, they believed, the former teaching of the Church as found, for instance, in Pope Leo XIII's encyclical *Arcanum*, Pope Pius XI's *Casti Connubii*, and Pope Pius XII's various addresses to obstetricians and midwives. They argued that the text should be revised along the lines of those already approved magisterial documents. Browne further argued that the certain teaching of the magisterium is that the primary end of sexual intercourse is procreation and the mutual love and help of the spouses is a secondary end. This teaching should be made clear in the text.

The neo-Thomist position was first articulated by Cardinal Leger of Montreal, who spoke after Ruffini. Leger argued that there was great doubt among the married faithful and their confessors about the Church's teaching on birth control, and many theologians were suggesting a more in-depth investigation of the fundamental principles of the teaching on marriage. More weight should be given, he argued, to the conjugal love of the spouses, which both signified and effected their intimate union. Suenens followed Leger and also asked for a more in-depth analysis of the fundamental principles related to marriage and that the communion of the spouses should be given an equal status with procreation as an end of marriage. In response to press reaction to his speech, he later had to issue a statement that he was not calling for a change in Church teaching but only for a more in-depth analysis of it.[44] Archbishop Staverman of Indonesia, speaking on behalf of the Indonesian bishops, argued that, since marriage is a historical reality, it evolves like any other historical reality and that, therefore, the Church cannot be content with simply repeating its past teachings. To do so would, as was already happening, cause the Church to lose its pastoral effectiveness. Cardinal Alfrink of Utrecht argued that the two ends of marriage were not separate. "It is not a conflict between two separate values, for without the love and fidelity of the spouses, recreated though 'the cult of love' (as our schema rightly says), the motive of procreation is in moral danger."[45] It became clear that, with respect to the question of the ends of marriage, which had implications for the question of birth control, the general opinion of the fathers was in the neo-Thomist direction. That opinion, however, kept coming up against the removal of any debate on birth control from the council

---

[44] See *Acta Synodalia*, 3/6, 381.
[45] Ibid., 83–84.

and its restriction to the pontifically-established birth control commission. We must, therefore, consider that commission and its deliberations.

At the instigation of Cardinal Suenens, whose ultimate intent was that an adequate document on Christian marriage be brought before the council for debate, Pope John XXIII withdrew the question of birth control from council discussion and restricted it to an expert commission he established to study the question. The commission was confirmed and enlarged by Pope Paul VI until it ultimately had seventy-one members, not all of whom attended its meetings or voted.[46] The final episcopal vote took place in answer to three questions. In answer to the question "Is contraception intrinsically evil?," nine bishops voted "No," three voted "Yes," and three abstained. In answer to the question "Is contraception, as defined by the Majority Report, in basic continuity with tradition and the declarations of the Magisterium?," nine bishops voted "Yes," five voted "No," and one abstained. In answer to the question, "Should the Magisterium speak on this question as soon as possible?," fourteen answered "Yes," one answered "No."[47] A preliminary vote of the theologians who were advisors to the Commission, in response to the question "Is artificial contraception an intrinsically evil violation of the natural law?" had resulted in a count of fifteen "No" and four "Yes" answers.[48] Both a majority report and a minority report were then submitted to Paul VI who, professing himself unconvinced by the arguments of the majority, and probably also sharing the concern of the minority report that the Church could not repudiate its longstanding teaching on contraception without undergoing a serious blow to its overall moral authority, approved the minority report in his encyclical letter *Humanae Vitae*. The differential between the two groups is easily categorized.

The minority report, which became the controverted part of the encyclical, argued that "each and every marriage act must remain open to the transmission of life" (HV 11). As we have already noted, Paul VI was the first to state officially the Church's teaching in this way. The tradition had always been that it is *marriage* itself, and not each and every act of intercourse in marriage, that is to be open to procreation, and that is what the majority report argued. It asserted that "human intervention in the

---

[46] Clifford Longley, *The Worlock Archive* (London: Chapman, 2000), 232.

[47] Robert McClory, *Turning Point: The Inside Story of the Papal Birth Control Commission and How Humanae Vitae Changed the Life of Patty Crowley and the Future of the Church* (New York: Crossroad, 1995), 127.

[48] Ibid., 99.

process of the marriage act *for reasons drawn from the end of marriage itself* should not always be excluded, provided that the criteria of morality are always safeguarded."[49]

The differential in the two positions was created by adherence to two different models of marriage, the minority report being based on the traditional procreative institution model, the majority report being based on an emerging interpersonal union model that had its origins in the 1930s and was embraced by the council.[50] Richard McCormick commented in 1968 that "the documents of the Papal Commission represent a rather full summary of two points of view. . . . The majority report, particularly the analysis in its 'rebuttal,' strikes this reader as much the more satisfactory statement."[51] That judgment continues to be the judgment of the majority of Catholic theologians and the vast majority of Catholic couples, because they adhere to the same interpersonal model on which the majority report was based. So much so that in 2006, Margaret Farley could offer the judgment that, "In much of Catholic moral theology and ethics, the procreative norm as the sole or primary justification of sexual intercourse is gone."[52] Over four decades after *Humanae Vitae*, despite a concerted minority effort to make adherence to *Humanae Vitae* a test case of genuine Catholicity, the debate between the procreative and interpersonal models continues in the Church and is far from resolved.

Conclusion

A summary of the approach to marriage and sexual activity in the modern period of Catholic theology and teaching is easy to present. The modern period represents yet one more development in Catholic theology and, to a lesser extent, in magisterial teaching. The major development in the Catholic theological approach to marriage is the recovery of the two purposes of marriage and sexual intercourse articulated in Genesis, the relational and procreational, and a rearranging of their rela-

---

[49] Cited by Robert Blair Kaiser, *The Politics of Sex and Religion* (Kansas City: Leaven Press, 1985), 260–61. See also Longley, *Worlock Archive*, 233.

[50] See Michael G. Lawler, "Catholic Models of Marriage," in *Marriage in the Catholic Church: Disputed Questions* (Collegeville, MN: Liturgical Press, 2002), 27–42.

[51] Richard A. McCormick, *Notes on Moral Theology: 1965–1980* (Lanham, MD: University Press of America, 1981), 164.

[52] Margaret A. Farley, *Just Love: A Framework of Christian Sexual Ethics* (New York: Continuum, 2006), 278.

tive priorities. Since Clement, Augustine, and Aquinas, the procreational end became established in Catholic teaching as the *primary end* of sexual intercourse and the relational became relegated to a *secondary end*. Beginning with Pius XI's *Casti Connubii* and culminating in the Second Vatican Council's *Gaudium et Spes*, these two purposes of sexual intercourse have been equalized, so that neither is prior to the other. Pope Paul VI's *Humanae Vitae* tried to change the terms of the debate over marriage and sexual intercourse by teaching officially for the first time in Catholic history that "each and every marriage *act* must remain open to the transmission of life," but that judgment is controverted by the vast majority of Catholic believers and, "in much of Catholic theology and ethics, the procreative norm as the sole or primary justification of sexual intercourse is gone." With the reestablishing of the relational purpose for marriage and sexual intercourse, the judgment about the morality of any sexual act is now made by Catholic ethicists, not on the basis of the *act* alone, but on the basis of the place of the act within its *relational* context.

It is the constant teaching of the Catholic Church that a marriage between two Christian believers is a sacrament. Two issues are embedded in that claim. First, what is the human matrix of the sacrament? What is the human conduct that is elevated by grace to the level of sacrament of the covenant between Christ and his Church? Second, that human matrix, *Gaudium et Spes* suggested, is the mutual love of the spouses from which all the other meanings of their marriage have their origin and in which they are embedded. Though it did not deal in any detail with the sacrament of marriage, *Gaudium et Spes* did illuminate its matrix. Marriage, it taught, is "a community of love . . . an intimate partnership of marital life and love" (GS 47–8). The mutual love of the spouses is of the very essence of their human marriage; it is also, therefore, of the very essence of their sacrament of marriage.

If marriage is rooted ultimately in the mutual love of the spouses, it is rooted proximately in their "irrevocable personal consent" (GS 48) that ritually expresses that love. In 1970, the Sacred Roman Rota, the supreme marriage tribunal of the Catholic Church, removed all doubt about the centrality of mutual love in constituting both marriage and the sacrament of marriage. They ruled that "where marital love is lacking, either the consent is not free, or it is not internal, or it excludes or limits the object which must be integral to have a valid marriage." They concluded that "the lack of marital love is the same as lack of consent. Marital love has juridical force here because the defendant despised the total communion of life *which primarily and of itself constitutes the object of the marriage contract*."[53] In our day, both marriage and the sacrament of marriage are situated in a matrix which every loving spouse can recognize. In cooperation with the grace of God, spouses cocreate their marriages by freely consenting to one another as lovers in a sacred covenant for the whole of life, in which they give and accept gifts of love as warrants of their mutual gifts of self. It is this mutual, covenantal, and marital love—ritually expressed in their exchange of consent in the wedding ceremony and in a thousand acts of loving action throughout their lives—that provides the human matrix that is taken up and transformed into sacrament.

The Council has no doubt that marriage and conjugal love "are by their very nature ordained to the generation and education of children" but that "does not make the other ends of marriage of less account." Marriage "is not instituted solely for procreation" (GS 50). The intense debate which took place throughout the long and tortuous development of Schema XIII and which continued to the very end in the council itself makes it impossible to claim that the council's refusal to speak of a hierarchy of ends in marriage was the result of oversight. It was the result of an intensely deliberated and explicit choice of the Catholic Church in council. Any doubt was removed in 1983 by the publication of the revised *Code of Canon Law*, frequently referred to as the Second Vatican Council's final document. Marriage, the new *Code* decrees, "is ordered to the well-being of the spouses and to the procreation and upbringing of children" (Can 1055, 1), with no specification of any hierarchy among these ends. The Catholic Church changed its law about marriage to be in line with its new theology of marriage, moving beyond the narrow, traditional, juridical essence to embrace in the essence of marriage the mutual love and communion of the spouses. The great Protestant theologian Karl Barth once complained that the traditional doctrine of Christian marriage, both Catholic and Protestant, situated marriage in juridical rather than in theological categories.[54] The good news for Barth and for all Christian spouses seeking to live out in Christ their intimate partnerships of life and love is that the Catholic Church at the Second Vatican Council corrected that grave imbalance.

---

[53] Cited from Paul F. Palmer, "Christian Marriage: Contract or Covenant?," *Theological Studies* 33, no. 3 (September 1972): 647, emphasis added.

[54] Karl Barth, *Church Dogmatics* (Edinburgh: Clark, 1961), III, 4, 186.

Questions for Reflection

1. Catholic sexual morality is summed up in two magisterial principles. First, Pope Paul VI's teaching that "each and every marriage act must remain open to the transmission of life;" second, the Congregation for the Doctrine of the Faith's teaching that "any human genital act whatsoever may be placed only within the framework of marriage." What is the ultimate origin of these teachings and is this a strange origin for Catholic teachings? What are the implications of this teaching for moral sexual activity in the twenty-first century?

2. The Pontifical Biblical Commission teaches that the biblical texts are bound to the societies in which they originate. "Consequently, the scientific study of the Bible requires as exact a knowledge as possible of the social conditions distinctive of the various milieus in which the traditions recorded in the Bible took place." This is a clear statement of the historicity of the biblical texts. How do you understand this statement and what are its implications for reading the Bible?

3. Compare and contrast the teaching of Augustine and Thomas Aquinas that procreation is the primary good or end of sexual intercourse with that of Pope Pius XI who taught that mutual love can be said to be the "chief reason and purpose of marriage" if marriage is looked at in a broader sense as "the blending of life as a whole and the mutual interchange and sharing thereof." What did Von Hildebrand, Doms, and Pope Pius XII add to this debate?

4. How did the Second Vatican Council's document *Gaudium et Spes* change the Catholic theological approach to marriage?

Chapter Five

Being Christ-ian and the Service of Love and Justice

Introduction

"The joys and the hopes, the griefs and the anxieties of the men of this age, especially those who are poor or in any way afflicted, these too are the joys and the hopes, the griefs and anxieties of the followers of Christ" (GS 1). Thus did the Second Vatican Council open its Pastoral Constitution on the Church in the Modern World. The statement allows for both a weak and a strong meaning. The weak meaning is that many of those poor and afflicted are Christians, ostensibly followers of Christ. The strong meaning is that Christ-ians[1] are those who are genuine and active believers and who not only *say* "Lord, Lord" but also *do* the will of their "Father who is in heaven" (Matt 7:21). Among the many things Christ-ians are called to do, the document repeats again and again, is that they must minister to the poor and afflicted of every race, color, and religious persuasion, and do so precisely because they are followers of the Christ who so ministered in his time and his place. A year before the publication of *Gaudium et Spes* (1964), the council had published its majestic new image of Church, the people of God, all the baptized, laity and clergy, together (LG 9–18). "It has pleased God to make men holy and save them not merely as individuals without any mutual bonds, but by making them into a single people, a people which acknowledges him in truth [that is, in actions as well as in words] and serves him in holiness" (LG 9). That communal, perhaps family, image of Church will be a vital root throughout *Gaudium et Spes* in its claim that "God intended the earth and all that it contains for the use of every human being and

[1] We are fully aware of the contrived nature of this word. We use it throughout to underscore the demand made on those who say they are followers of the Christ to live a life like Christ, a life that acknowledges reciprocation between God and the poor and excluded, and act accordingly.

people." We shall return to this claim as we proceed through this chapter. In using the goods of the earth, therefore, "a man should regard his lawful possessions not merely as his own but also as common property in the sense that they should accrue to the benefit of not only himself but of others." That is so true in the people of God that "if a person is in extreme necessity, he has the right to take from the riches of others what he himself needs"[2] (GS 69).

The opening and closing sections of *Gaudium et Spes* reveal what it intends to be about. The opening chapter seeks to develop an anthropology, a description of man in his essence. This anthropology, however, is more than simply historical, philosophical, or psychological; it is theological. It takes its direction from revelation to clarify the human and human existence.

We wish to highlight three claims critical to understanding the anthropology of *Gaudium et Spes*, which is the foundation for the whole Constitution and for the theology it propagates. First, "man was created to the image of God" and was appointed by God as "master of all earthly creatures (Gen 1:26; Wis 2:23) that he might subdue them and use them to God's glory" (Eccl 17:3-10). Second, "God did not create man as a solitary. For from the beginning 'male and female he created them' (Gen 1:27). . . . By his innermost nature man is a social being, and unless he relates himself to others he can neither live nor develop his potential" (GS 12). God "has willed that all men should constitute one family and treat one another in a spirit of brotherhood" (GS 23) (this teaching will be at the root of much of the analysis of this chapter). Third, Christ who is "'the image of the invisible God' (Col 1:15) is Himself the perfect man." This perfect man "fully reveals man to man himself and makes his supreme calling clear" (GS 22). His incarnation creates a solidarity between God and man and among men and women themselves. All of this is subsumed and rearticulated in summary at the closing of the document: "Mindful of the Lord's saying: 'By this will all men know that you are my disciples, if you have love for one another' (John 13:35), Christians cannot yearn for anything more ardently than to serve the men of the modern world ever more generously and effectively." That service offered "generously and effectively" is a key to understanding what is required, for "not everyone who cries 'Lord, Lord' will enter into

---

[2] The ancient universal principle that "in extreme necessity all goods are common, that is, all goods are to be shared" requires interpretation in the concrete for any action to be moral. See Thomas Aquinas's explanation in *Summa Theologiae* II–II, 66, 7.

the kingdom of heaven, but those who do the Father's will . . . [and] the Father wills that in all men we recognize Christ our brother and love Him effectively in word and deed" (GS 93). Everything that follows in this chapter is to be understood in the light of these conciliar teachings.

"The dignity of the human person and the common good," writes Pope Francis in his first Apostolic Exhortation, *Evangelii Gaudium* (The Joy of the Gospel), "rank higher than the comfort of those who refuse to renounce their privilege" (EG 218).[3] It is a firm statement of Catholic social teaching: the dignity of all human persons, the priority demands of the common good, and the preferential option for the poor.[4] It has become easy to assume that since the theological principles, the body of thought, and the call to action subsumed in the phrase "Catholic social teaching" came to prominence in the twentieth century, the reality itself came into existence only in that era. Kenneth Himes's definition of Catholic social thought as "the explicitly formulated theories of economic, political, and social life that are expressed in papal, conciliar, and other episcopal documents," coupled with his listing of those documents as beginning with Pope Leo XIII's *Rerum Novarum* and ending with Pope John Paul II's celebration of its hundredth anniversary in *Centesimus Annus*, lent some support to this assumption.[5] Several influential works under the general rubric of "One hundred years of Catholic social thought" had earlier lent further credence to the assumption that Catholic social teaching came into existence only with *Rerum Novarum*,

---

[3] Pope Francis, *Evangelii Gaudium,* http://www.vatican.va/holy_father/francesco /apost_exhortations/documents/papa-francesco_esortazione-ap_20131124_evangelii -gaudium_en.html, accessed April 4, 2014.

[4] The phrase "preferential option for the poor," which has been common currency in discussions of Catholic social thought for the past twenty years, gained its preeminence as a result of two conferences of Latin American bishops, the first at Medellín in Colombia in 1968, the second at Puebla in Mexico in 1979. Medellín adumbrated the phrase, "preferential option for the poor"; Puebla adopted it explicitly. Among the signs of authentic Christian evangelization are "preferential love and concern for the poor and needy" (Puebla, Final Document, no. 382). Latin American bishops pledged themselves "to make clear through our lives and attitudes that our preference is to evangelize and serve the poor" (Puebla, Final Document, no. 707). "A preferential option for the poor represents the most noticeable tendency of religious life in Latin America" (Puebla, Final Document, no. 733). The Puebla Conference is analyzed in its contextual depth in John Eagleson and Philip Scharper, eds., *Puebla and Beyond* (Maryknoll, NY: Orbis Books, 1979).

[5] Kenneth R. Himes, *Responses to 101 Questions on Catholic Social Teaching* (Mahwah, NJ: Paulist Press, 2001), 7–8.

though John Coleman acknowledges the reality that "Catholic social thought is much older than one hundred years. Its roots go back to the life and words of Jesus."[6] Though a legitimate theological argument can be offered that Catholic social thought as defined by Himes concretizes the Catholic social thought that preceded in light of the political, economic, and social issues of the past two centuries, this chapter is not about Catholic social thought in that restricted sense. The assumption that the past hundred or so years are all there is to Catholic social teaching is seriously, and ultimately disastrously, mistaken. *Gaudium et Spes* is testimony to that.

This chapter is about Catholic social teaching in a more historically radical sense, rooted in documents that long antedate the last one hundred years and the papal theology written in them. Catholicism is a religion of the Book, a "textualized religion,"[7] that assigns theological priority to its canonical writings in the Bible that it takes to be the very word of God. This chapter argues that Catholic social thought in its deepest roots and fullest flowering grows from the word of God and could not be clearer. The biblical God, and the Christ whom God sent to reveal God's self, is a God of love and justice and in real historical time stands preferentially on the side of the poor and oppressed, those whom Jorg Rieger calls "the underside"[8] and those who, Pope Francis argues, "are no longer society's underside or its fringes or its disenfranchised—they are no longer even part of it. The excluded are not the 'exploited' but the outcasts, the 'leftovers'" (EG 53). All who would be truly Christ-ian and "perfect as your heavenly Father is perfect" (Matt 5:48) have no option but preferentially to do the same. This imperative of Christ-ian discipleship is so central to the Gospel and beyond debate, it is astonishing that among the many preparatory commissions and documents preparing for the Second Vatican Council, there was not one that felt it necessary to prepare a document on the Church in the Modern World. *Gaudium*

---

[6] John A. Coleman, ed., *One Hundred Years of Catholic Social Thought* (Maryknoll, NY: Orbis Books, 1991), 2. See also David J. O'Brien and Thomas A. Shannon, eds., *Catholic Social Thought: The Documentary Heritage* (Maryknoll, NY: Orbis Books, 1996); Donal Dorr, *Option for the Poor: A Hundred Years of Catholic Social Teaching* (Maryknoll, NY: Orbis Books, 1992).

[7] George Lindbeck, "Barth and Textuality," *Theology Today* 43, no. 3 (October 1986): 361.

[8] Jorg Rieger, *Remember the Poor: The Challenge to Theology in the Twenty-First Century* (Harrisburg: Trinity Press International, 1998), 1–5.

et Spes grew out of that lacuna at the urging of Cardinal Suenens of Malines, Belgium.

The Church, then, or the people of God in *Lumen Gentium*'s preferred term, is almost by definition a Church of the poor. More so, Francis—both saint and pope—insist, it is a poor Church. Since his election, Francis has pointed out in both word and illuminating deed the scandal of debilitating poverty in a world of plenty and the obligation of those who have riches to share with those who have not. "The right to have a share of earthly goods sufficient for oneself and one's family," *Gaudium et Spes* teaches, "belongs to everyone," and "all are obliged to come to the relief of the poor, and to do so not merely out of their superfluous goods" (GS 69).[9] Pope John XXIII, just before the council in September 1962, declared that the "obligation of every man, the urgent obligation of the Christian man is to reckon what is superfluous by the measure of the needs of others, and to see to it that the administration and the distribution of created goods serve the common good."[10] The final document of the Second Vatican Council, *Gaudium et Spes*, whose painful birth we traced in an earlier chapter, was greatly influenced by these ancient and modern judgments. It was, of course, even more influenced by the sacred Scripture, the word of God.

The Bible and the Demands of Love and Justice

"It has pleased God," the Second Vatican Council taught, "to reveal himself and to make known the mystery of his will . . . through deeds and words that are intrinsically connected: the works performed by God in the history of salvation show forth and confirm the doctrine and realities signified by the words; the words for their part proclaim the works and bring to light the mystery they contain" (DV 2). The God of Jews and Christians is a God of actions, a God who speaks and acts efficaciously, a God whose word is also happening and event. Every confession of belief in God is rooted in historical happenings and events. The most radical

---

[9] See Basil, *In illud Lucae*, PG 31, 263; Lactantius, *Divinarum Institutionum*, Liber 5, *PL* 6, 565; Augustine, *Enarratio in Ps CXLVII, 12, PL* 37, 192; Gregory the Great, *Regulae Pastoralis Liber*, Pars 3, chap. 21, *PL* 77, 87; Bonaventure, *In IV Sent.*, d. 15, ad 2, q. 1, de superfluo; there is an ancient Catholic principle, "In extreme necessity all goods are to shared," but see Aquinas's explanation of how that principle is to be applied in *S.T.* II–II, 66, 7.

[10] *Acta Apostolicae Sedis* 54 (1962): 682.

of these events for Jews was the great Exodus from Egypt, comprising their experience of slavery in Egypt, their liberation from Egypt under Moses, their wandering in the desert, and their settlement in the land where "milk and honey flow" (Deut 26:9). The response of biblical faith to God's saving action, the revelation in turn of Israel's righteousness, is other actions, the observance in real time of God's commandments. When we ask in what actions that righteousness is to be concretized, the Bible universally leaves us in no doubt.

Yahweh, the God of Israel, intervenes in history in signs and wonders to reveal not only God's power, but also that God's power is in defense of the defenseless poor and oppressed. Yahweh is "father of the fatherless and protector of widows. . . . God gives the desolate a home to dwell in; God leads out the prisoners to prosperity; but the rebellious dwell in a parched land" (Ps 68:6-7). To know this God is not, as it is in Greece, to know *that* God is and *what* God is; it is to love God and act like God. In Gustavo Gutierrez's accurate judgment, "to know God as liberator is to liberate, is to do justice,"[11] always remembering how Yahweh intervened in Egypt to achieve liberation for Israelite slaves. That memory and the actions in history it demands return again and again.

> You shall remember that you were a slave in Egypt and the Lord your God redeemed you from there; therefore I command you to do this. When you reap your harvest in your field and have forgotten a sheaf in the field, you shall not go back to get it; it shall be for the sojourner, the fatherless, the widow; that the Lord your God may bless you in all the works of your hands. When you beat your olive trees, you shall not go over the boughs again; it shall be for the sojourner, the fatherless, the widow. When you gather the grapes of your vineyard, you shall not glean it afterwards; it shall be for the sojourner, the fatherless, the widow. You shall remember that you were a slave in the land of Egypt; therefore, I command you to do this. (Deut 24:18-22)

What Jesus, for whom God's paradigmatic action in the New Testament was raising him from the dead and revealing his righteousness, would later advance as a reciprocal relationship between God and "the least of these my brethren" (Matt 25:40) has always been embedded in his Jewish tradition as a reciprocal relationship between God and the poor.

---

[11] Gustavo Gutierrez, *The Power of the Poor in History* (Maryknoll, NY: Orbis Books, 1983), 8.

The prophets consistently linked these two and proclaimed that to truly know and love God demands action against the injustice and oppression perpetrated against God's poor. Jeremiah, for instance, proclaimed this prophetic message.

> Hear the word of the Lord all you men of Judah who enter these gates to worship the Lord. Thus says the Lord of Hosts, the God of Israel. Amend your ways and your doings and I will let you dwell in this place. . . . For if you truly amend your ways and your doings, if you truly execute justice one with another, if you do not oppress the alien, the fatherless, the widow, or shed innocent blood in this place, and if you do not go after other gods to your own hurt, then I will let you dwell in this place, in the land that I gave of old to your fathers forever. (Jer 7:2-7)

The reciprocation could not be made clearer: knowledge and love of God is proved in practice by action on behalf of justice for the underside, Francis's "excluded," who are the poor and the oppressed. The Book of Proverbs offers an axiomatic statement about this reciprocative preferential option for the poor: "He who mocks the poor insults his creator" (Prov 17:5). *Gaudium et Spes* insists that, with respect to this reciprocation, "before the judgment seat of God each man must render an account of his own life, whether he has done good or evil" (GS 17).

Isaiah's messianic formulation of the intimate connection between God and justice for the underside or excluded leads us into the New Testament, for Luke's Jesus chooses it for commentary in his home synagogue of Nazareth.

> The Spirit of the Lord God is upon me, because the Lord has anointed me to bring good tidings to the afflicted; he has sent me to bind up the brokenhearted, to proclaim liberty to the captives and the opening of the prison to those who are bound; to proclaim the year of the Lord's favor and the day of vengeance of our God; to comfort all who mourn; to grant to those who mourn in Sion—to give them a garland instead of ashes, the oil of gladness instead of mourning, the mantle of praise instead of a faint spirit, that they may be called oaks of righteousness . . . for I the Lord love justice, I hate robbery and wrong. I will faithfully give them their recompense and I will make an everlasting covenant with them. (Isa 61:1-8)

This predilection for the poor and the oppressed, Isaiah prophetically proclaims, will be characteristic of the coming Messiah, the ultimately righteous one of Israel. That the Messiah has come in Jesus is proclaimed in Luke's Jesus commentary on the text: "Today this scripture has been fulfilled in your hearing" (Luke 4:21).

The confession of the followers of Jesus was and is that he is the promised Messiah, in Greek the Christ (Mark 1:1; Matt 1:1), the one anointed by God "to bring good tidings to the afflicted." The gospels symbolize his messianic anointing in the passage that narrates his baptism by John the Baptizer, the descent of the Holy Spirit upon him, and his designation as "beloved son" (Mark 1:9-11; Matt 3:13-17; Luke 3:21-22). Immediately following his anointing he proclaims the advent of the kingdom or reign of God (Mark 1:15), the nature of which is the full import of Luke's use of the Isaiah text cited above: "Today this scripture has been fulfilled in your hearing": the reign of God is a reign of justice in favor of the poor, the underside, the excluded. Jesus' proclamation of this reign, not only in words but more importantly in actions, is precisely what led him, first, to his death on the cross and, then, to his resurrection by God (1 Cor 15:4; Rom 6:4 and 8:4; Col 2:12; Acts 2:24, 32; 3:15). For the entire body of his disciples dispirited by his death, and not just for the two on the road to Emmaus, "their eyes were opened" (Luke 24:31) by his resurrection, in which God verified both that the words and actions of Jesus were right with God and that he was, indeed, the "holy and righteous one" (Acts 2:14).

The eyes of Jesus' followers were so well and truly opened by his resurrection that, ultimately, they confessed not only that he was the Christ, the holy and righteous one sent by God, but also that he was God in human form, God made man full of grace and truth, God pitching his tent among God's people (John 1:14). The universal biblical reciprocation between God and the poor reaches an unsurpassable personification and high point in Jesus who, in Gutierrez' pregnant phrase, is "God become poor."[12] It is in his life on behalf of his poor, excluded sisters and brothers, that Jesus is finally recognized as God's beloved Son. It is in their lives on behalf of his poor, excluded sisters and brothers, that Christ-ians too will be recognized as God's daughters and sons, for Jesus "clearly taught the sons of God to treat one another as brothers" and sisters (GS 32).

Like any good Jew of his time Jesus continued both to uphold the reciprocal relationship between God and the poor and to insist that to know and love God is to act against injustice perpetrated against the poor. Matthew makes his position clearest in his Sermon on the Mount:

[12] Ibid.

"Not everyone who *says* to me 'Lord, Lord' shall enter the kingdom of heaven but the one who *does* the will of my Father who is in heaven" (7:21). The disciples who responded to Jesus' invitation to "follow me" (Mark 1:17; Matt 4:18), and that includes every person today who claims to be a Christ-ian, upheld the same reciprocal relationship and insisted that it is to be lived not in words but in action. Again, Matthew makes it clearest in his powerful final judgment scene.

> Then he will say to those at his left hand "depart from me you cursed into the eternal fire prepared for the devil and his angels; for I was hungry and you gave me no food, I was thirsty and you gave me no drink, I was a stranger and you did not welcome me, sick and in prison and you did not visit me." Then they also will answer, "Lord, when did we see you hungry or thirsty or a stranger or naked or sick or in prison and did not minister to you?" Then he will answer them, "Truly I say to you, as you did it not to one of the least of these, you did it not to me." (Matt 25:41-45)

Matthew's final comment is a chilling woe for those who, both then and today, do not recognize the reciprocation between God and the underside and excluded, and a blessing for those who do: "they will go into eternal punishment, but the righteous into eternal life" (Matt 25:46). The righteousness God and His Christ demand of their follow-ers is not easy for, "although he was made by God in a state of holiness, from the very dawn of history man abused his liberty at the urging of personified evil. . . . Therefore man is split within himself. As a result, all of human life, whether individual or collective, shows itself to be a dramatic struggle between good and evil, between light and darkness" (GS 13). It is the great mystery of sin. Christ-ians, however, share in the promise of their Christ who is "the true light that enlightens every man coming into the world" and gives them "power to become children of God; who were born, not of blood nor of the will of the flesh nor of the will of man, but of God" (John 1:9-12).

James, as radically Jewish as Jesus and Matthew, has his own formula-tion of the reciprocation between God and the poor. "What does it profit, my brethren, if a man says he has faith but has not works? Can his faith save him? If a brother or sister is ill-clad and in lack of daily food, and one of you says to them, 'Go in peace, be warmed and filled' without giving them the things needed for the body, what does it profit? So faith by itself, if it has no works, is dead" (Jas 2:14-17). *Gaudium et Spes* has its own formulation of this sentiment, borrowed from twelfth-century

Gratian:[13] "Feed the man dying of hunger, because if you have not fed him you have killed him" (GS 69). Martin Luther sparked a long and false debate between Lutherans and Catholics about the respective values of faith and good works, as if Lutherans valued *only* faith and Catholics valued *only* good works. That debate has now been formally laid to rest by the agreement between Lutherans and Catholics articulated in their *Joint Declaration on the Doctrine of Justification*. The theological reality is that Luther and the theologians who followed him never doubted that faith is proved in action; in other words, that faith must work; and the Catholic Church never doubted that faith concretized in works is necessary for salvation.[14]

Christ, Service, and Communion

There is another Christ-ian pattern highlighted throughout the New Testament, which is intimately related to the universal reciprocation between God, God's Christ, and God's least. That pattern is the pattern of service to others, especially to the poor and the excluded, which Jesus exemplifies in his life and unceasingly strives to inculcate in his disciples. The synoptic Christ articulates the perspective unequivocally: "The Son of Man came not to be served but to serve and to give his life as a ransom (redemption) for many" (Mark 10:45; Matt 20:28). *Diakonia*, service, is Christ's way of relating to others; service of others is what he strives to inculcate in his disciples of every generation. He instructs them patiently that those who have authority over the Gentiles lord it over them. "But it shall not be so among you. Whoever would be great among you must be your servant, and whoever would be first among you must be the slave of all" (Mark: 10:42-44; Matt 20:25-7). *Gaudium et Spes*'s interpretation of that perspective is that "The fundamental purpose of this productivity must not be the mere multiplication of products. It must not be profit or domination. Rather, it must be the *service* of man, and indeed of the whole man, viewed in terms of his material needs and the demands of his intellectual, moral, spiritual, and religious life. And when we say man, we mean every man whatsoever [and surely every woman and child] and every group of men, of whatever race and from

---

[13] Gratian, *Decretum*, chap. 21, dist. LXXXVI.

[14] Henry Denzinger and Adolf Schönmetzer, eds., *Enchiridion Symbolorum Definitionum et Declarationum de Rebus Fidei et Morum* (Fribourg: Herder, 1965), nos. 1529 and 1532.

whatever part of the world" (GS 64). How far Christians are from being Christ-ians today is summed up in another statement from *Gaudium et Spes*. "If the demands of justice and equity are to be satisfied, vigorous efforts must be made . . . to remove as quickly as possible the immense inequalities which now exist" (GS 66). Those immense inequalities are starkly highlighted by the fact that "while an enormous mass of people still lack the absolute necessities of life, some, even in less advanced countries, live sumptuously or squander wealth. Luxury and misery rub shoulders" (GS 63). Present day Christians must shoulder a great deal of blame for this situation. It would appear that they have not understood or, perhaps, have chosen to ignore Jesus' clear teaching.

John's paschal supper narrative highlights this Christ-ian emphasis on service, an emphasis that has been somewhat obscured liturgically by the Catholic emphasis on the transformation of bread and wine in the eucharistic supper. The narrative describes Jesus' washing of his disciples' feet, a prophetic action that reveals Jesus' will to be remembered as servant and challenges those who remember him at the supper to be and do the same. Lest this point be missed (as it has been regularly missed in Christian history), John's Jesus underlines the challenge in his final testament. "I have given you an example that you also should do as I have done to you" (John 13:15). Jesus, he of right action and righteousness, who lived a life of neighbor-love (Lev 19:18; Mark 12:31) in service to others, challenged his disciples, then and now, to do the same. Xavier Léon-Dufour interprets this foot washing as symbolically integral to Jesus' paschal meal, to the Christian Eucharist that derives from it, and to the character of both as memorial meals.[15] We are arguing here that it is integral, too, to the way Christ-ians, committed to the reciprocation between God and the poor underside, are to live their lives in real time after celebrating Eucharist together in memory of the Christ. Included in that memory are Jesus' death and his transformation in resurrection. Through that resurrection, Christ-ians are taught, "the riddles of sorrow and death grow meaningful. Apart from His gospel they overwhelm us. Christ has risen, destroying death by His death. He has lavished life on us, so that, as sons in the Son, we can cry out in the Spirit: Abba, Father (cf. Rom 8:15; Gal 4:6)" (GS 22). Christ-ians are called, in preparation for their final resurrection, to transform the lives of their sisters and brothers of the poor underside.

---

[15] Xavier Leon-Dufour, *Sharing the Eucharistic Bread: the Witness of the New Testament*, trans. Matthew O'Connell (New York: Paulist Press, 1987), 82–95.

Pope John Paul II, in his important letter on the lay faithful, teaches that "communion is the very mystery of the Church" (*Christifideles Laici* [On the Lay Faithful] CL 18). The CDF cites with approval the pope's words to the bishops of the United States: "the concept of communion lies at the heart of the Church's self-understanding."[16] These opinions echo the judgment of the 1985 Roman Synod[17] and of the secretary of the Second Vatican Council's Central Theological Commission that its vision of Church as communion was the council's most important teaching.[18] The Church *is* a communion;[19] communion describes its very essence. "One of the salient features of the modern world is the growing interdependence of men one on the other, a development very largely promoted by modern technical advances. Nevertheless, brotherly dialogue among men does not reach its perfection on the level of technical progress, but on the deeper level of interpersonal relationships. These demand a mutual respect for the full spiritual dignity of the person. Christian revelation contributes greatly to the promotion of this communion between persons" (GS 23). That communion is intended to be among all men but, certainly especially, among all Christ-ians in the Church. Communion is a common word in the Catholic tradition but, in the recent tradition, it has not been used to describe the Church. Rather, it has been used as an expression for receiving the Body of Christ in Eucharist.[20] The two uses of the term, however, are not unconnected, and Paul was the first to enunciate their connection. "The cup of blessing which we bless, is it not a communion in the blood of Christ? The bread which we break, is it not a communion in the body of Christ? Because there is one bread, we who are many are one body, for we all partake of the one bread" (1 Cor 10:16-17). The Second Vatican Council taught this explicitly. "Truly partaking of the Body of the Lord in the breaking of the Eucharistic bread, we are taken up into communion with Him and with one another" (LG 7). That statement is important for the reciprocative communion between God

---

[16] See *Catholic International* 3 (1992): 761.

[17] See its Final Report, *The Church, in the Word of God, Celebrates the Mysteries of Christ*, II, C, 1.

[18] Gerard Philips, *L'Eglise et son mystere au IIe Concile du Vatican* (Paris: Desclée, 1966), I, 7, 59 and II, 24, 54, 159.

[19] See Jerome Hamer, *The Church Is a Communion* (New York: Sheed and Ward, 1964); Michael G. Lawler and Thomas J. Shanahan, *Church: A Spirited Communion* (Collegeville, MN: Liturgical Press, 1995).

[20] See Henri de Lubac, *Corpus Mysticum: l'eucharistie et l'église au moyen age* (Paris: Aubier, 1944).

and the excluded underside and between all Christ-ians in the Church, as well as for the argument of this chapter.

Participation in Eucharist leads to communion not only with God in Christ but also with the body of believers, the Church. The reality of communion in the Church is an essentially eucharistic reality, in both a weak and a strong sense. The weak sense is Holy Communion in the sacramental Body of Christ in and through sacramentally transformed bread and wine. The more important strong sense is that the eucharistic meal is the sacrament, that is, both the sign and the instrument[21] of the communion of believers, not only with their Christ but also with one another.

It was and is because the disciples of Jesus share food and drink in his name that they were and are made one in communion. That relationship is already evident in the earliest Jerusalem church, which devoted itself to "the apostles' teaching and *koinonia*" (Acts 2:42) and "had everything in common (*panta koina*)" (Acts 4:32). Paul makes clear that communion is not just between the members of a local altar community but reaches out to embrace all the churches, telling us in his original Greek that the poor churches in Macedonia and Achaia "have been pleased to make *koinonian*" for the church at Jerusalem (Rom 15:26; see 2 Cor 8:4) and praising "the generosity of your *koinonias*" (2 Cor 9:13). Such genuine communion among disciples sharing the eucharistic meal, Paul argues, is a necessary precondition for genuinely celebrating the Lord's Supper. When there is no such communion between believers, as there was not at Corinth, neither is there communion with the Christ whom they *say* they confess as Lord. In such circumstance, Paul judges, "it is not the Lord's Supper that you eat" (1 Cor 11:20). That judgment ought not to come as a surprise given the final Judge's declaration that "as you did it not to one of the least of these you did it not to me" (Matt 25:45). When there is no communion with the least in the body of believers, neither is there communion with Christ and Christ's God. Leaning on this notion of communion, *Gaudium et Spes* teaches that in our contemporary world "it grows increasingly true that the obligations of justice and love are fulfilled only if each person," contributes to the common good, "according to his own abilities and the needs of others" (GS 30).

---

[21] See Michael G. Lawler, *Symbol and Sacrament: A Contemporary Sacramental Theology* (Omaha: Creighton University Press, 1995). See David N. Power, *The Eucharistic Mystery: Revitalizing the Tradition* (New York: Crossroad, 1992), 30–32.

The theologians who have most detailed the connection between ritual Eucharist, ecclesial communion, and communional Christ-ian life are liberation theologians.[22] What came to be known as liberation theology was spawned in the barrios of South America on behalf of the multitudinous poor in its various countries. Liberation theologians correctly interpreted the biblical data we have considered as a preferential option for the poor, and enunciated this option first as a theological doctrine which later was verified as an ecclesial doctrine of the South American Catholic Church. It is not a surprise that an Argentinian Pope Francis would manifest this doctrine in his papal actions and words. The doctrine of the preferential option for the poor came to preeminence as a result of two conferences of Latin American bishops, the first at Medellín in Colombia in 1968, the second at Puebla in Mexico in 1979. Medellín adumbrated the phrase *preferential option for the poor*, Pueblo explicitly adopted it. Among the signs of authentic Christ-ianity, the bishops taught, are "preferential love and concern for the poor"; they pledged themselves "to make clear through our lives and attitudes that our preference is to evangelize and serve the poor"; they also taught that a "preferential option for the poor represents the most noticeable tendency of religious life in Latin America."[23] Medellín and Puebla, we should note, came shortly after the Second Vatican Council and *Gaudium et Spes* was an acknowledged influence on them. Questions are being asked today about the words and novel actions of Pope Francis with respect to a Church of the poor and a poor Church. The answers lie openly for those with eyes to see in *Gaudium et Spes*, Medellín, and Puebla.

An Asian liberation theologian, Tissa Balasuriya, writes of Eucharist that it is "spiritual food in so far as it leads to love, unity, and communion

[22] We do not wish to pursue this thought in this chapter, but we do wish to state that we are always puzzled by the absence of a homegrown Catholic American liberation theology despite the existence of a multitudinous underside and excluded in American life: people of color, women, immigrants from whatever nation, gays and lesbians, people with disabilities, the poor, the homeless. There is an obvious need for an American-based theology of liberation, a need to which the Protestant works of Frederick Herzog and James Cone respond. Cone opined that Herzog was the only white theologian to reorder theological principles in the light of the oppression of black people, one of the obvious American "signs of the times" so prized by the Second Vatican Council.

[23] Puebla Final Document, nos. 382, 707, 733. The Puebla Conference is analyzed in contextual depth in John Eagleson and Philip Scharper, eds., *Puebla and Beyond* (Maryknoll, NY: Orbis Books, 1979).

among persons and groups. Today this requires love among persons and *effective* action for justice. The Eucharist must also lead us to a response to the suffering of the masses, *often caused by people who take a prominent part in the Eucharist.* Unless there is this twofold dimension of personal love and societal action, the eucharist can be a sacrilege."[24] The phrase we have underscored, and which is demonstrable throughout the Christian world without debate, illustrated the Second Vatican Council's confession that the Church is a Church of sinners in her membership and is, therefore, "at the same time holy and always in need of being purified" and renewed in its commitment to the Christ and to the God he reveals (LG 8). It is a sad commentary on the Church that several liberation theologians so dedicated to the poor and excluded were condemned for teachings contrary to Church doctrine, though their condemnations were later lifted thanks to the influence of Pope John Paul II. Pope Francis speaks out of the biblical tradition, the best of the Church tradition, and *Gaudium et Spes* when he teaches that "alleviating the grave evil of poverty must be at the very heart of the Church's mission. It is neither optional nor secondary."[25]

Eucharist is not the only sacrament with embedded ethical demands: they all have such embedded demands. Alfred North Whitehead characterized the function of symbol in these words: "it makes connected thought possible, while at the same time it automatically directs action."[26] The prophetic symbol that is sacrament is no different.[27] It makes connected Christ-ian thought possible and it directs Christ-ian action. The sacramental symbols of baptism and confirmation, for instance, not only ritually inform Christians about the death and resurrection of Jesus the Christ and the presence of Christ's Spirit among them, but also present a radical challenge to prophetic Christ-ian action. It is not enough for Christ-ians to ritually proclaim and celebrate new life in Christ through the Spirit, they must also live that new life by living a life that is like the life of Christ and is animated by the Spirit of Christ. This call to Christian action is embedded in the sacrament's character as *prophetic* symbol.

---

[24] Tissa Balasuriya, *The Eucharist and Human Liberation* (Maryknoll, NY: Orbis Books, 1979), 22, emphasis added.

[25] See Bishop Robert W. McElroy, "A Church for the Poor," *America* 209, no. 11 (October 21, 2013): 13.

[26] Alfred North Whitehead, *Symbolism: Its Meaning and Effect* (New York: Putnam's, 1959), 74.

[27] See Lawler, *Symbol and Sacrament*, 5–28.

More importantly for Christ-ians, as we have seen several times already, it is embedded in the Gospel of Christ, for "not everyone who *says* to me 'Lord, Lord' shall enter the kingdom of heaven, but whoever does the will of my Father who is in heaven" (Matt 7:21). Part of that Christ-ian doing, to underscore once more, is the doing of love and justice for the Father's poor and excluded.

"This communitarian character is developed and consummated in the work of Jesus Christ. For the very Word made flesh willed to share in the human fellowship. . . . In His preaching He clearly taught the sons of God to treat one another as brothers. In His prayers he pleaded that all His disciples might be 'one'" (GS 32). The ethical demand for love, justice, and service for the poor underside, and for all women and men, is embedded in Christian sacraments because it is first of all embedded in incarnation, the theological term in which Christ-ians express the reality of Christ. In incarnation, Dermot Lane comments, "the gulf between heaven and earth, between God and man, between the supernatural and the natural, between the sacred and the secular . . . has once and for all been overcome so that now we can glimpse heaven on earth, God in man, the supernatural in the natural, the sacred amidst the secular."[28] The Second Vatican Council articulated this incarnational idea by teaching that "a secular quality is proper to laity," in the sense that "laity, by their very vocation, seek the kingdom of God by engaging in temporal affairs and by ordering them to the plan of God" (LG 31). John Paul II insists that this secular quality is to be understood *theologically* and not simply sociologically. He teaches that the term *secular* is to be "understood in the light of the act of God, the Creator and Redeemer, who has handed over the world to women and men so that they may participate in the work of creation, free creation from the influence of sin, and sanctify themselves in marriage or the celibate life, in a family, in a profession, and in the various activities of society" (CL 15). One of the activities of society and real Christ-ians today is the service of love and justice for the poor underside.

The inseparable connection between participation in Christ-ian *sacrament* and Christ-ian life in real time is a firm and ancient theological position in the Church. Already in the third century, Cyprian of Carthage argued that putting on Christ in baptism is meaningless unless it is followed by a Christ-like life. "To put on the name of Christ and not

---

[28] Dermot Lane, *The Reality of Jesus* (New York: Paulist Press, 1975), 137.

continue along the way of Christ, what is that but a lie?"[29] If we have put him on, "we ought to go forward according to the example of Christ."[30] In the twentieth century John Paul II agrees: initiation into communion in the Church is initiation into the mission of the Church. "Communion gives rise to mission and mission is accomplished in communion" (CL 32). The communion that is the mission of the Church, we have already argued, is twofold: it is the communion of believers with one another and the communion of believers with Christ and Christ's God. Those two communions are reciprocal, the one depending on the other, and they are celebrated, proclaimed, and made real in Eucharist and are intended to be lived outside Eucharist in real time Christ-ian lives. It is not difficult to see how this sharing in the Church, the Body of Christ, shares also in the ancient reciprocation between God and God's least, the easily ignored poor and excluded.

Jesus and Family

There is another gospel tradition related to the question of Catholic social thought, a recurring, disturbing, and therefore usually ignored tradition about Jesus' attitude to the family life of his day. Mark reports that Jesus was preaching and healing and that his family, concerned about his conduct which impinged on their honor, came "to restrain him." When told "your mother and your brothers are outside asking for you," Jesus responded with a question: "Who is my mother? Who are my brothers?" The contemporary American answer is clear: his biological mother and brothers, waiting outside, seeking to restrain activity for the sake of family honor, are his mother and his brothers. That, however, is not the answer Jesus gives. His answer is more expansive and other-embracing than the biological answer. Looking around at those in the circle around him, he declared: "Here are my mother and my brothers. Whoever does the will of God is my brother, my sister, and my mother" (Mark 3:31-33).

"As the first-born of many brethren and through the gift of His Spirit, [Jesus] founded after his death and resurrection a new brotherly community composed of all those who receive Him in faith and in love. This He did through His Body, which is the Church. Thus everyone, as members one of the other, would render mutual service according to the different gifts bestowed on each" (GS 32). The followers of Jesus

---

[29] *De Zelo et Livore* 12, *PL* 4, 646.
[30] *De Bono Patientiae* 9, *PL* 4, 628.

are like one big family, but there is a caveat to be heeded. The extended biological or blood family was the source of honor and status in first-century Mediterranean society. It was also "the primary economic, religious, educational, and social network."[31] To sever connection to that family was to lose connection to everything that was social and, in that corporate culture, personal. Yet Jesus suggests a move away from that family to another, surrogate family in which kin is created not by blood but by belief in and loyalty to the God preached by Jesus. The true holy family, he suggests, is not his biological family but the surrogate, fictive-kin family composed of believers loyal to God. This is made clearer in a Lucan parallel in which, in response to a woman who proclaims his mother blessed, Jesus declares "blessed rather are those who hear the word of God and obey it" (Luke 11:27-28). The "blessed" language here is honor language. The woman proclaims the traditional honor due to the mother of an honorable son; Jesus responds that for him and his followers true honor derives not from fidelity to one's blood kin but from fidelity to God and God's word.

Earlier in his gospel, Luke highlighted the issue of breaking with one's biological kin group (Luke 9:57-62). He taught that the followers of Jesus would lead a deviant lifestyle to the extent that they might live away from their family home (vv. 57-58). He recorded that Jesus rejected a family obligation of the highest order, "leave the dead to bury their dead" (v. 62). "There can be no doubt about the radical quality of the break that following Jesus requires nor about Luke's understanding of its cost."[32] A fictive-kin family of brothers and sisters in Christ is not to eliminate the blood-kin family but to transcend it and embrace a larger, more universal family. The cost of such a move is high and is underscored later in the gospel. "If anyone comes to me and does not hate his father and his mother, wife and children, brothers and sisters, even his own life, he cannot be a disciple of mine" (14:26).

Jesus does not demand such a socially suicidal sacrifice without offering some reassurance. Peter asks about the reward to be expected from such countercultural behavior. "We here have left our belongings to become your followers." The implication is clear. Look what we have done for you; what will you do for us? Jesus replies that they will receive "manifold more in this age, and in the age to come eternal life"

[31] Bruce J. Malina and Richard L. Rohrbaugh, *Social Science Commentary on the Synoptic Gospels* (Minneapolis, MN: Fortress Press, 1992), 202.
[32] Ibid, 345.

(Luke 18:28-30). There is little good news here for the blood family. A forlorn mother in Gerd Theissen's fictional-scholarly account of Jesus' life puts the attitude of parents bluntly. "He corrupts the young people. It all sounds fine; blessed are you who weep for you will laugh. But what does he actually do? He makes parents weep over lost sons. He promises everything will change. But what actually changes? Families are destroyed because children run away from their parents."[33] The bad news here for blood families is balanced by the good news or gospel that blood families are to be transcended to create a larger surrogate, fictive-kin family that embraces all not included in the biological family: the poor, the "lepers" of whatever color or sexual orientation, the sinners who dishonor the family, many of whom, to repeat, "take a prominent part in the Eucharist," indeed all who "hear the word of God and obey it" (Luke 11:28). That word of God, remember, in that society in which Jesus lived and preached, included the reciprocation between God and the poor underside. Nothing has changed for Christ-ians today.

Jesus appears to be teaching clearly in these passages that God and grace are embedded not in a particular family structure, whether it be ancient Israelite or contemporary American, but in the following of Jesus. "Follow me," he invites (Mark 1:17), join my surrogate, fictive-kin family and be blessed not by belonging to this or that honorable family but by hearing the word of God and keeping it. In the earliest Christian tradition that following of Jesus was called discipleship and the gathering of disciples was called *ekklesia tou theou*, the Church of God (1 Cor 10:2; 10:32: 11:22; 15:9; Gal 1:13). Many today, called baptized nonbelievers, appear to equate being a disciple of Christ with simply being ritually born into this ecclesial family in baptism, with little attention being paid either to the word of God or the following of Jesus. That equation, *Gaudium et Spes* teaches, is seriously misconstrued.

> This split between the faith which many profess and their daily lives deserves to be counted among the more serious errors of our age. Long since, the prophets of the Old Testament fought vehemently against this scandal [see Isaiah 58:1-12] and even more so did Jesus Christ Himself in the New Testament threaten it with grave punishments" [see Mark 7:10-13; Matt 23:3-23]. (GS 43)

---

[33] Gerd Theissen, *The Shadow of the Galilean: The Quest of the Historical Jesus in Narrative Form* (Philadelphia: Fortress Press, 1987), 71.

The Church, that is, the people of God, can heal this scandal and the disunity among Christ's followers, "for the promotion of unity belongs to the innermost nature of the Church, since she is, 'by her relationship with Christ, both a sacramental sign and an instrument of intimate union with God, and of the unity of all mankind'" (LG 1; GS 42). This is one more place where *Gaudium et Spes* assumes the new ecclesiology advanced by *Lumen Gentium*.

Being Christ-ian means much more than being baptized. It means following Jesus, structuring one's life like the life of Jesus, a life that God verified in resurrection as a life right with God and, therefore, righteous. That life, as we have seen, is doubly characterized: it grasps reciprocation between God and the poor and excluded and is a life of service to them. Living such a life, and only living such a life, is what makes an individual, a family, or a Church Christ-ian. We are in total agreement with evangelical theologian Rodney Clapp when he asserts that "the Bible is centrally and first of all the *story* of Israel and Jesus."[34] That an individual, a family, or a church will be Christian, he suggests, is determined not by any ancient or contemporary social structure, but by its being faithful to the biblical story of God revealed in Christ. We agree completely. Being Christ-ian is defined by living a Christ-ian life. By extending biological family into surrogate, fictive-kin family of all who hear the word of God and obey it, Jesus is embracing into his family all those dishonorable outsiders traditionally excluded from family of his time: the poor, the sinners, the lepers, the scorned and oppressed. His talk of a fictive-kin family of God is just another way to talk of the traditional reciprocation between God and the poor underside. Catholic social thought as described in *Gaudium et Spes* and as rooted in its biblical origins assigns righteousness to all who hear the word of God and obey it; they are the true holy family of God and as such are to be treated with love and justice. A reflection on this family of God completes this chapter.

The Family of God

Israelite self-understanding was rooted in their covenant with God. To covenant is to consent and to promise so that both parties, equal or unequal in other respects, are equally committed to one another solemnly and radically. It is thus that God and Israel commit themselves

[34] Rodney Clapp, *Families at the Crossroads: Beyond Traditional and Modern Options* (Downer's Grove, IL: InterVarsity Press, 1993), 15, emphasis in original.

to one another in covenant. When the Egyptian slaves reached Sinai, God instructed Moses what to say to the people: "You have seen what I did to the Egyptians and how I bore you on eagles' wings and brought you to myself. Now, therefore, if you will obey my voice and keep my covenant, you shall be my own possession among all peoples." All the people answered together and said: "All that the Lord has spoken we will do" (Exod 19:4-8). This foundational covenant, which solemnly ratifies the reciprocation between God and the poor slaves from Egypt and establishes them as "a people [a family] holy to the Lord your God" (Deut 7:6; 14:2; 26:5-9), is neither forgotten nor abandoned by the followers of Jesus. It is, rather, transformed to be rooted in Jesus. *Gaudium et Spes* invites all Christ-ians to commit to that same covenant, people, and extended family.

There are no covenants, as there are no contracts, without stipulations, and the Jewish and Christian covenants with God are no different. There are endless stipulations, but they all spring from the same root, the two commandments on which "depend all the law and the prophets" (Matt 22:40). These commandments are clear in Jewish Torah. The first embraces relationship with the covenant God: "You shall love the Lord your God with all your heart, and with all your soul, and with all your might" (Deut 6:4). The second embraces relationship with the covenanted people of God, brothers and sisters in God's family: "You shall love your neighbor as yourself" (Lev 19:18). When tested about the greatest commandment, Jesus, righteous Jew that he was, has no hesitation in citing these Torah commandments (Mark 12:28-34; Matt 22:34-40; Luke 10:25-28) and making them stipulations also for those who would covenant in his ecclesial family. His statement in Luke tells all: "Do this and you shall live" (25:28). *Gaudium et Spes* stands firmly in this ancient biblical tradition. "Love for God and neighbor is the first and greatest commandment. Sacred Scripture, however, teaches us that the love of God cannot be separated from love of neighbor" (GS 24). Good news, indeed, for the poor underside.

There is a caveat to be heeded here. In its contemporary American usage love almost always means romantic love, a strong, passionate *feeling* for another person. That is not what New Testament *agape*-love, neighbor-love means, at least not exclusively. *Agape* is more radical than feeling-love which is frequently about oneself; it is love that *wills* and *does* the good of another for the other's sake. That is the love the Bible commands for Christ-ians: willing and active love, compassionate and forgiving love, persevering and steadfast love. The Bible may not, as we have argued, have much to tell us about family structures, but it does have a great deal to tell us about relational *processes* that make it possible for two or four or one hundred people to live together in extended family, peace, and communion. The recipe it offers sounds a lot like the famous Beatles song, "All you need is love." The caveat is that biblical, Christ-ian love evinces a preferential option for the poor and voiceless excluded. John Wesley puts the point beyond debate. Since the love of God is universal and unrestricted, so also is Christ-ian neighbor love universal and unrestricted.[35] Christ-ians are to love, not only their spouses, not only their families, not only their neighbors, but all people, especially those who are not always easy to love: the least, the poor, enemies, the excluded underside. It may not be possible to feel love for them, but Christ-ians, like Christ, can will good to them and love them.

Pope John Paul II put this same argument in his usual personalist terms, stressing *interdependence* among the hierarchy of values and teaching that, when interdependence is appreciated, the "correlative as a moral and social . . . 'virtue' is *solidarity*." This solidarity "is not a vague feeling of compassion or shallow distress at the misfortune of so many people . . . [but] a *firm and persevering determination* to commit oneself to the common good—to the good of all and of each individual because we are *all* really responsible for *all*" (SRS 38; emphases in original). Following a well-marked magisterial trail of recent decades, he later underscored this solidarity as "a love of preference for the poor" (SRS 42)[36] and proposed as a motto for our time *opus solidaritatis pax*, "peace as the fruit of solidarity" (SRS 39). It is not without relevance to the present discussion that peace and communion are regularly linked and even used synonymously.[37]

[35] John Wesley, "A Plain Account of Genuine Christianity," in *John Wesley*, ed. Albert Outler (New York: Oxford University Press, 1964), 184.

[36] See also *Economic Justice for All* (Washington, DC: United States Catholic Bishops, 1986), 90a, 260, 600, and 637.

[37] The conjunction and equivalence of peace and communion is an ancient one. In his many troubles Athanasius, bishop of Alexandria, proudly claimed that more than five hundred bishops accepted him in *koinonia kai agape*, communion and love (*Apologia Contra Ariano*, PG 25, 281), and that the bishops of Egypt were united among themselves and with him in *agape kai eirene*, love and peace (*Epist. Encyclica*, PG 25, 225). It is clear from the contexts that *koinonia, eirene,* and *agape* form a connected cluster signifying what we have called throughout *communion*. The connection continues in the present in the papal practice of addressing encyclical letters to "Patriarchs, Primates, Archbishops . . . at peace and in communion with the Apostolic See."

The Church, the fictive-kin family of sisters and brothers in Christ, Pope Paul VI taught, "has an authentic secular dimension, inherent in her inner nature and mission, which is deeply rooted in the mystery of the Word incarnate and realized in different forms in her members."[38] The Christian doctrine of the incarnation of God in Jesus constructs a bridge over the gulf between God and humans. The Christian Church, founded and rooted in Jesus, enlivened by his Spirit, and charged to continue his mission, minsters to maintain that bridge. It, therefore, must also be incarnate everywhere in human life. That theological doctrine explains why Pope John Paul II teaches that the lay faithful are possessed of a "secular character," and why he insists that character is to be understood in a *theological* and not just a sociological sense. The world, John Paul means, is both the place and the means in and with which lay Christians fulfill their Christ-ian vocation. God, he explains explicitly, "has handed the world over to women and men so that they participate in the work of creation, free creation from the influence of sin, and sanctify themselves" in the various activities of society (CL 15). The reference could not be clearer. Christ-ians are to sanctify themselves by immersion in their community. They are to live in their community and "permeate and perfect [it] with the spirit of the gospel."[39] A major and fundamental part of that gospel is the reciprocation it proclaims between God and the poorest underside.

The calling of Christians, we have argued, is theologically summed up in the following of Christ, in living a Christlike life in the world. That is not to be understood as asserting that the laity have no role in the sacred, for they have, or that clerics have no role in the secular, for they have. It is merely to state what the Christian churches have taken for granted through the centuries, namely, that lay women and men work in the world of real-time reality, that they people the professions and the factories, the schools and the hospitals, the offices, the fields, and the homes. It is to state that they are called, as faithful followers of Christ, to incarnate Christ in these everyday places and thereby bring the Gospel of neighbor-love, reconciliation, compassion, forgiveness, justice, and salvation in Christ directly to the world. It is precisely because that is their calling as Christians that four great fourth-century bishops and fathers of the Church, two in the East and two in the West, could argue as they argued.

---

[38] Paul VI, *Acta Apostolicae Sedis*, 64 (1972): 208.

[39] *Code of Canon Law*, 225, 2. The revised *Code of Canon Law* (1983) is frequently referred to as the final document of the Second Vatican Council.

Basil, the fourth-century bishop of Caesarea, wrote to the rich of his day, "Who is avaricious? One who is not content with those things which are sufficient. Who is a robber? One who takes the goods of another. Are you not avaricious? Are you not a robber? You who make your own the things you have received to distribute . . . that bread which you keep belongs to the hungry; that coat which you preserve in your wardrobe to the naked; those shoes which are rotting in your possession to the shoeless; that gold which you have hidden in the ground to the needy. Wherefore, as often as you were able to help others and refused, so often did you do them wrong."[40] John Chrysostom, fourth-century Patriarch of Constantinople, offers a similar argument.[41] In the West, Ambrose, bishop of Milan, argues in the same vein. "Not from your own do you bestow upon the poor man, but you make return from what is his. What has been given in common for the use of all you appropriate to yourself alone. The earth belongs to all, not to the rich. . . . You are, therefore, paying a debt, not bestowing what is not due."[42] The great Augustine of Hippo offers an almost identical argument.[43] Though all these ancient bishops were consummate rhetoricians, these texts cannot be interpreted as mere rhetoric. Their consonance with the words of Jesus the Christ, already considered, make them authentic Christ-ian interpretation.

Conclusion

Pope John Paul II draws attention to a temptation that Christians "have not always known how to avoid," the temptation to separate faith from life, to separate "the gospel's acceptance from the actual living of the gospel in various situations in the world" (CL 2). What the pope implies is that, to be responsive and faithful to their vocation to follow Christ, Christ-ians need to reach out in active love to all the women and men around them, always and preferentially the poor and excluded. This chapter underscores that the demand to do so does not come from fourth-century Basil and Ambrose, nor from thirteenth-century Aquinas, nor

---

[40] Basil the Great, *Hom in Illud Lucae,* 1, PG 31, 275–78.

[41] John Chrysostom, *De Virginitate,* 68, PG 48, 584–85.

[42] Ambrose, *De Nabuthe Jezraelita,* 1, 53, PL 14, 747.

[43] Augustine, *Sermo L,* 1, PL 38, 326. "God commands sharing, not as being from the property of those he commands but as being from his own property, so that those who offer something to the poor should not think they are doing so from what is their own."

from nineteenth-century Leo XIII, nor from twentieth-century John XXIII, all of whom do no more than interpret the ancient traditional demand for the situations of their time and place. No, the demand comes from the original Jewish and Christian tradition that accepts a reciprocation between God and God's People, especially between God and God's least, the underside poor and excluded. Pope Francis, a faithful interpreter of the Second Vatican Council and especially of *Gaudium et Spes*, states it pointedly: "How can it be that it is not a news item when an elderly homeless person dies of exposure, but it is news when the stock market loses two points? This is a case of exclusion. Can we continue to stand by when food is thrown away while people are starving? This is a case of inequality" (EG 53). *Gaudium et Spes* itself, however, must have the last word.

> Mindful of the Lord's saying: "By this will all men know that you are my disciples, if you have love for one another" (John 13:35), Christians cannot yearn for anything more ardently than to serve the men of the modern world ever more generously and effectively. . . . Not everyone who cries, "Lord, Lord," will enter into the kingdom of heaven, but those who do the Father's will and take a strong grip on the work at hand. Now, the Father wills that in all men we recognize Christ our brother and love Him effectively in word and in deed. By thus giving witness to the truth, we will share with others the mystery of the heavenly Father's love." (GS 93)

Questions for Reflection

1. What does it mean to say that Catholic social thought goes back to the life and words of Jesus?

2. What does it mean to be Christ-ian? How is social justice an essential part of the Christ-ian vocation?

3. What does Scripture, both Old and New Testaments, teach about the poor and the responsibility to the poor?

4. What is the relationship between Eucharist and Catholic social teaching?

5. What is the relationship between ecclesiology, a particular understanding of the Church (e.g., hierarchical or communal), and Catholic social teaching?

6. List and explain examples of people who are the "exploited" in the world. What is our responsibility to these people individually, communally, nationally, and internationally? Share examples on how individuals can effect social change.

7. What is liberation theology? What would liberation theology look like in your country? What issues would it need to address to realize the common good?

8. How has Pope Francis contributed to Catholic social teaching?

Chapter Six

The Political Community and Peacebuilding

This final chapter reflects on *Gaudium et Spes*'s insights on the role and function of the Church in political life[1] and promoting peace in a politically, socially, and economically turbulent world. We consider each in turn.

I. The Church and the Political Community

Gaudium et Spes presents a short chapter on "The Life of the Political Community" (GS 73–76), an essential consideration on the relationship between the Church and the modern world. Exploring this chapter and drawing insight from other Church documents on the Church and the political community, we address two issues: First, the role and function of the Church and the political community and the interrelationship between the two in promoting human dignity and the common good; second, the role and function of the laity in the Church and the political community.

A. The Role and Function of the Church and the Political Community

Gaudium et Spes is concerned with defining human dignity and the common good, providing a theological justification for those definitions, and exploring questions of "special urgency" that must be addressed in order to facilitate their attainment. The life of the political community is an issue of special urgency for the Church since it "regards the indi-

---

[1] For an excellent treatment on the relationship between the Church and the political community, see Kenneth R. Himes, *Christianity and the Political Order: Conflict, Cooptation, and Cooperation* (Maryknoll, NY: Orbis Books, 2013). We draw from his work throughout this section.

vidual State as its partner,"[2] and the political community formulates laws and policies and constructs infrastructures that either promote or frustrate human dignity and the common good. *Gaudium et Spes* notes that the political community exists "for the sake of the common good, in which it finds its full justification and significance, and the source of its inherent legitimacy. Indeed, the common good embraces the sum of those conditions of the social life whereby men, families and associations more adequately and readily may attain their own perfection" (GS 74). Pope John Paul II emphasized that the welfare of the person in community is the essential criterion for all political regimes, programs, systems, laws, and policies (*Redemptor Hominis* 17). This criterion indicates that a well-functioning political community must recognize a coherent and comprehensive definition of human dignity and the common good and seek to promote laws and policies and construct infrastructures that promote and facilitate attaining human dignity and realizing the common good. As definitions of human dignity and the common good evolve and change (as they have evolved and changed throughout the history of the Church), so too, laws, policies, and infrastructures must evolve and change in the political community to reflect this evolution.

Gaudium et Spes teaches that there is common ground between the institutional Church and the political community in that both must seek to promote human dignity and the common good. However, their respective roles and functions in promoting those two areas are distinct. The Church must maintain a balance in its relationship with political life. On the one hand,

> it is always and everywhere legitimate for [the Church] to preach the faith with true freedom, to teach her social doctrine, and to discharge her duty among men without hindrance. She also has the right to pass moral judgments, even on matters touching the political order, whenever basic personal rights or the salvation of souls make such judgments necessary. (GS 76)

This means, in part, that "the role and competence of the Church being what it is, she must in no way be confused with the political community, nor bound to any political system. For she is at once a sign and a safeguard of the transcendence of the human person." On the other hand,

---

[2] Herbert Vorgrimler and Oswald von Nell-Breuning, "The Life of the Political Community," in *Commentary on the Documents of Vatican II*, vol. 5, ed. Herbert Vorgrimler (New York: Herder and Herder, 1969), 316.

"the political community and the Church are mutually independent and self-governing" (GS 76). The Church is not a political party, and the political community is pluralistic and must not self-identify with any particular religious institution.

Though the political community is autonomous and independent from any religious institution, there is inauthentic and authentic political freedom. Inauthentic political freedom is that freedom which espouses relativism, based on the idea "that all conceptions of the human person's good have the same value and truth" (Note 3).[3] Relativism denies any universals or objective truths regarding human dignity or the common good. Authentic political freedom must be "concerned with very concrete realizations of the true human and social good in given historical, geographic, economic, technological and cultural contexts" (Note 3). The concrete realizations of human dignity and the common good allow for plural perspectives on the definitions of these concepts and plural perspectives on how these are to be realized in laws, policies, and infrastructures in particular historical, geographic, economic, technological, and cultural contexts. This particularity is not, *eo ipso*, synonymous with relativism. Rather, it recognizes the complexity of the political community and the challenges of pluralistic perspectives in formulating and constructing laws, policies, and infrastructures that are within the parameters of these definitions. Those parameters must be determined by universal principles and their application through the will of the discerning public exercising their informed consciences and rights and responsibilities in the political processes.

Although there is no single model for the interrelationship between the Church and the political community, Kenneth Himes proposes five criteria that should guide it. First, the Church should influence politics through persuasion, not coercion. This means that threats of ecclesial sanctions toward politicians or voters who disagree with particular Church teachings (e.g., on abortion or same-sex marriage) are inappropriate within this relationship. The focus should be on presenting foundational principles, grounded in reason, that persuade people to see the truth of those principles and their plausible application that defends human dignity and promotes the common good in various contexts. Sec-

---

[3] CDF, "Doctrinal Note on Some Questions Regarding the Participation of Catholics in Political Life," http://www.vatican.va/roman_curia/congregations/cfaith /documents/rc_con_cfaith_doc_20021124_politica_en.html, accessed February 4, 2014. Hereafter, "Note."

ond, the Church should have proper respect for the authentic autonomy and pluralistic perspectives of other actors and public institutions. There should not be a moral or intellectual triumphalism in the Church's perspective for how the political community should be organized or the laws, policies, or infrastructures that should be implemented. Third, the Church's focus must be to promote human dignity and the common good—not to defend narrow sectarian perspectives or institutional agendas. The principles of human dignity and the common good allow for prudential judgments on how to implement those principles in laws and policies, which may differ among people of good will with different perspectives. The political process should provide an infrastructure to debate the merits of those differences and to work toward and realize human dignity and the common good by building consensus. Fourth, "in matters of law and policy the Church's aim should be to protect public order." We take this to mean that, although the Church must respect law and policy, it can speak out against law and policy that it perceives as a threat to human dignity and the common good, and strive to affect constructive change while respecting just political processes. Finally, the Church should defend its political perspectives using language grounded in reason accessible to all human beings of good will, rather than relying on language from revelation.[4] This is a natural law approach to political discourse that relies on *recta ratio* (right reason), holistically understood to include the intellectual, affective, psychological, cultural, historical, and relational dimensions of the human person to discern the content of natural law. Appealing to universal principles of natural law to promote human dignity and the common good can help avoid accusations of sectarianism and religious politicking.

B. The Role and Function of the Laity in the Church and the Political Community

Not only are there important distinctions between the role and function of the institutional Church and the political community as they work toward realizing human dignity and the common good, but there are also distinct roles for laity in relation to the Church and the political community. *Gaudium et Spes* notes that "the faithful will be able to make a clear distinction between what a Christian conscience leads them to

---

[4] Himes, *Christianity and the Political Order*, 289.

do in their own name as citizens, whether as individuals or in association, and what they do in the name of the Church and in union with her shepherds" (GS 76). This distinction recognizes a fundamental change in the worldview from Popes Leo XIII and Pius XII, who conceived of the State as Christian or a Catholic denominational state, to the worldview of the council fathers, who recognized a pluralistic society as normal. With this evolution in worldview comes an evolution in the proper role and function of the faithful in relation to the political and ecclesial communities.[5] In the political realm, what the faithful do or do not do guided by Christian conscience may be distinct from what they do or do not do "in the name of the Church and in union with her shepherds."

As citizens in the political community, the faithful must exercise a unique type of political engagement, "one shaped by the moral convictions of well-formed consciences and focused on the dignity of every human being, the pursuit of the common good, and the protection of the weak and vulnerable" (FC 14),[6] while doing so in a pluralistic context where laws, policies, and infrastructures are shaped and formulated within that context. Regarding morally flawed laws, the US bishops note that "the process of framing legislation . . . is subject to prudential judgment and 'the art of the possible.'" The "art of the possible" recognizes the moral complexity of the political community and the legislative process and seeks to implement universal principles prudentially, in a way that will promote human dignity and the common good in terms of laws, policies, and infrastructures, and limit violations of human dignity and the common good. Creating a just community is a complex and gradual process.

Canon Law notes that, as members of the Church, in union with their shepherds, the faithful must have *obsequium religiosum* (religious respect) of intellect and will to authoritative teaching of the pope and bishops, even when they are not proclaiming a doctrine by a definitive act or infallibly. Religious respect means there is a presumption of truth toward authoritative teaching, but there can be legitimate dissent from such teachings if there are serious and well-founded reasons. While *Gaudium et Spes* recognizes the lay faithful have a right and moral obligation to

[5] Herbert Vorgrimler and Oswald von Nell-Breuning, "The Life of the Political Community," 323–24.

[6] United States Conference of Catholic Bishops (USCCB), "Forming Consciences for Faithful Citizenship" (Washington, DC: USCCB Publishing, 2011), http://www .usccb.org/issues-and-action/faithful-citizenship/upload/forming-consciences-for -faithful-citizenship.pdf. Hereafter, FC.

fulfill their civic duties "guided by a Christian conscience," there is debate about what constitutes a well-formed Christian conscience and how this is to be exercised in the political process. Two particular considerations on the laity and their responsibilities to the political community are relativism and the types of Church teaching that inform consciences.

1. Conscience and Relativism

In its "Doctrinal Note on Some Questions Regarding the Participation of Catholics in Political Life," the Congregation for the Doctrine of the Faith, while affirming the authority of the Christian conscience in public life, and the obligation to participate in that life, raises concerns about cultural relativism, "which sanctions the decadence and disintegration of reason and the principles of the natural moral law" (Note 2). Relativism masquerades as a defense of ethical pluralism, which denies the existence of "moral law rooted in the nature of the human person." It denies the existence of universals and that the "good" can be defined as human dignity, human flourishing, human fulfillment, or a similar cognate. The moral law rooted in the nature of the human person affirms the existence of universals and asserts that the "good" can be defined as what facilitates, and does not frustrate, attaining human dignity. This leaves unanswered the question, however, whether there is a homogenous definition of human dignity and a homogenous set of norms that facilitate its attainment, or plural definitions of human dignity and of norms that facilitate its attainment? The Note warns against a false tolerance, motivated by relativism and an incorrect sense of autonomy, whereby Catholics "are asked not to base their contribution to society and political life . . . on their particular understanding of the human person and the common good" (Note 2). A subsequent statement seems to recognize particular, and plural, understandings of the human person and of the common good when the Note warns of "*a conception of pluralism that reflects moral relativism*" (Note 3; emphasis added), implying that there is a conception of pluralism that does not reflect moral relativism. Such a pluralism coincides with Lonergan's perspectivist epistemology that we explained in chapter three.

The faithful can agree that the good and the right are defined in terms of human dignity and the common good, but there are plural and evolving definitions of these latter two concepts. The faithful also recognize that there are plural civic definitions of human dignity and the common good. Formulating and justifying laws, policies, and infrastructures in the political realm that facilitate, and do not frustrate, attaining human dignity or the common good must be done utilizing political processes, recognizing that there will be partial truths and disagreements on specific definitions of human dignity and of the common good and the particular laws, policies, and infrastructures that facilitate or frustrate their attainment. These disagreements, however, we repeat, are not to be automatically labeled as expressions of relativism; rather they may reflect a perspectival objectivism. Relativism does not recognize universal definitions of human dignity or the common good; perspectival objectivism recognizes plural, partial, and evolving definitions of human dignity and the common good. Such perspectival objectivism is well within the parameters of the doctrinal Note's conception of pluralism that *does not* reflect moral relativism and a pilgrim Church in search of practical ethical truth within the context of a political community.

2. The Formation of Conscience and Voting Responsibly

Gaudium et Spes notes the authority of a well-formed conscience that must guide the faithful in exercising their civic duty. The USCCB suggests seven key themes drawn from Catholic social teaching that should inform the faithful's consciences to participate in the civic realm: "The Right to Life and the Dignity of the Human Person; Call to Family, Community, and Participation; Rights and Responsibilities; Option for the Poor and Vulnerable; Dignity of Work and the Rights of Workers; Solidarity; and Caring for God's Creation" (FC). The challenge for the faithful when exercising their civic duty is twofold. First, these themes may, and often do, come into conflict with one another when considering voting on a particular law or for a particular candidate. So, while President Obama's Affordable Care Act provides a basic right to health care for millions of the 47 million people in the US who do not have health insurance, and thus fulfills an important aspect of the theme of rights and responsibilities (health care is a basic need that "is universally binding on our consciences") (FC 25),[7] the so-called "contraceptive mandate," which requires insurance coverage for contraception, sterilization, and abortifacients, is seen by some to violate an aspect of the theme "Call to Family, Community, and Participation." In a pluralistic culture with complex political mechanisms, prudence must guide the faithful in mor-

[7] Ibid., n. 25.

ally navigating these tensions. Prudence, the virtue which "enables us 'to discern our true good in every circumstance and to choose the right means of achieving it' . . . shapes and informs our ability to deliberate over available alternatives, to determine what is most fitting to a specific context, and to act decisively" (FC 19). To exercise one's conscience prudentially, we can draw guidance from the US bishops' pastoral letter, *The Challenge of Peace*, which indicates various levels of Church teaching and the complexity of applying those teachings in the political realm.

The bishops write:

> We do not intend that our treatment of each of these issues [arms race, contemporary warfare, weapons systems, negotiating strategies] carry the same moral authority as our statement of universal moral principles and formal Church teaching. Indeed, we stress here at the beginning that not every statement in this letter has the same moral authority. At times we reassert universally binding moral principles. . . . At still other times we reaffirm statements of recent popes and the teaching of Vatican II. Again, at other times we apply moral principles to specific cases.
>
> When making applications of these principles we realize—and we wish readers to recognize—that prudential judgments are involved based on specific circumstances which can change or which can be interpreted differently by people of good will.[8]

The bishops recognize that Church teaching operates at various levels of moral authority and a well-formed conscience must distinguish between these levels in the process of prudentially discerning a specific response to a public policy issue. *Gaudium et Spes* recognizes "the permanent binding force of universal natural law and its all-embracing principles" (GS 79). An example of a universal principle noted by the CDF's "Note" is "a correct understanding of the human person" (Note 3). It is one thing to claim that "a correct understanding of the human person" is a universal principle; given plural and particular definitions of the human person and the complexity and ambiguity of the political realm, it is quite another to say *how* this understanding can be incarnated in public policy. There are plural understandings of the human person or human dignity, and plural understandings of norms, laws, policies, or infrastructures that facilitate attaining human dignity. This does not

---

[8] National Conference of Catholic Bishops, *The Challenge of Peace: God's Promise and Our Response* (Washington, DC: United States Catholic Conference, 1983), nos. 9–10.

mean, however, that all definitions of the human person are morally legitimate. There are parameters, guided by universal principles, for what constitutes a particular definition of human dignity or the common good.

For example, any definition of human dignity which proposes that one person can own another person (i.e., slavery), would be rejected based on "a correct understanding of the human person." Within those parameters, however, and in light of the distinct role and function of the political realm, since "politics are concerned with very concrete realizations of the true human and social good in given historical, geographical, economic, technological and cultural contexts . . . a plurality of acceptable policies and solutions arises" (Note 3). While pluralism exists internally within the Catholic Church, it is more complex and expansive externally in the political realm.

The second challenge with exercising one's civic duty is to distinguish between the common good and what John Courtney Murray labeled the "public order." All people and institutions are responsible to contribute to the common good to realize human dignity. The State is only concerned with "public order," which includes three goods: public justice, public peace, and public morality.[9] Public justice protects rights and provides an infrastructure for resolving conflicts between competing rights; public peace preserves order and tranquility through structures and institutions; public morality is a minimalist moral code to protect freedom, preserve order, and to ensure the stability and functioning of social life. Public order is necessary for the common good, but it is not sufficient. It has a minimalist moral code and attempts to ensure as much individual freedom as possible, without threatening public order.

When exercising their civic duty, the faithful must apply universal principles to the public order. This application allows for plural interpretations where they can reach different conclusions on the most appropriate way to implement those principles and must consider the complexity of the political realm. In cases, for example, where flawed laws currently exist (e.g., abortion legislation), "the process of framing legislation to protect life is subject to prudential judgment and 'the art of the possible'" (FC 32). Again, prudential judgment allows for plural responses in the application of universal principles. The bishops wisely note that "Decisions about political life are complex and require the

---

[9] John Courtney Murray, "The Problem of Religious Freedom," in J. Leon Hooper, ed., *Religious Liberty: Catholic Struggles with Pluralism* (Louisville: Westminster John Knox Press, 1993), 145.

exercise of a well-formed conscience aided by prudence" (FC 31). A well-formed conscience distinguishes between various levels of Church teaching and the complexity of the sociopolitical, cultural, historical context to implement that teaching.

Given the complexity of the relationship between Church and State and the various roles and responsibilities of the faithful in relation to the Church and exercising their civic responsibility to the State, we offer the following guidelines to the faithful to navigate these relationships. First, the faithful should inform their consciences through the teachings of the Church and human reason on a variety of ethical issues that arise in the civic realm. Second, they should have *obsequium religiosum* (religious respect) of intellect and will to Church teaching. This means that the faithful should understand the teaching, its history and foundations, and the values it is trying to protect. Third, the faithful must recognize that within the civic realm, there is a distinction between the common good and public order. This distinction means that, while the Church does teach universally binding moral principles, these principles must be interpreted and applied in the concrete to the civic realm. As we have seen, the interpretation and application of universal principles, such as a correct understanding of the human person, is pluralistic depending on one's perspective and the partial definition of a complex and multidimensional reality. When applying such principles to the civic realm, the faithful can come to very different prudential judgments in that application. They must also recognize the complexity of the civic realm and the conflict between the application of principles within this realm. In light of this conflict, the faithful must prioritize principles and prudentially judge how such principles might be most fully realized within this complex reality. This process is more an art than a science and relies heavily on the virtue of prudence. Finally, the faithful may often have recourse to the principle of the "art of the possible" when exercising their civic responsibilities.

Not only does *Gaudium et Spes* provide guidelines for the Church and the faithful to engage in the political process, in its final chapter it also extends those guidelines to peace and war. It is to that chapter we now turn.

II. The Church on Peace and the Avoidance of War

On the eve of his announcement to the College of Cardinals his intent to convene Vatican Council II, Pope John XXIII confided to his secretary, "the world is starving for peace. If the Church responds to its Founder and rediscovers its authentic identity, the world will gain" (PT 221). Christiansen describes John XXIII's pontificate as "a new 'optimistic' Vatican politics of peace."[10] Though John XXIII passed away before the promulgation of *Gaudium et Spes*, his hope and vision for a politics of peace is evident throughout the *Pastoral Constitution*, especially chapter five, "The Fostering of Peace and the Promotion of a Community of Nations."

A. The Sources of Moral Knowledge: Reading the Signs of the Times

Catholic moral theology lists four sources of moral knowledge: Sacred Scripture, tradition, reason, and human experience. *Gaudium et Spes* draws from these various sources in its formulation and justification of a response to building peace and avoiding war in light of "the signs of the times."

1. Scripture

The first biblical passage cited in chapter five is taken from Matthew's Sermon on the Mount and highlights the centrality of peace to the Gospel. *Gaudium et Spes notes*, "the artisans of peace are blessed 'because they will be called the sons of God'" (Matt 5:9). Later in the text, it cites the complementary Old Testament Zion text on peacemaking: "They shall beat their swords into plowshares and their spears into pruning hooks; one nation shall not raise the sword against another, nor shall they train for war again" (Isa 2:4) (GS 78). How are we to interpret the beatitude on peacemakers in the Sermon on the Mount and what are its normative implications on war and peace on the fiftieth anniversary of *Gaudium et Spes*?

Joachim Jeremias submits four models for interpreting the meaning of the Sermon on the Mount.[11] The first model is the "perfectionist conception." This is a legalistic model in greatest continuity with the

---

[10] Drew Christiansen, "Commentary on *Pacem in Terris* (Peace on Earth)," in *Modern Catholic Social Teaching: Commentaries and Interpretations*, ed. Kenneth R. Himes (Washington, DC: Georgetown University Press, 2005), 218.

[11] Joachim Jeremias, *The Sermon on the Mount* (New York: Oxford University Press, 1961). See also Lisa Sowle Cahill, *Love Your Enemies: Discipleship, Pacifism, and Just War Theory* (Minneapolis, MN: Fortress Press, 1994), 26–30; Himes, *Christianity and the Political Order*, 318–19.

Old Testament and sees obedience to, and fulfillment of, the law as the highest calling. This perfectionist conception of peacemaker has often needed to be tempered by realist considerations of the sin of the world and complex social and political interrelationships. The second model for interpreting the meaning of the Sermon on the Mount is the "theory of the impossible ideal." According to this model, peacemaking is the impossible ideal that humanity should always strive for, but will always fall short of. Peace only comes with the kingdom; only God can redeem and save humanity. The third model is the Sermon as an "interim ethic." There is an immediacy to the moral demands of the Sermon, which reflect the expectations of Christ's imminent return. According to this model, peacemakers are radical pacifists who fulfill Christ's command to seek peace and to love enemies.

All three of the above models share a common vision of the Sermon as law, and the requirements of the Beatitudes, such as the role of peacemakers, as fulfilling the dictates of the law through command, pedagogical encouragement, or eschatological fulfillment. The fourth model, which Jeremias prefers, views the Sermon on the Mount not as law but as Gospel. The law emphasizes human efforts to do their utmost to fulfill the law; the Gospel emphasizes God's effort and unconditional gift of love to humanity and invites humanity to recognize, embrace, and become this gift—to become Christ's presence to others through ongoing conversion. The process of becoming peacemakers and "turning swords into ploughshares and spears into sickles" is a gradual process that exists in the tension between the already and not-yet of the kingdom. Violence and war are sometimes an unfortunate part of this interim period.

2. Tradition

Tradition, the handing down of Scripture, interpreted and reinterpreted in light of the lived and living experience of the Christian community in space and time, reflects different models of interpretation of the Sermon on the Mount and the beatitude on peacemaking at different points in history. Thinking on peacemakers, peace, and war has evolved, and this evolution provides insight into *Gaudium et Spes* and more recent Church teaching on peace and war.[12]

---

[12] This brief historical survey of the just war tradition draws from the following authors: Cahill, *Love Your Enemies*; Thomas A. Shannon, *What Are They Saying about Peace and War?* (New York: Paulist Press, 1983); and Thomas Massaro and Thomas

a. The Early Church: Pre-Constantine

The early Christian community expected the imminent Parousia or second coming of Christ. Initially, Christianity was a sect made up largely of people of the lower socioeconomic class who were focused on Jesus' second coming, attaining salvation, and living in a way to realize that objective. It was not concerned with government, the state, politics, or war.[13] In fact, the idolatry and immorality of soldiers within the military made military service unattractive and a violation of many Jewish and Christian precepts.[14] As a result, the implications of war and violence did not preoccupy the Christian conscience and there was a perception of the separation between the sacred and secular realms. This perception is reflected in Justin Martyr's writing that he prays for both emperor and empire, yet claims that the Christian community currently lives in fulfillment of the messianic period predicted in Isaiah 2:4.[15] It is also reflected by Tertullian, who seems to absolutely exclude military service, since there "is no agreement" between human and divine masters. He elaborates: "Even if soldiers came to John and got advice on how they ought to act, even if the centurion became a believer, the Lord, by taking away Peter's sword, disarmed every soldier thereafter. We are not allowed to wear any uniform that symbolizes a sinful act."[16] Origen asserts that Christ absolutely forbids any type of killing, even against the greatest sinner. Christians "fight as priests and worshippers of God while others fight as soldiers."[17]

Taken as a whole, the early Church promoted nonviolence and pacifism as mandated by the Gospel. Though it recognized the legitimacy of government and military to defend the empire, there was somewhat of a dualistic perspective between the earthly and heavenly realms. This perspective gradually changed as the early Christian movement expanded and began to include Christian converts who were already in the military. The most profound changes occurred as a result of the

---

A. Shannon, *Catholic Perspectives on Peace and War* (Lanham, MD: Rowman & Littlefield, 2003).

[13] Massaro and Shannon, *Catholic Perspectives*, 7.

[14] Dennis Hamm, *Building Our House on Rock: The Sermon on the Mount as Jesus' Vision for Our Lives as Told by Matthew and Luke* (Frederick, MD: The Word Among Us Press, 2011), 230.

[15] Ibid., 231.

[16] Louis J. Swift, *The Early Fathers on War and Military Service*, Message of the Fathers of the Church, vol. 19 (Wilmington, DE: Michael Glazer, 1983), 41–42.

[17] Ibid., 55.

shift in status of Christianity within the empire. With that shift came the Christian formulation and justification of the just war criteria.

b. The Early Church: Post-Constantine and the Just War Tradition

As the Christian movement grew in numbers, it grew also in the diversity of its membership, including converts from the political and military realms. The separation between the earthly and heavenly realms gradually diminished when social roles and religious commitments became more intermixed. This diminishment reached a climax and caused a fundamental reconsideration of the relationship between the sacred and secular realms—and between views on peace and war—when Constantine legalized Christianity in 313 and Theodosius made it the official religion of the empire in 381. These events fundamentally transformed the relationship between Christianity and the State, the Christian movement being transformed from a persecuted to a privileged religious entity. With this transformation came a reconsideration of the relationship between the heavenly and earthly realms in general, and the implications of Christian belief for living in a turbulent, and often violent, empire, in particular. Citizens and public officials who were Christian had to balance the dictates of Christian discipleship, which heretofore had been largely committed to nonviolence and pacifism, with their responsibilities, either in the military or as public officials, to protect citizens and empire from violent and invading forces. Two influential figures who had a profound development on the just war tradition emerged in this context to address this dilemma.

St. Ambrose, a governor of a province in northern Italy and, later, bishop of Milan, witnessed both violence against the empire by invading barbarians and violence against the Christian faith by heresies like Arianism. Out of this context Ambrose constructed an ethic of war to justify securing the empire's boundaries and protecting its people and to combat heresy, protect doctrinal orthodoxy, and make converts.[18] To do so, he drew from two sources: the Jewish Scriptures and its depiction of military campaigns in the name of Yahweh, and Cicero, who had developed a type of just war theory in his *De Officiis*. Here, Cicero puts forth central criteria for when, and on what grounds, war can be justified. War can be justified to promote peace, protect the innocent, and avenge violations of justice. It can be waged as long as there is a formal

---

[18] Shannon, *What Are They Saying about Peace and War?*, 12–13.

declaration or demand for redress preceded by an appropriate warning. An important point to note with St. Ambrose is that he drew from both sacred and secular sources to formulate a response to the ethical challenges that national and international conflicts pose to the vision of Christianity grounded in peace.[19] The attempt to separate the sacred and secular realms reflected in the earlier tradition and the implications of this separation for Christians' involvement in the world could not be maintained after the peace of Constantine and the realization that Christians and Christianity played central roles in both the sacred and the secular, including the political and military realms.

Augustine, one of the greatest theologians of all time, recognized the interrelationship between these two realms, the heavenly city and the earthly city.[20] While we only find true and eternal peace in the heavenly city, we can find partial peace in the earthly city. Peace in the earthly city is dependent on maintaining or restoring relationships. Sometimes war is necessary to maintain or restore the just relationships necessary for peace. In the *City of God*, Augustine notes: "A just war . . . is justified only by the injustice of an aggressor, and that injustice ought to be a source of grief to any good [person], because it is human injustice."[21] Seeking to restore justice was Augustine's justification for declaring and participating in war. Elsewhere, he elaborated on this principle: war must be waged only under a ruler's authority; it must be conducted justly; and clergy cannot participate in it.[22]

With the principle for just war firmly established by Augustine, Aquinas affirms and expands on this principle. In his *Summa Theologiae*, Aquinas summarizes his three conditions for a just war. "First, the authority of the sovereign by whose command the war is to be waged. . . . The second condition is that hostility should begin because of some crime on the part of the enemy. . . . The third condition is rightful intention, the advancement of good or the avoidance of evil."[23] Only legitimate rulers, who have exhausted all other options and intend to preserve or restore justice, can wage a just war. The conduct of the war must be guided by the moral order and must not take retribution or revenge for injustices suffered, but must seek to restore order.

---

[19] Ibid.; Massaro and Shannon, *Catholic Perspectives*, 10.

[20] See Cahill, *Love Your Enemies*, 55–80.

[21] St. Augustine, *City of God, Books XVII–XXII*, trans. Gerald G. Walsh and Daniel J. Honan, The Fathers of the Church: Saint Augustine (Washington, DC: The Catholic University of America Press, 1954; paperback repr. 2008), Book 19, Chap. 17.

[22] Shannon, *What Are They Saying about Peace and War?*, 13–14.

[23] Aquinas, *S.T.* II–II, q. 40, a. 1–4.

These conditions were eventually expanded and formulated into criteria for judging whether or not going to war can be justified (*jus ad bellum*) and how war should be conducted (*jus in bello*). The *jus ad bellum* criteria are: 1. There must be a just cause; 2. war must be declared by a legitimate authority; 3. with a right intention; 4. as a last resort; 5. with a reasonable probability of success; and 6. with proportionality between the end sought and the destructive means to realize that end. The *jus in bello* criteria are: 1. Proportionality between end and means; and 2. noncombatant immunity.[24] In a period of nuclear, biological, and chemical weapons, many question whether or not the criteria of proportionality and noncombatant immunity can ever be fulfilled and, if they cannot be fulfilled, what revisions of the just war criteria are necessary to justify war?

c. *Pacem in Terris* and *Gaudium et Spes*

John XXIII introduced profound developments into the just war tradition and developed five themes in *Pacem in Terris* that shaped contemporary Catholic teaching on war and peace and were affirmed, and developed, in *Gaudium et Spes*.[25] First, *Pacem in Terris* marked a fundamental shift in language to "rights talk." While discussion of human rights is evident throughout the Catholic tradition, such talk was viewed with suspicion during the Enlightenment period, which saw a shift in focus from the institution to the individual, from the sacred to the secular, from faith to reason. The Church perceived this period and its promotion of individual human rights as liberalism's threat to sacred reality and the authority of the Church, and rights language was largely abandoned in Church discourse. The claims of human rights and the primacy of conscience, for example, were subordinated to the imperatives of the institutional Church in Pius IX's *Syllabus of Errors*. *Pacem in Terris* marked a fundamental shift in the recent tradition from "staunch opposition to modern rights and freedoms to activist engagement in the global struggle for human rights." Hollenbach notes that "this shift was one of the most dramatic reversals in the long history of the Catholic tradition."[26]

---

[24] See National Conference of Catholic Bishops, *The Challenge of Peace: God's Promise and Our Response, A Pastoral Letter on War and Peace* (Washington, DC: U.S. Catholic Conference, 1983), pars. 80–110.

[25] Christiansen, "Commentary on *Pacem in Terris*," 227–32. See, also, J. Milburn Thompson, *Introducing Catholic Social Thought* (Maryknoll, NY: Orbis Books, 2010), 121–22.

[26] David Hollenbach, "Commentary on *Gaudium et Spes* (Pastoral Constitution on the Church in the Modern World)," in *Modern Catholic Social Teaching*, 280.

All human rights entail corresponding duties and responsibilities. Combined, rights, duties, and responsibilities seek to realize and promote the common good. The common good, "the sum of those conditions of social life which allow social groups and their individual members relatively thorough and ready access to their own fulfilment, today takes on an increasingly universal complexion and consequently involves rights and duties with respect to the whole human race. Every social group must take account of the needs and legitimate aspirations of other groups, and even of the general welfare of the entire human family" (GS 26). Socialization, i.e., "a social process in which technological and other social changes lead to more complex patterns of social interaction, expressed in new forms of association and richer patterns of organizational interaction,"[27] informed by the social sciences, recognizes the ongoing complexity of realizing the common good and serves as a corrective to the individualism that is often associated with modern rights language. Socialization also recognizes the complex relationships, internally and externally, among governments and nations, that often lead to conflict.

Pacem in Terris proposed human rights as the foundation for civil authority (PT 61) and *Gaudium et Spes* proposed them as the foundation for peace (GS 81). Peace can only be realized through the protection and promotion of human rights and human dignity in community that seeks and promotes the common good. As Pope John XXIII emphasizes, "it is agreed that in our time the common good is chiefly guaranteed when personal rights and duties are maintained" (PT 60). When human rights are threatened or violated by one's own or another state, violent resistance may be justified as a last resort to such threats or violations. "Governments cannot be denied the right to legitimate defense once every means of peaceful settlement has been exhausted" (GS 79). And yet, *Pacem in Terris* cautions, "in this age of ours which prides itself on its atomic power, it is irrational to believe that war is still an apt means of vindicating violated rights" (PT 127). *Gaudium et Spes* recognizes that, in changing historical, social, scientific, and technological circumstances, the potential use of atomic (chemical and biological) weapons poses an urgency which compels us "to undertake an evaluation of war with an entirely new attitude" (GS 80). It proclaims that war can be a means to vindicate violated rights and restore justice to build a lasting peace, but it must be proportional to the violation suffered. *Gaudium et Spes*

---

[27] Ibid., 279.

also applauds those who renounce the use of violence to vindicate the violation of rights, "provided that this can be done without injury to the rights and duties of others or of the community itself" (GS 78). This qualification recognizes that, while pacifistic resistance is an option for oneself, even to the point of suffering violations of basic human rights, one cannot impose this option on others who do not freely choose it and, as a national policy, pacifism could endanger the overall stability and well-being of a country, making it vulnerable to the unjust aggression of other nations.[28]

The second theme is that individual conscience has primacy over State authority and sovereignty, especially when it is a question of recognizing and respecting human rights. *Pacem in Terris* recognizes the long held tradition that governmental authority and laws derive from God when they are in accordance with natural law and right reason. When such authority or laws are against right reason, they violate natural law, are unjust, and have no binding force on conscience (PT 48, 49, 51, 61). The authority of conscience and legitimate disagreement with a government or law is extended in *Gaudium et Spes* to pacifism and the right of conscientious objection for the individual, *even in the case of a just war.* "We cannot fail to praise those who renounce the use of violence in the vindication of their rights and who resort to methods of defense which are otherwise available to weaker parties too . . ." (GS 78). And, "it seems right that laws make humane provisions for the case of those who for reasons of conscience refuse to bear arms, provided however, that they accept some other form of service to the human community" (GS 79; CCC 2311). These statements on pacifism and conscientious objection are in stark contrast to Pius XII's statement ("a Catholic citizen cannot invoke his own conscience in order to refuse to serve and fulfill those duties the law imposes") and mark an evolution in tradition.[29] Pacifism is not an obligation; but it is an option for individuals who, following their consciences, choose conscientious objection rather than bearing arms in a just war.

[28] James V. Schall, ed., *Out of Justice, Peace: Joint Pastoral Letter of the West German Bishops; Winning the Peace: Joint Pastoral Letter of the French Bishops* (San Francisco: Ignatius Press, 1984), no. 201.

[29] Pius XII, "Communism and Democracy: 1956," in *The Major Addresses of Pope Pius XII*, vol. 2, ed. Vincent A. Yzermans (St. Paul, MN: North Central, 1961), 225.

3. Reason and Experience

The next three themes from *Pacem in Terris*, which influenced *Gaudium et Spes*, draw from the "signs of the times" and reason and experience as sources of moral knowledge. In the midst of the cold war and nuclear proliferation, the Cuban missile crisis, the Vietnam war, and numerous civil wars throughout the world, as well as the relatively recent experience of the impact of the atomic bomb and indiscriminate killing of noncombatants, *Pacem in Terris*'s third theme highlighted the irrationality of war in the modern period and demanded an end to the arms race. It taught that armed force as a means to procure peace is a violation of the principles of right reason, which requires "truth, justice and vigorous and sincere co-operation" to build lasting peace and to create a just world (PT 114).

Pacem in Terris was optimistic about the capacity to recognize the irrationality of war as a solution to conflict, asserting that people today "are becoming more and more convinced that any disputes which may arise between nations must be resolved by negotiation and agreement, and not by recourse to arms" (PT 146). This conviction is due in large part to the "terrifying destructive force of modern weapons" (PT 127). *Gaudium et Spes* recognized and affirmed the irrationality of war, focusing on the destructive capacity of modern weapons, the complexity of the modern world and international relations, and the reality of terrorism and guerilla warfare, which often target noncombatants. Throughout tradition, especially since Augustine, war was seen as a last resort to restore peace and justice. With scientific and technological developments that produce atomic, nuclear, biological, and chemical arms capable of incredible and indiscriminate destruction, and the potential use of these weapons by countries as well as terrorist organizations in the form of "dirty bombs," even as a last resort, the use of such weapons, from a rational perspective, are an irrational option and fundamentally violates the just war criteria of noncombatant immunity and proportionality. It is difficult, if not impossible, to limit the use of these and other modern weapons to ensure noncombatant immunity (including the more recent use of drones, which inflict substantial "collateral damage") and there is substantial risk of escalation and retaliation, which is often directed toward noncombatants.

The irrationality of war extends to the arms race and the call for disarmament. Although stockpiling arms can act as a deterrent, it creates a culture of fear, undermines trust, and wastes intellectual, environmental, and economic resources that could be invested in creating economic and social stability by promoting trust and redirecting resources. *Pacem in Terris* notes that "this process of disarmament be thoroughgoing and complete, and reach [humans'] very souls" (PT 113). To reach humans' very souls, merely reducing and eliminating arms, though necessary, is not sufficient. There must be fundamental conversion in perspective that sees the connection between the arms race and a culture of violence, distrust, fear, animosity, disarmament, and a culture of nonviolence, trust, harmony, and reconciliation. It is this change in perspective that has the potential to build lasting peace. The change will require commitment at various levels, individually, communally, nationally, and internationally. *Gaudium et Spes* sums this up well. "Peace must be born of mutual trust between nations rather than imposed on them through fear of one another's weapons. Hence everyone must labor to put an end at last to the arms race, and to make a true beginning of disarmament, not indeed a unilateral disarmament, but one proceeding at an equal pace according to agreement, and backed up by authentic and workable safeguards" (GS 82).

What is necessary to insure an evolution of perspective and transformation from war preparation to peacebuilding is an "effective system of mutual control" to model, ensure, and, if necessary, enforce such a perspective through nonviolent means, the fourth theme of *Pacem in Terris*. A system of mutual control highlights the need to develop an international community to set policy for disarmament and establish guidelines and treaties to build trust between nations. Such a policy requires the free "consent of all nations" and "must operate with fairness, absolute impartiality, and dedication to the common good of all peoples" (PT 138). It is important to note that the international community extends beyond military concerns and disarmament and is fundamentally committed to realizing the common good. Its "special function . . . must be to evaluate and find a solution to economic, social, political, and cultural problems which affect the universal common good" (PT 140). *Gaudium et Spes* affirms the need for international organizations to establish peace and eliminate those things which lead to wars, *especially injustice* (GS 83). To eliminate the discord that leads to war, we must build peace, and we build peace by creating a more just society.

The intrinsic link between peace and economic, social, and cultural development, the fifth theme, is integral to Catholic social teaching and contemporary teaching on war and peace. The idea that development is necessary for peace was introduced in conciliar discussions by Manuel Larrain, bishop of Talca, Chile,[30] and taken up by Pope Paul VI

---

[30] René Coste, in Willem Schuijt, "History of *Gaudium et Spes*," in *Commentary on the Documents of Vatican II*, vol. 5, ed. Herbert Vorgrimler (New York: Herder and Herder, 1969), 330. See Himes, *Peacebuilding*, 272.

in *Populorum Progressio*, where he asserts that "development is the new name for peace" (PP 76). Paul VI explains,

> peace is not merely the absence of war. Nor can it be reduced solely to the maintenance of a balance of power between enemies. . . . Instead, it is rightly and appropriately called 'an enterprise of justice.' . . . Peace results from that harmony built into human society by its divine Founder, and actualized by men as they thirst after ever greater justice. (PP 78)

Reflecting on Paul's assertion, the German bishops wisely note, "in order to build up peace, we must above all remove the causes of discord in the world which lead to war, i.e., primarily the injustices."[31] *Gaudium et Spes* proposes norms that should guide regional and international organizations to foster peace and realize a genuine and universal economic order (GS 85).

First, developing nations should "seek the complete human fulfillment of their citizens as the explicit and fixed goal of progress" by using their own resources and foreign aid responsibly and sharing them equitably. Second, advanced nations must facilitate developing nations in this process, by providing aid, debt relief, and negotiating trade, for instance, that is formulated to advance the well-being and development of developing countries, rather than to exploit their resources. Third, the international community should oversee and stimulate economic growth for all countries, based on the principle of subsidiarity, to allow for thorough and fair access to economic markets. This would involve trade, for example, that limits subsidies that give an unfair advantage to developed countries in the world market. Fourth, economic and social structures must be reformed, but such reform must be holistically developed balancing spiritual and temporal needs (GS 86). The focus of these norms is on economic development and has implications for addressing the huge disparities between developed and developing countries and within countries. Addressing these disparities is a fundamental requirement to work toward a stable and lasting peace.

Pacem in Terris heavily influences *Gaudium et Spes* and the Catholic peace tradition by focusing on human rights, the primacy of conscience, the irrationality of war in light of modern weapons, the call to develop an international body to pursue the common good, and the intrinsic link

---

[31] Schall, *Out of Justice, Peace*, no. 118.

between ending violence and pursuing peace through development. Fifty years after *Gaudium et Spes*, what do the signs of the times require for the Church's ongoing call for "an evaluation of war with an entirely new attitude"?

B. The Signs of the Times: Fifty Years After Gaudium et Spes

1. "New Wars," Just War and Development

The first consideration for the signs of the times is the evolving nature of war itself and, concurrently, the nature of peace within that evolving context. Mary Kaldor refers to "new wars," caused by "a revolution in the social relations of warfare" in the twentieth and twenty-first centuries, which must be understood in the context of globalization, the "intensification of global interconnectedness."[32] These wars pose challenges for interpreting and applying traditional just war criteria, especially the criterion of legitimate authority and who or what body has the authority to declare war.[33] Bryan Hehir comments that the concept of the sovereign state, considered an essential entity for discerning the just war criterion of legitimate authority, even though it remains a basic unit within world politics, does not entail the absolute autonomy that it once did.[34] This autonomy is constrained by globalization, the intensification of interrelationships between governments, laws, policies, economies, and cultures. The new wars are shaped by this new reality and are often internal or civil wars. However, these wars "involve a myriad of transnational connections so that the distinction between internal and external, between aggression (attacks from abroad) and repression (attacks from inside the country), or even between local and global, are difficult to sustain."[35] These new wars include wars in Eastern Europe, the Arab Spring's civil wars, terrorist attacks in developing and developed countries, and the

---

[32] Mary Kaldor, *New and Old Wars: Organized Violence in a Global Era* (Stanford, CA: Stanford University Press, 1999), 3.

[33] For a detailed study investigating the question of authority in the just war tradition, see Anthony F. Lang Jr., Cian O'Driscoll, and John Williams, eds., *Just War: Authority, Tradition, and Practice* (Washington, DC: Georgetown University Press, 2013).

[34] J. Bryan Hehir, "Religion, Realism, and Just Intervention," in *Liberty and Power: A Dialogue on Religion and U.S. Foreign Policy in an Unjust World*, ed. J. Bryan Hehir, et al. (Washington, DC: Brookings Institute Press, 2004), 14.

[35] Kaldor, *New and Old Wars*, 2.

wars in Iraq and Afghanistan. The means of conducting new wars include advances in technology such as drones, biological and chemical weapons directly targeting noncombatants, cyber war, and the potential and threatening use of "dirty bombs."

A second consideration is that new wars challenge the interpretation and application of traditional just war criteria. For example, in the case of the present civil war in Syria and State-sanctioned repression, including the use of chemical weapons on innocent civilian populations, who has the authority to respond to these injustices militarily, and what are the limitations for conducting such a response? What is the international community's responsibility to intervene in situations where there are blatant and horrendous human rights violations? What should be done when an international authority, such as the United Nations Security Council, is hamstrung in issuing a consensus statement of response to an unjust war due to political and economic interests of permanent voting members, such as Russia and China, who have absolute veto power on a resolution in the Security Council? How should such conflicts be resolved in order to restore justice and peace? Pope Francis called for a day of prayer and fasting for peace in Syria and opposes any military response against Syria for its use of chemical weapons against its own people. "War begets war, violence begets violence." Is a nonviolent response mandated by the just war tradition or can violence be used as a last resort "to rescue the innocent and establish justice"?[36] Who is the legitimate authority to make such a determination?

Also, since 9/11 and with the advent of the "war on terror," how and on what criteria do we determine a "just cause" for military intervention? In the war on Iraq in 2003, the Bush administration put forth preemptive or preventive use of force as a just cause. Preemption or anticipatory use of force, according to the US bishops, may be morally permissible if there is a clear, immediate, and grave danger or threat.[37] There is, however, a lack of clarity on the criteria for evaluating the nature of the danger and gravity of the threat, which would justify a preemptive or anticipatory

---

[36] United States Bishops, "The Harvest of Justice is Sown in Peace," in *Peacemaking: Moral and Policy Changes for a New World*, ed. G.F. Powers, D. Christiansen, and R.T. Hennemeyer (Washington, DC: USCC Publishing Services, 1994), 318.

[37] See Gerard F. Powers, "An Ethical Analysis of War against Iraq," http://www.usccb.org/issues-and-action/human-life-and-dignity/global-issues/middle-east/iraq/paper-entitled-an-ethical-analysis-of-war-against-iraz-by-gerard-powers-2002-12.cfm, accessed April 4, 2014.

use of force. As has become clear in the case of the Bush administration's decision for a preemptive strike against Iraq, the justification was based on false—if not fabricated—intelligence and questionable motives. Although the bishops do recognize the legitimacy of preemptive use of force in certain situations, determining those situations requires a politically, economically, militarily neutral international community to formulate and apply criteria for making such judgments.

Finally, the new and old approaches to war require tremendous economic, intellectual, cultural, and environmental resources to develop, maintain, and improve the world military complex, which continues to wreak havoc and destruction on peoples and economies throughout the world. In the United States, the military budget nearly doubled since 9/11, from $287 billion in 2001 to $530 billion in 2011. If one adds in benefits for veterans, military spending accounts for 23.5 percent of the federal budget. To put this in perspective, the following are some examples of federal expenditures on nonmilitary programs in 2011: social security (20 percent); Medicare, Medicaid, and Children's Health Insurance Program (21 percent); Safety Net Programs (13 percent); Education (2 percent); Science and Medical Research (2 percent). On a world scale, the United States spends more on its military than the next highest thirteen countries combined, which include China, Russia, the UK, and France.[38] Such a high percentage of federal budgets invested in the military limits resources that could be invested in social programs and development. Recently in the United States, the Republican majority in the House of Representatives proposed and passed a bill cutting SNAP (Supplemental Nutrition Assistance Program) funding by $40 billion over the next ten years, though the bill has not yet passed the Democratic-led Senate. A drastic cut to social programs such as SNAP and exponential increases in military spending are examples of how investment in the military complex impedes development. While maintaining a military is necessary in the current world climate, has such astronomical investment created, or can it create, a more just and peaceful society? Current expenditures on the military demonstrate that from national and international political perspectives, we continue to invest more heavily in the military to ensure a false sense of peace and stability than in development. The lack

---

[38] See Brad Plumer, "America's Staggering Defense Budget, in Charts," *Washington Post*, January 7, 2013, http://www.washingtonpost.com/blogs/wonkblog/wp/2013/01/07/everything-chuck-hagel-needs-to-know-about-the-defense-budget-in-charts/, accessed April 4, 2014.

of investment in development, including social programs and foreign aid, and the increasing disparity between rich and poor throughout the world are of growing concern and, from the Church's perspective, are key factors for violence and civil unrest.

Recent Church teaching realizes a strong correlation between violence, poverty, and the gap between rich and poor.[39] *Gaudium et Spes* states, "If peace is to be established, the primary requisite is to eradicate the causes of dissension between men. Wars thrive on these, *especially on injustice*" (GS 83; emphasis added). Paul VI notes, "excessive economic, social, and cultural inequalities among peoples arouse tensions and conflicts, and are a danger to peace" and a temptation to violence (PP 76, 30). John Paul addresses the disparity between rich and poor and its correlation with violence and asserts, "People excluded from the fair distribution of goods originally destined for all could ask themselves: why not respond with violence to those who treat us first with violence" (SRS 10)? Commenting on the world situation in the wake of 9/11, the USCCB notes that "grinding poverty amidst plenty" is a source "of deep resentment and hopelessness which terrorists seek to exploit for their own ends."[40] Pope Francis recently commented that "inequality is the root of social ills" (EG 202) and we must say "no to the inequality which spawns violence" (EG 59–60). Inequality is one of the greatest threats to peace since, "in the end, a peace which is not the result of integral development will be doomed; it will always spawn new conflicts and various forms of violence" (EG 219).

2. New Directions in War, Peace, and Peacebuilding in the Twenty-First Century

This entirely new attitude to an evaluation of war has been articulated by popes, bishops, theologians, and laypeople since Vatican II. Drawing from these perspectives, we conclude with some general recommendations for peacebuilding in the twenty-first century in terms of perspective, method, structures, and norms.

---

[39] See Todd David Whitmore, "The Reception of Catholic Approaches to Peace and War in the United States," in *Modern Catholic Social Teaching* (Washington, DC: Georgetown University Press, 2005), 514–15.

[40] USCCB, "Living with Faith and Hope after September 11," http://www.usccb .org/issues-and-action/human-life-and-dignity/september-11/a-pastoral-message -living-with-faith-and-hope-after-september-11.cfm, accessed April 4, 2014.

a. Changing Perspectives:
From Just War to Peace and Peacebuilding

The perspective on just war has gradually shifted from a presumption in favor of war, to a presumption against war with an emphasis on non-violence and, more recently, peacebuilding. Himes attributes this gradual shift to three papacies: Pius XII, John XXIII, and Paul VI.[41] Though Pius XII supported traditional just war theory, he considerably narrowed the parameters of just cause for going to war to defense against aggression. John XXIII asserted that there is a general shift in perspective, especially with the advent of atomic weapons, that disputes between States should not be resolved by recourse to conflict; war should truly be a last resort after all alternative approaches to resolve a conflict have been exhausted. Paul VI's speech to the United Nations encapsulates this evolution and sets a clear agenda for the shift from just war to peacebuilding. "No more war, war never again! Peace, it is peace which must guide the destinies of peoples and of all humankind."[42] The Second Vatican Council and Catholic social teaching affirmed this perspective on peace and peacebuilding and a substantial amount of theological literature has developed to articulate it.

Peace, Paul VI proclaims, "is not simply the absence of warfare." While the absence of warfare is necessary for peace, it is not sufficient. The biblical concepts of *shalom* in the Hebrew Scriptures and *eirene* in the New Testament indicate both a perspective on peace and what that perspective implies concretely. The perspective on peace is shaped by the reality that we are in covenant with God, who brings interior peace through redemption. Concretely, we seek to share that peace through love of God, neighbor, and self.[43] This means, in part, that peace is realized when we strive to recognize and realize human dignity by creating a just society. Human dignity is a holistic concept that includes the biological, emotional, psychological, spiritual, and relational dimensions of the human person. A just society promotes human dignity by creating and supporting laws, policies, and infrastructures that facilitate, and do not frustrate, attaining human dignity. To realize peace requires peacebuilding.

---

[41] Kenneth R. Himes, "Peacebuilding and Catholic Social Teaching," in *Peacebuilding: Catholic Theology, Ethics, and Praxis*, ed. Robert J. Schreiter, R. Scott Appleby, and Gerard F. Powers (Maryknoll, NY: Orbis Books, 2010), 279–83.

[42] Paul VI, "Address to the General Assembly of the United Nations Organization, 4 October, 1965," *AAS* 57, no. 5 (1965).

[43] See Himes, "Peacebuilding," 268–71.

Peacebuilding may be defined as "that mode of conflict transformation that strives to comprehend the *longue durée* of a conflict—its full temporal, transgenerational range—and forge 'solutions' commensurate with the deep historical rootedness of the inhumane personal, social, economic, and political relationships fueling the deadly violence."[44] Peacebuilding utilizes all levels of social and religious institutions—local, national, and international. It draws from interdisciplinary resources—economic, political, social, cultural, and religious—to construct a comprehensive and comprehensible strategy to eliminate those aspects that prevent peace and create and sustain those aspects that build peace. Peacebuilders attempt to address those aspects that lead to violent conflict, including economic, political, social, cultural, and religious aspects. The peacebuilding perspective requires a method to justify that definition, structures to facilitate attaining it, and norms to guide the process.

b. Method: Just War or Peacebuilding?

We fully agree with theologians such as Thomas Shannon who assert that "peace be the beginning premise rather than the conclusion of one's methodology"[45] for reflecting on peace and war. If peace is the conclusion of one's methodology, then the focus is on attaining peace by means that too easily include recourse to violence and war. Early in its history, the just war tradition recognized that the State could only justify violence in order to realize justice. But as the just war tradition evolved, the concept of justice expanded and the method sometimes accepted war as an inevitable reality, focusing on formulating and justifying criteria for when war was justified and how war was to be conducted. If peace is the beginning premise of one's methodology, then there is a presumption against war and the focus is on building and sustaining peace and formulating and justifying norms for peacebuilding. Both just war and peacebuilding methods utilize the four sources of moral knowledge (Scripture, tradition, secular disciplines of knowledge, and experience), yet the selection, interpretation, prioritization, and integration of those sources varies depending on perspective—just war vis-à-vis peacebuilding—and determines the formulation, justification and application of norms for addressing peace and war.

---

[44] R. Scott Appleby, "Peacebuilding and Catholicism: Affinities, Convergences, Possibilities," in *Peacebuilding*, 3.

[45] Shannon, *What Are They Saying about Peace and War?*, 112.

There is evidence of a changed perspective and methodological shift in Church documents and theological literature on just war and peacebuilding. Although *Gaudium et Spes* follows the just war tradition to a certain extent, it reflects the gradual shift in Church documents from a focus on just war and criteria for going to war and conducting war to peacebuilding and a presumption against war. It notes that "peace is not merely the absence of war. . . it is rightly and appropriately called an enterprise of justice . . ." and "is likewise the fruit of love, which goes beyond what justice can provide." All Christians are called "to join with all true peacemakers," and "to practice the truth in love" (Eph 4:15) to bring about peace (GS 78). True and lasting peace is attained through development, according to *Populorum Progressio*. In his 2005 World Day of Peace address, John Paul II asserts that "peace is a good to be promoted with good."[46] We seek peace through the good of development. The German bishops sum up well this shift in focus in Church teaching. "We Christians must translate and incorporate this potential for Christian peace into political action on behalf of peace so that the demands of Jesus in respect of nonviolence and loving one's enemy will thereby achieve validity in social and political structures."[47]

There is evidence of this evolution in perspective and method on just war and peacebuilding in the theological literature. One method, what we call the just war method, represented by authors such as George Weigel[48] and Michael Novak,[49] supports the just war tradition and peace as the conclusion of its method. This method strongly disagrees with the presumption against war. It emphasizes tradition that focuses on just war, reason and experience that indicate political and military instability throughout the world, justifies the need for heavy investment in the military with the "new war," the war on terror, and uses Scripture that emphasizes the authority and autonomy of the State, established by God, and its right to sovereignty and self-defense. This method tends to narrowly define just war theory as a "theory of statecraft," which belongs

[46] John Paul II, "Do not Be Overcome with Evil, but Overcome Evil with Good," World Day of Peace Message (January 1, 2005), no. 1.

[47] Schall, *Out of Justice, Peace*, no. 49.

[48] George Weigel, "Moral Clarity in a Time of War," *First Things* (January 2003) http://www.firstthings.com/article/2008/01/001-moral-clarity-in-a-time-of-war-30; and *Tranquillitas ordinis: The Present Failure and Future Promise of American Catholic Thought on War and Peace* (New York: Oxford University Press, 1987).

[49] Michael Novak, "An Argument That the War against Iraq Is Just," *Origins* 32 (2003): 593–98.

primarily, if not exclusively, to the political realm, limits the moral relevance of the Beatitudes in this realm, and distinguishes just war theory from broader theological reflections that include covenantal relationship with God *and* neighbor, and emphasizes maintaining a strong military to maintain peace, rather than becoming peacemakers through development. Critics of this method and the normative conclusions that are drawn from it point out that within this perspective and method there is an explicit rejection of economic rights and Catholic social teaching that justifies those rights, which may constitute formal dissent from Church teaching on social justice.[50]

Another method, what we call a peacebuilding method, represented by scholars such as Kenneth Himes, David Hollenbach, Lisa Sowle Cahill, Charles Curran, and Tobias Winright, emphasizes peace as the premise of this method. The peacebuilding method emphasizes the tradition that focuses on peace and peacebuilding, especially since Vatican II. It also emphasizes reason and experience that demonstrate how lack of development threatens peace, the need for heavy social, political, and economic investment in development that fosters human dignity and the common good, and the use of Scripture that emphasizes the Christian vocation to become peacemakers and responsible for the poor and oppressed, especially those who suffer from violent conflict, as a means to build peace through nonmilitary means. While this method recognizes a limited use of force, for example in legitimate self-defense, it supports recent Catholic teaching on a presumption against war. We find the latter method to be more in line with recent Church teaching on peace and war and investigate structures that can realize this perspective and norms that facilitate attaining it.

c. Structures

John Paul Lederach, a Mennonite sociologist, has worked extensively on Catholic peace initiatives since 1989 and suggests that the "ubiquitous presence" of the Catholic Church and its hierarchical structure is one of its strongest and most influential contributions to peacebuilding.[51] He

---

[50] Whitmore, "The Reception of Catholic Approaches," 514; see also his, "John Paul II, Michael Novak, and the Differences between Them," in *Annual of the Society of Christian Ethics* 21 (2001): 215–32.

[51] John Paul Lederach, "The Long Journey Back to Humanity: Catholic Peacebuilding with Armed Actors," in *Peacebuilding*, 23–55.

divides this hierarchical pyramid into three different levels of leadership in the Church: high, middle, and community. At the highest level are bishops and bishops' conferences, which are highly visible individuals and organizations that propose initiatives, such as pastoral letters, and present top-down approaches to building peace. These public figures and institutional bodies and the statements that they issue have public and media exposure and a voice at the highest levels of power. That voice enables them to shape the discourse on peace, initiate strategies that will build a lasting peace, and promote dialogue with political and social leaders who can influence policy and structures to bring about peace. The middle level in the Church provides outreach and infrastructure for peacebuilding initiatives in the local church. This level consists of individual bishops and priests functioning within their own dioceses and the charitable, educational, pastoral, peace and justice programs and offices that serve as negotiators between the high and community levels to disseminate, coordinate, and implement peacebuilding initiatives. The community level consists of local priests and the faithful who initiate and carry out grassroots movements to facilitate increased responsibility and responsiveness to local conflicts and initiatives to build peace and, working with the other two levels, strategize to deconstruct structures that perpetuate violence, and construct structures that build peace.[52] Though he focuses his ubiquitous presence theory on Catholic-majority countries, Lederach extends his theory also to countries where there is a significant Catholic presence. With the election of Pope Francis, this presence and the Catholic voice for building peace is being projected and heard in a way it had not been projected and heard in the papacies of John Paul II and Benedict XVI. Though the message of the need for development to create and sustain peace is consistent among the three popes, Francis's method of delivery and emphasis has drawn worldwide attention among Catholics and non-Catholics alike, which will serve well the strategy of, and commitment to, peacebuilding.

As peacebuilder, the Church must also recognize its own failure in realizing and building peace and collaborating with evil. The atrocities in Rwanda and the complicity of priests and faithful at the community level in the genocide that slaughtered 800,000 Tutsis and moderate Hutus, as well as the hesitancy to speak out against violence and injustices in other parts of the world at the highest level, indicate that the Church

---

[52] Ibid., 29–31.

must continue a holistic approach to peacebuilding both externally and internally. A holistic approach to peacebuilding includes addressing the root causes of war and violence as well as causes of sexual, gender, environmental, ethnic, political, and developmental violence and injustices. It also includes norms that facilitate peacebuilding.

d. Norms and Principles: Catholic Social Teaching, Peacebuilding, and *Jus Post Bellum*

An important aspect of *Gaudium et Spes*'s "fresh appraisal of war," Hollenbach notes, is that "the norms of just war are to be interpreted very strictly."[53] With the advent of modern technology and the development and proliferation of weapons of mass destruction, there has been an ever-increasing strictness in Church documents in interpreting and applying the just war criteria in ways that would justify war in the name of justice, as well as an ever-increasing resistance to violence as a justifiable option. If we shift the perspective to peace as our point of departure, then we can better grasp Jeremias's interpretation of the Beatitudes, which calls us to become peacemakers as individuals, families, communities, and nations. The Beatitudes call us to conversion, both individually and communally. Shifting to the perspective of peace as our point of departure calls for all of us to name those structures, policies, and laws that inhibit peace by perpetuating injustice, and to work to transform them in the name of peace. The result of this shift in perspective is that it shifts the methodology from a narrow focus on war and the avoidance of war to a broader consideration of peace and peacebuilding through development. It gives new urgency to the Beatitude on becoming peacemakers and challenges "all people of good will" to strategize on how to recognize and realize human dignity and the common good. It also shifts the types of principles or norms, from just war criteria to principles or norms that build peace through development and, in cases of justified violence, *jus post bellum*, to justice after war. We conclude with a list and description of these principles and norms, though we acknowledge that this list is by no means complete.

Catholic social teaching provides four basic principles to facilitate building peace through integral human development and the common good. We addressed some of these principles in chapter five. Here, we

---

[53] Hollenbach, "Commentary on *Gaudium et Spes*," 283.

merely indicate how they apply specifically to peacebuilding. Perhaps the first and foundational principle for peacebuilding is solidarity. Solidarity recognizes the interrelationship and interdependence of all human beings; we *are* our brother's and sister's keepers. The responsibility for our neighbor applies to individuals, communities, and nations. Individually, we must build peace through our actions, character and relationships, sharing our gifts, talents, and resources to facilitate the common good. Communally, we must support policies, laws, and legislators that build a culture of equality and focus on meeting the basic needs (e.g., economic, educational, healthcare) of the most vulnerable in society. Nationally, it requires that wealthier nations assist less developed nations and that less developed nations work toward development that shares limited resources fairly and equitably. Pope Francis highlights the responsibilities of wealthier countries to poorer countries in terms of solidarity, and approvingly cites Pope John Paul II's claim that "peace is an *opus solidaritatis*," a work of solidarity.[54] Solidarity requires greater investment in caring for neighbor through responsible development and less investment in protecting neighbor by preparing for armed conflict.

Second, peacebuilding requires social justice, a more equitable distribution of goods to meet the basic human needs of all people. When 24,000 people die each day due to extreme poverty, this indicates that we have a long way to go to reach social justice. Pope Francis notes that social justice "requires the realignment of relationships between stronger and weaker peoples."[55] In terms of peacebuilding, this requires that more developed nations shift resources from war preparation to social development within its own borders and humanitarian aid in less developed countries. Such a shift can also reduce competitive investment between countries in the arms race and free up resources for other countries to invest in social justice and development.

Third, subsidiarity or participatory justice states "it is an injustice and at the same time a grave evil and a disturbance of right order to transfer to the larger and higher collectivity functions which can be performed and provided for by lesser and subordinate bodies" (QA 79). The cooperation between various levels within the Church that Lederach

---

[54] Pope Francis, "World Day of Peace: Fraternity, the Foundation and Pathway to Peace" (1 January 2014) http://www.vatican.va/holy_father/francesco/messages /peace/documents/papa-francesco_20131208_messaggio-xlvii-giornata-mondiale -pace-2014_en.html, accessed April 4, 2014.

[55] Ibid., no. 4.

envisions in his "ubiquitous presence," and the cooperation between the Church and secular communities and organizations, captures well the principle of subsidiarity. Subsidiarity empowers all people at every level—high, middle and community—to participate in peacebuilding efforts and confronts, challenges, and deconstructs structures that limit and frustrate these efforts.

Fourth, the preferential option for the poor, which John Paul II describes as a "special form of primacy in the exercise of Christian charity, to which the whole tradition of the Church bears witness" (SRS 42), contextualizes the principle of solidarity. While all people must be treated with dignity and respect to realize integral human dignity, the poor have a unique and urgent claim to solidarity because of their poverty. The poor include economically, socially, and culturally oppressed people. It also includes those who are victims of violence in just or unjust wars. Peace must be built on solidarity, justice, subsidiarity, and a preferential option for the poor. As Pope Francis notes, "In the end, a peace which is not the result of integral development will be doomed; it will always spawn new conflicts and various forms of violence" (EG 219).

Peacebuilding seeks to build peace through integral human development and the prevention of war. It also seeks to restore peace in the aftermath of war. Michael Schuck proposes three principles for *jus post bellum*.[56] The first is repentance among all members of a military conflict, victors and vanquished alike. War is never cause for celebration; it should be an occasion for humility and thoughtful reflection on how to move forward in a spirit of peace and reconciliation. The second principle is honorable surrender, which insures the protection of basic human rights and proscribes punitive or degrading measures against the vanquished. The third principle is restoration, which prescribes that victors remove the remnants of war (e.g., landmines) and help to rebuild infrastructure and proscribes neglect or exploitation of the vanquished.

Since Schuck's article, there has been a great deal of literature on *jus post bellum* principles. Himes summarizes this literature, adding three principles for peacebuilding. The first is "just cause for war's termination," which means that a war must seek to realize the just cause that brought a military force into conflict. To end the conflict before the just cause is met or to extend it beyond the just cause is unjust. The second

---

[56] Michael Schuck, "When the Shooting Stops: Missing Elements in Just War Theory," *Christian Century* 101 (1994): 982–84.

principle is "rehabilitation and reform," which means that those responsible for initiating an unjust conflict are to be held accountable and that infrastructural transformation, political, economic, and social, take place to correct unjust structures that perpetuate violence. The third principle is "victors' duties to the defeated," which includes a commitment to restoring peace through justice. This duty will vary depending on the type of military intervention, e.g., a humanitarian intervention or a response to aggression.[57]

Daniel Philpott has recently proposed "political reconciliation" as a model for political restoration of right relationship after massive injustices suffered in war. Political reconciliation is a holistic approach to building justice and restoring political order through justice, mercy, and peace, drawing from Christianity, Judaism, and Islam. This proposal builds on the peacebuilding tradition and consists of six practices: "1) building socially just institutions; 2) acknowledgement; 3) reparations; 4) apology; 5) punishment; and 6) forgiveness."[58] These practices complement well the peacebuilding tradition and move it forward in the twenty-first century.

III. Conclusion

Gaudium et Spes and the recent Catholic tradition mark a fundamental shift in the tradition from just war to peacebuilding. We conclude with a quote from Pope Francis's homily at a peace vigil for Syria, which articulates well the call for peacebuilding in the twenty-first century. "'Peace expresses itself only in peace, a peace which is not separate from the demands of justice but which is fostered by personal sacrifice, clemency, mercy and love' (World Day of Peace Message, 1975). Forgiveness, dialogue, reconciliation—these are the words of peace, in beloved Syria, in the Middle East, in all the world! Let us pray for reconciliation and peace, let us work for reconciliation and peace, and let us all become, in every place, men and women of reconciliation and peace! Amen."[59]

---

[57] Himes, "Peacebuilding," 285–87.

[58] Daniel Philpott, *Just and Unjust Peace: An Ethic of Political Reconciliation* (New York: Oxford University Press, 2012), 171.

[59] Pope Francis, "Homily at Peace Vigil," September 7, 2013, http://en.radiovaticana .va/news/2013/09/07/pope_francis:_homily_at_peace_vigil/en1-726626, accessed April 4, 2014.

Questions for Reflection

1. Explain the role and function of the Church in relation to the political community.

2. Apply Himes's five criteria to guide the relationship between the Church and political community to recent elections. Were these criteria recognized and respected by leadership within the Church during the most recent election process? Explain.

3. Explain the role and function of the faithful in relation to the Church and the political community. Since no political candidate or public policy fully realizes definitions of human dignity or the common good, but frequently has partial realizations of these definitions, how should the faithful inform their consciences to vote responsibly?

4. Explain how Church teaching has evolved in its understanding of the just war tradition.

5. Explain the relationship between violence and poverty. How can development impact violence, according to Church teaching?

6. What is the impact on the just war tradition if peace is the beginning premise rather than the conclusion of one's methodology?

7. What is peacebuilding? How can peacebuilding be realized methodologically, structurally, and normatively? Explain.

8. Discuss specific strategies for individuals and communities to become peacebuilders?

Index

koinonia, 150, 159

Lactantius, 122, 142
laity, 2, 3, 10, 18, 21, 34, 38, 46, 47, 52, 57, 60, 69, 70, 101, 107
Lambeth Conference, 124
Lane, Dermot, 3, 38, 153
Lateran II, 87
Lateran III, 87
Lawler, Michael, G., 84, 86, 89, 111
Lederach, John Paul, 192, 193, 195
Lefebvre, Archbishop, 25, 29
Leger, Cardinal, 132
Leo XIII, Pope, 9, 27, 105, 132, 140, 162, 168
Léon-Dufour, Xavier, 148
Liberation Theology, 69, 151
literary forms, 17, 97, 99, 116, 117
Lonergan, Bernard, 80–84, 91, 112, 113, 169
longue durée, 190
Lumen Gentium, 2, 3, 6, 21, 30–34, 37, 38, 40, 48, 61, 88, 101, 138, 142, 149, 152, 157

magisterium, 75, 76, 80–90, 95, 99, 102–6, 114, 124, 132
Majority Report, 133
Malines Schema, 5, 21, 23–25, 40, 128, 142
Manicheans, 122, 131
marriage, 8, 9, 19–30, 35, 36, 51, 71, 73, 112–37, 153, 166
Martin Luther, 147
Massingale, Bryan, 84, 110
Mater et Magistra, 21, 28
materialism, 25, 125
McCormick, Richard, A., 88, 101, 103, 134
McDonagh, Enda, 50
Medellín, 151
metaethics, 7, 73,77, 78, 79, 82, 111
methodological, 6, 10, 13, 71–74, 80, 90, 92–97, 107–10, 191

Middle Ages, 1, 2, 45, 103, 113
Minority Report, 133, 134
Mixed Commission, 5, 20, 22, 27, 30, 35, 128
modernist, 44
Montini, Cardinal, 36; *see also* Paul VI, Pope
Moore, George, E., 77
Murray, John Courtney, 14, 45, 172

natural, 2, 3, 33, 38, 55, 56, 78, 87, 92, 93, 95, 108, 113, 114, 117, 123, 125, 126, 127, 133, 153, 167, 169, 171, 181
natural law, 64, 71, 76, 77, 79, 94, 110, 138, 148
Navarette, Urban, 124
neo-Augustinian, 4, 6, 9, 14, 18, 19, 27, 33, 36, 39, 79, 80, 106, 112, 128, 131
neoscholastic, 43, 44
neo-Thomist, 4, 6, 14, 16, 18, 19, 33, 36, 39, 44, 79, 80, 112, 113, 132
new theology, 13, 128, 136
nihilism, 72, 77
noncombatants, 182, 186
noninfallible, 86–90, 103, 104
Noonan, John, 82, 106
normative ethics, 77, 111
norms, 6, 7, 8, 13, 73–94, 103–14, 169, 171, 184, 188, 190, 192, 194
Novak, Michael, 117, 191, 192
nuclear weapons, 15, 22, 69

Obama, Barack, 170
objective, 4, 8, 18, 19, 35, 71–86, 90, 113, 128, 166, 176
objectivism, 7, 79, 82, 84, 85, 170
obsequium religiosum, 88, 89, 90, 168, 173
O'Malley, John, 17, 42, 45, 52, 54, 61
On the Active Presence of a Servant Church of the Lord among Men of Good Will, 24